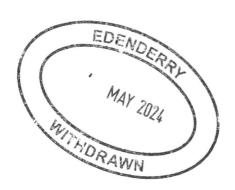

Robert Llewellyn is an actor, novelist, screenwriter, comedian and TV presenter, best known for *Red Dwarf*, *Scrapheap Challenge*, *Carpool* and *Fully Charged*. He drives an electric car and writes under a rack of solar panels in Gloucestershire.

By the Same Author

The Reconstructed Heart
The Man in the Rubber Mask
Thin He Was and Filthy-Haired
Therapy and How to Avoid It (with Nigel Planer)
The Man on Platform 5
Punchbag
Sudden Wealth
Brother Nature
Behind the Scenes at Scrapheap Challenge
Sold Out
News from Gardenia
News from the Squares
News from the Clouds

Some Old Bloke

Recollections, Obsessions
and the Joys of Blokedom

Robert Llewellyn

Unbound

Unbound

6th Floor Mutual House, 70 Conduit Street, London W1S 2GF

www.unbound.com

Text design by Ellipsis, Glasgow

Illustration p.vii © Louis Pascoe

A CIP record for this book is available from the British Library

ISBN 978-1-78352-602-4 (trade hbk)
ISBN 978-1-78352-601-7 (ebook)
ISBN 978-1-78352-603-1 (limited edition)

Printed in Great Britain by CPI Group (UK)

For Reg and Brenda

Some old bloke

The Plaque

Early one morning in May 2013 I received a text from the comedian Ross Noble.

Ross is a lovely fellow and he wanted me to be on his telly programme, although this flattering request was imbued with a microdot of low-status subtext.

This was very much a last-minute thing. He wanted me on his show but not later in the year or three months ahead as might be expected with a traditional TV production.

No, he wanted me to be there that day.

The text from Ross had an air of panic about it: they couldn't get any properly famous celebrity at such short notice, so they tried me.

I'm not suggesting that I'm under constant pressure to make public appearances, but I can, occasionally, be quite busy.

On the morning I got the text from Ross I was under enormous pressure to feed the chickens and put the rubbish out, so I replied, 'Yes.'

Then I looked in the bathroom mirror.

The slightly backlit reflection confirmed that I was (then) a fifty-seven-year-old bloke, and while that could be – and often is – a depressing realisation, on this particular morning I was gently elated at how lucky I'd been.

I'd been around the block a bit, but I'd never spent a night in a hospital, never had to wear a uniform or fight in a war.

I'd never been challenged to survive a post-apocalyptic Armageddon, zombie apocalypse or a tsunami; I hadn't experienced starvation or been put in prison for my opinions; I hadn't been oppressed or brutalised because of my gender or the colour of my skin.

If, as the writer and doctor Abraham Verghese argues, 'geography is destiny', then I've been lucky from the get-go.

Of Indian heritage, Verghese was born in Ethiopia, had to flee the civil war when he was a kid, and went to America with his family. There he studied medicine, worked as a doctor in India, went back to America and became a writer.

His destiny was very much defined by geography; he is part of the massive diaspora of many people around the world.

I didn't have any of that. I'm a white-skinned bloke born in a European country where my antecedents had been living for, who knows, possibly thousands of years.

However, the acknowledgement of coming from where I do, being my age and acknowledging my privilege is, I will argue, very important.

It's a political stance and it seems quite rare among my peers.

There are many men living in developed Western countries the same age as me who, it would seem, feel hard done by. They might express this disappointment through fake jocularity to disguise the fury and frustration they feel inside.

A certain Mr Farage is a good example.

Miserable, moaning, self-pitying whingers who still see the world as their grandfathers would have done. Being 'British' and proud to wave a flag. Lamenting the passing of our world-power status, wasting a fortune on nuclear weapons, the list goes on. Men my age.

No, I don't want to be a miserable old bloke. Blaming other people for everything, puffed up and pompous, bullying and pig ignorant.

In contrast to this miserable anger, and I say this with some pride, I acknowledge that I have been lucky.

For a start I'm still alive and I can walk, bend down and pick things up – okay, that activity involves a bit of grunting but I can still do it.

I'm also lucky because I'm a white man living in Europe, as opposed to, say, a black woman living in Somalia or an old Indian man living in Maharashtra begging for food at a dusty train station.

Sure, my life has been tough at times. I've cried myself to sleep on occasion, I've had disappointments, humiliations and failures, but they have generally turned out to be my own fault.

A plus to the six decades under my expanded belt is that I've learned a few useful things along the way, quite a bit about gearboxes, laundry, transmission systems, the importance of equality between genders, single socks, brake callipers, tolerance of people different from myself, vegetable gardening, parenting, hydraulic diggers, love, baking cakes, limited slip differentials, reading my children bedtime stories, asynchronous electric motors, self-awareness, building bonfires, battery-management software, bed-making and one or two things about being a bloke.

For the last few years I have been trying to reclaim the word 'bloke'. It's a very common word in both the UK and Australia. For me, it denotes a man in late middle age, a bit knackered, a bit broken down by life, but still willing to get stuck in.

Commonly used terms such as 'good bloke' or a 'nice bloke' indicate it's generally a positive term.

Being a bloke is a great privilege and should be recognised as such by those who have had blokedom bestowed upon them.

If you are male and live long enough, you can be fairly certain that at some stage in the latter portion of your life, you will have blokedom so bestowed.

The generally accepted idea is that a male baby gradually develops into a boy, then into a teenager or adolescent and then at some point you sort of become a man.

Eventually.

It takes a while.

In fact it seems to be taking longer and longer.

My grandfather's generation went to school until they were about twelve and then became adults. Bosh. Just like that.

A thirteen-year-old apprentice dressed the same way as adults. They had jobs and apparently didn't think any more about it.

My father's generation went to school a little bit longer but then became adults immediately after they left their education, an elite minority going to university, the overwhelming majority into the armed forces or a full-time job.

The armed forces were a big thing for both my father and grandfather. My paternal grandfather Percy fought in the First World War, lost an eye but somehow survived.

My father Reginald fought in the Second World War, flew Halifax and Wellington bombers on thirty-six missions over occupied Europe and survived.

The pressure on them to be 'adults' at a very early age is pretty much impossible for us to imagine now, but it was clearly concrete and insurmountable at the time.

I can now see I was an adolescent-man well into my mid-thirties. I wasn't 'mature'. I didn't conform to any of the traditional male roles that were laid down for me during my education.

You could call this deliberately fostered immaturity and I was fully aware of the fact. I articulated it at the time. I didn't want to grow up and be an adult because all the role models I saw of grown-up adult men seemed to me to be rather negative.

Grown-ups, 'proper men', men who wore suits or uniforms always seemed a bit bitter, cynical, sexist, racist, homophobic and managed to consistently blame others for what appeared to me to be their own failings.

I didn't want to be like that so I decided to stay an adolescent.

I maintain that there were positive elements to this determination. It helped me keep a fresh and open attitude to the world and, most importantly, to people who weren't like me.

I'm not trying to claim this was easy and that I'm naturally such a beneficent, open and empathetic person that a universal understanding of the entire human condition was second nature to me. Far from it.

I sometimes found it hard to understand the difficulties faced by women, black people, disabled people, gay people. They were different to me, I didn't know what they wanted from life, they were a bit frightening. The only thing I learned as a young man was that I could accept that they often did face rather more difficulties than I did.

To make this understanding more challenging, I also had to accept that because I was born white and male I was, by default, part of the problem.

No fun in that.

I became aware of a thing called patriarchy. It's a term liberally bandied about in arguments, but it exists. We live in a patriarchy; it's been around for centuries, it's the foundation of much of our societal structure and legal system, and it often defines our view of the world.

So, like many, I had inherited an uncomfortable mantle from my forefathers, white men who implicitly 'knew' they were better than anyone else on the planet and behaved accordingly.

If you accept that by fate of birth you are part of the problem, life can get very complicated. As some of you may know from your own experience, this is often an annoying and tiresome minefield to negotiate.

However, it helped me stop seeing anyone who wasn't like me as being 'the problem', which, let's face it, folks, is the traditional white male position.

That's the positive side of refusing to grow up and be a mature man.

The negative side, and one that I found very difficult to accept, was that I was emotionally incapable of committing to anyone or anything.

I would ebb and flow in my passions and beliefs; I was an emotional reactionary even if I was struggling to avoid being a political one.

I was a teenage man for much longer than was healthy for me, or for society in general. I struggled endlessly with what it meant to be a man, or indeed how to be a man and not support the patriarchy. I never felt comfortable or happy with the role; I was always attracted to men who were, like me, emotional children. Impulsive, funny, unpredictable, insecure, feckless and delightful but hopeless as supporting and stable partners.

I thought I would change when I became a father. I'll give myself a break because I really did try but I was fairly hopeless.

I survived, just. My marriage survived, just.

My children survived – actually, they survived quite well and have gone on to be wonderful adults who don't hate me that much, which, considering everything, is a result.

We all got through it, then something rather wonderful happened.

Around the age of fifty-five I became a bloke.

As soon as I became a bloke I relaxed. Possibly because of some long-buried biological determinant, I finally knew how to be the thing I was.

All through my life I've never been sure how to be anything. I've tried so many different roles and I've always failed, but being a bloke has just come naturally.

On the morning Mr Noble texted me, I think I was right to feel lucky as I drove to Northampton in my plug-in hybrid car.

I'd only met Ross once before when he recorded an episode of *Carpool* with me. I took him to the shops and he made me laugh with ease.

Ross was in Northampton filming an episode of his TV series *Freewheeling,* in which he travels the country using Twitter as his source of inspiration.

He had asked the Twitterati if any famous people had been born in Northampton and the suggestions came flooding in. Not including, as I recall, Francis Crick, the co-discoverer of the structure of the DNA molecule in 1953, although he was born in the town.

No, the suggestions were Alan Carr, the comedian; Tim Minchin, the uber-talented musician and comedian – yes, I know he's Australian but he was born in Northampton; and Matt Smith, the eleventh Doctor Who.

Oh yes, and me.

The plan was that Ross would get a plaque made up, the sort of thing they attach to houses in London where the great and good once lived. He then planned to carry out a classic unveiling ceremony; he was very excited about it.

I was born on 10 March 1956, second son to Reginald and Brenda.

Reg died in 1997 and Brenda in 2001 so they never lived to witness this glorious moment. I thought about them as I drove through the gentle rolling countryside that slightly overcast morning. It's not that I don't normally think about them –

they're my mum and dad, I think about them a lot – but obviously they were a fairly major part of the 'where I was born' story.

The house I was born in is on a pleasant tree-lined avenue that overlooks the rather lovely Abington Park in the northern section of Northampton.

I'd seen the house many times as a child; my parents moved out of it when I was about six months old so I don't remember living there, but my mother, of whom there will be more later, had said to me on many occasions, 'There will be a plaque on that house one day, my lad,' as we drove past the house in her Hillman Imp in the 1960s.

As a seven-year-old I had no idea what she meant.

Now, fifty-plus years later, I recalled that comment with a wry grin.

My mum was right. Sort of.

I pulled to a halt and parked a couple of hundred metres from the house, got out of the car and stretched.

The stretches were accompanied by repressed grunting. At my age it takes a moment or two to straighten up after an hour and a half in a car.

I checked my flies, pulled my jacket straight and walked towards the little crowd that had gathered outside the house.

This was the house where I came into the world. Apparently, I was 'a difficult birth', which was the only information I ever got from my mother.

There are small black-and-white photographs of my parents and my older brother taken in the back garden of the property dating from around the time of my arrival. My dad dressed in a smart suit holding me, a little baby wrapped in a white shawl, my mother wearing a big pleated 1950s skirt, looking fairly brain-dead and exhausted.

According to my dad, I cried non-stop for the first three years of my life.

If you are lucky enough to believe in a kind of Buddhist rein-carnation, circle-of-life type thing, you could interpret this non-stop wailing as the result of some innate understanding of where I'd landed and the concomitant despair that realisation unleashed. Instead of being the child of a tribe in Borneo, or the offspring of a family of academics in Sydney, Australia, or the handsome son of a scuba diver on the Mediterranean coast of France, I was the son of a building society branch manager and an amateur watercolourist in Northampton.

Thankfully, I don't have any such beliefs, but the short walk from the car to the house allowed me to reflect on my life in a more intense way than I normally indulge in.

I had to send a text to one of the researchers on Ross's show as I approached. This was all going to be shot 'as live' and I had no idea what was going to happen.

There were maybe thirty people crowded around the front of the house. As I approached, Ross shouted, 'Here he is, ladies and gentlemen,' and he grabbed me and pulled me into the very small front garden.

Now, I'm not going to pretend I'm not used to being in front of the camera. I've been on the telly on and off since 1985, which, according to my low-level grasp of mathematics, is more than thirty years, but stumbling about in the very crowded front garden with Ross Noble constantly rambling to the camera was a bit unusual.

He has enormous energy and I didn't have a moment to reflect as he introduced me to the mayor of Northampton and a row of civic dignitaries.

I suddenly felt hugely self-conscious when I saw my sister Elizabeth in the crowd, looking on with mild amusement and a healthy pinch of 'Who does my tosser of a brother think he is?'

I was introduced to a huge man who played rugby and a woman who looked alarmingly like Tina Turner.

I then had to get up on a stage with Ross. I say 'stage', but I'm being generous: it was a plank of wood supported by two kitchen chairs resting on uneven gravel.

Behind me, on the front wall of the house, was a very make-shift set of wooden blinds held up with tape and string.

'We wanted to get a curtain but we didn't have time so we borrowed some kitchen blinds from the neighbours,' Ross explained to the crowd before us.

After a count of three I had to gently pull up the blinds and reveal my plaque that was held onto the wall with tape and Black-tack.

For those of you not familiar with this product, Black-tack is Blu-tack pro: it's the same idea but a lot stickier, and it's black.

The plaque read:

Robert Llewellyn, 1956–
Actor, writer, comedian lived here.

My eye was drawn to the small gap after the date. It was probably only for a second but that moment now feels like it was an hour.

1956–

One day, it will be possible to fill the second figure in. I can't imagine the date but obviously it's going to happen. I'm going to die. I'm going to actually be dead, to be no more.

To experience even a shallow moment of epiphany while standing in front of thirty people in the garden of the house you were born in is not a sensible plan; it was a fleeting thump in the chest but it stayed with me.

I want to make it clear that I don't now and never have had any fear of being dead. I don't worry about it. I have even gone as far as to try and worry about it to see if it will give me insight into religious belief.

Like nationalism, team sports and gambling, religion and the fear of being dead have remained a mystery to me my entire life.

Why would anyone be interested in watching young men run around on grass kicking a ball? Why would anyone put a coin in a machine with the frail hope that more coins will come out and they'll be rich? Why would anyone go to the bother of making up stories about what happens after you die and then build a belief system on it?

It's important to make the distinction between dying and being dead. Like any mortal creature I have a natural aversion to the process of dying. I don't want to die, I have fear of the pain that may precede being dead, but once I'm dead, that's it. I'm dead. There is nothing more.

Clearly this attitude hasn't been common among large swathes of the human race for the past ten thousand years. We've exhibited an endless fascination with being dead, with heaven and hell, with being rewarded in the afterlife for the suffering we've endured on this earth.

Maybe it's because my life – when compared to that of an Anglo-Saxon peasant who was born in, say, 1156 – has been one of rampant luxury, ease, comfort and very low levels of danger.

That may make me complacent about being dead, or it could be that the Anglo-Saxon peasant was uneducated and believed all the tosh the Church who lived off his toil told him because he had no other source of information.

Anyway, I don't fear being dead but I don't particularly want to die, just yet.

As soon as the plaque was revealed, Ross dragged me off the makeshift stage and the woman who looked like Tina Turner climbed up and sang 'Simply the Best!' without accompaniment, and she did it alarmingly well.

She was swiftly followed by a group of three young men in Mexican Mariachi outfits who sang a funny song, their fake moustaches falling off as they did so.

The small crowd loved it, they clapped and cheered, and in all fairness I was a bit of a sideshow. This was Ross Noble's gig and he was wonderful.

That was it, I can't have been in that front garden for more than ten minutes. In the chaotic few moments that followed, Ross thanked me, got on a terrifying-looking motorbike and roared off. The crew packed everything (including the plaque) into a couple of vans and followed soon after. I did an interview with a local paper, thanked the man who owned the house I was born in, and went off to have lunch with my sister.

My sister is one of the most grounded people I know. She has had to put up with her noisy brother her entire life, she is very private and doesn't seek shallow attention in the way I do.

We went to a pub very near where we both grew up. It was a bad choice; she'd suggested a much nicer place a little further away. I should always listen to my sister.

We sat down at a table and ordered. As soon as we were alone she said, 'Is this a normal day for you?'

I laughed. Of course it wasn't, but I had to admit that due to either my work choices or temperament, it wasn't that unusual. I then explained to my sister the experience I'd had when the plaque was revealed, the date I was born and the gap left for the date I was going to die.

'It really is all about you, isn't it?' she said with great kindness and understanding.

She was right, of course, and this wasn't the first time I'd heard the phrase, 'It's all about you, isn't it?'

I would only argue now that I'm not that fussed about it being all about me, it's nice when it is, as long as it's not too often, and it's genuinely fine when it isn't all about me in any way.

Another advantage of being a bloke: at my age, it's mostly all about everyone else.

Damn and Blast!

'Bloody teachers, blasted social workers, damnable fellow-travelling, leftie, do-gooder, scrounging, sandal-wearing, liberal hordes.'

These were the people my father raged against from about 1948 when he was demobbed from the RAF to the day he died in 1997.

To say Reginald was on the very far right of the political spectrum would be a gross understatement and yet he was a charming and popular figure among his peers. Bearing in mind, of course, that most of his peers were likely of a similar political outlook.

I disagreed with virtually everything he believed in, stood for, voted for and talked about, and I miss him every day.

I learned about being a man from him, which may explain a great deal. My happiest memories of him are from when I was very young. He was a wonderful dad when we were small kids. He must have spent a bit of time with us but my memories are fleeting and few.

He was born in 1922, and from the few photographs I've seen of him as a child he was clearly frail, as he suffered from serious asthma, but he grew into a hefty fellow in middle age. My dad was built like an ox, a big strong man from good Forest of Dean peasant stock. He had an impressive moustache and a clipped, middle-class accent that I now understand he would have developed later in life.

His natural accent would have had a Gloucestershire rolling R twang to it like his brother, my uncle Phil, exhibited. I assume, although I have no way of corroborating this, that he adopted his peculiar clipped received pronunciation during his time in the RAF.

The only fissure in his use of middle-class speech patterns was the word cucumber. We learned at a very early age to tease him about this.

For reasons now lost in the early 1960s, we had a sort of meal called 'tea' at five o'clock in the evening that consisted of cups of tea, a few sandwiches and either scones or a slice of cake. Basically sweet tea with sugar and flour-based products.

One of the most common sandwich fillings my mother used was cucumber, very thinly sliced and probably with the green skin removed.

'D'you want a sandwich, Dad?' we'd ask.

'What are they?' he'd ask as we passed the plate to him. The trick was to say nothing and he played along willingly. 'Oh queue-cumberrr.'

Later in life my dad developed into a proper old bloke, raging against what he then called 'fellow travellers' (nowadays, known on the right as 'libtards'), which included teachers, long-haired intellectuals and the Labour party, coal-miners and lazy, good-for-nothing immigrant layabouts sponging off the state.

Yes, he was possibly a little bit Faragey but with an amazing sense of humour. Come to think of it, that's what people say about Farage.

One of the things that fascinated me and still leaves me baffled was the barely concealed racism.

Actually, I'll modify that: it wasn't concealed at all within the family, it was more concealed during larger social events, such as my brother's wedding, family get-togethers and parties.

In 1974 I had a brief and sadly short-lived love affair with a black girl called Paulette. It was short-lived because I was nineteen and an idiot. The short-lived nature of the relationship wasn't her fault, although she was capable of being a little wild and crazy at times. It was the 1970s, it was the drugs, man.

Anyway, I can't remember the surrounding events. I think we were on our way to a party but on the way we dropped in at my parents' house in Oxfordshire.

As we rode along on the village bus, I warned Paulette that my mum was cool but my dad was an out-and-out racist. She said that was nothing new for her but could we not stop for too long.

When we arrived I was quite tense, my father opened the front door, ignored me completely and locked his gaze on Paulette.

His bushy eyebrows went up and he said, 'Hello, young lady,' rather like the 1950s 'Carry On' actor Leslie Phillips.

My dad was charming, giving the impression of a delightful, if slightly creepy, old letch.

We had a cup of tea with my mum and dad. My mother's face was a picture of discomfort, her smile was painful, she was clearly not happy about my choice of partner.

My father was all over Paulette like a cheap suit, asking about her family, what she was studying at college (catering) and where she hoped to work. He kept suggesting a hotel in Witney, the town where he worked, which was always looking for staff. It was all so obvious.

By the time we left, Paulette was laughing at all my dad's awful jokes and they were getting on like best buds. She gave him a peck on the cheek at the door and he promised never to wash his face again.

Seriously!

On the rest of the journey Paulette kept talking about my dad, what an amazing man he was, so funny, but my mum was a right bitch. It was all very awkward.

During a later and quite fraught phone call with my mother she denied that her reaction was racist. 'It's nothing to do with the colour of her skin, my lad. She wasn't even wearing a bra, she was a right little madam, and well you know it.'

For the following thirty years, my father would often ask if I was still in touch with the 'dusky maiden'.

What is that about? How can he be railing against 'darkies' invading his beloved country one minute and be flirting with one of them the next?

I will never understand that; I don't want to understand it.

Actually, of course I know exactly where that ghastly old colonial 'dusky maiden' stereotype comes from, and how horribly it patronises and objectifies women of colour. And I really don't like to think of my dad perving on Paulette in that way.

*

My father was stoical – not uncomplainingly so, just in his example. He worked hard and looked after us and, of course, for the most part when he was alive, I didn't appreciate it. I think my brother and sister may have done, but I rejected him from a very early age.

This rejection was with the compliance and encouragement of my mother. She didn't agree with him either.

Of course, now that it's far too late, I regret not trying to find common ground.

This is not to let him off the hook. Due to his upbringing and history and like so many of his contemporaries, he was an emotionally distant man who had little or no time for his children's needs other than the very obvious day-to-day necessities of food and shelter.

Once I entered adult life, my contact with him was minimal. He never asked me how the shoemaking was going, never once came to see me onstage, he never commented or asked me what I was doing on the telly.

The only time he might have found out anything about me was when I told him what I was up to, and even then, he showed minimal interest. I find this harder to understand now that I have children. I am almost unhealthily obsessed about their achievements and disasters.

Now they are young adults, I admit there are times when I wish I knew less about their traumas and difficulties because I often feel helpless and unable to assist them.

I know very little detail of my father's early life. He told us the occasional story, but what I've come to realise is that the thin young boy I saw in photographs was academically bright.

A natural at maths, he passed what I assume to have been the eleven plus, an exam you used to take at the end of primary school in the British Isles. He then attended Cheltenham Grammar School, which has since become Pates School, one of those incredibly high-achieving institutions that parents fret about getting their kids into.

Due to his mathematical prowess, something I singularly failed to inherit, at an early age, he was picked to be a navigator in the RAF at the outbreak of the Second World War. He sailed to New York in 1941 at the age of nineteen, trained as a co-pilot and navigator in Canada, came back to Britain and joined 192 Squadron, based at RAF Foulsham in Norfolk.

This, I later discovered, was one of the most secretive squadrons in the RAF. 192 Squadron didn't do bombing missions. The crew my father flew with – I met some of them at his funeral – flew night-time incursions into occupied Europe. A Wellington or Halifax bomber flying alone, the bomb bay packed with equipment and scientists trying to work out how German radar worked.

It was a simple solution: they flew into enemy airspace in the hope that a German fighter plane would try and shoot them down. At night, totally dark, freezing cold, in the air for eight or nine hours at a time. They used the equipment on board to try and read the radar signal coming out of the German fighters that seemed to be able to see British bombers in the dark.

The RAF eventually worked out ways to deceive German radar, which was years ahead of anything the allies had at their disposal.

The result of this research was that later in the war, my father, along with quite a few other air crews, would have flown over the English Channel at night dropping millions of strips of silver paper from their planes, which rendered the German radar signal useless, thus letting hundreds of heavy bombers enter enemy territory undetected.

Now, this sounds like he told us a great deal about his wartime experiences. There's me, sitting on his knee when I was five years old, listening to my dad explain what he did.

No, it never happened; he told us none of this.

He would occasionally sit in his special dad chair at teatime and do quite a convincing mime of flying over Germany, making the sound of the four engines on the Halifax, interspersed with the boom of anti-aircraft shells exploding all around. He'd say, 'Flying at twenty-five thousand feet over Bremerhaven with a bomb bay full of boffins.'

None of that meant anything until ten years after he died when I learned what he'd done during a BBC programme I made called *War Hero in My Family*.

The BBC researchers discovered all this information. Reg had signed the Official Secrets Act during the war and never divulged his wartime record, even though the ruling ran out in 1985, thirteen years before he died.

As soon as I discovered from a military historian that my father would have been in a plane crowded with scientists, the term 'bomb bay full of boffins' made total sense.

Of course, I can see now that Reg, with the incredibly intense experiences he'd had as a young man, might have had difficulty when his middle son grew up to be a bit of a long-haired, wishy-washy, fellow-traveller, sandal-wearing, namby-pamby peacenik hippie. It can't have been easy.

Our only method of communication during those periods was humour. He would be out in his beloved vegetable patch, rigorously ordered and weed-free. I'd tease him that the rows of carrot seedlings looked like soldiers of the Third Reich at the Nuremberg rally. He would then obligingly make a Heil Hitler salute and utter the immortal line, 'We fought on the wrong side in the war. That's what this country needs now, a bit of stiff upper-lip discipline.'

Marvellous.

I don't believe my father really did think he fought on the wrong side in the war. I truly hope not.

When he was in his final days, riddled with cancer at the age of seventy-five, I was lucky enough to be able to spend a lot of time with him in hospital.

Once, I was sitting by his hospital bed trying to think of something to say. Out of the blue he told me he was very proud of me. He'd watched me on TV and all his pals at the Witney Conservative Club thought *Red Dwarf* was very funny.

I could not believe my ears. This was the first time he'd ever mentioned *Red Dwarf* or indeed anything I'd ever done professionally. This was literally three days before he died.

I held his hand, the first time I could remember doing that since I was a very young child.

He smiled at me from behind the complex breathing apparatus, then, speaking in short bursts as he was having such difficulty breathing, he said, 'You're a good man. Look after your family, that's what matters.'

'Thanks, Dad,' I said. 'And I'm sorry I was such a pain in the arse when I was a teenager.'

'You were a fucking nightmare, m'lad,' he said with a toothless smile. His teeth were in a steel bowl on his bedside table.

An Afro-Caribbean nurse arrived at the bedside and she chatted and joked with my dad like they were old mates. She made sure he was feeling okay, stroked his bald head gently and smiled at me.

'My son,' said my dad nodding his head towards me. I almost choked up then. He was proud of me, his hideous son, and he was saying this to a black woman. Surreal doesn't begin to describe it.

When the nurse left, he leaned towards me slightly, drugged up to the eyeballs so his speech was a little slurred.

'They're fucking angels,' he said.

My concern must have been visible. I can't remember exactly what I thought, but I assumed he was hallucinating.

'Where?' I said.

'The nurses, you daft bugger. I'm not seeing fucking angels. I'm saying the nurses are fucking angels.'

I laughed. He couldn't, but he smiled.

He was, apart from the casually worn racism and the *Daily Mail* fury at perceived hypocrisy of anyone who wasn't a staunch Tory, a very funny man. He was still joking when I visited the following day when he could barely take a breath.

When I arrived he asked me how my daughter was. Holly was just over a year old at the time and she'd been a little poorly. We didn't know what was up but I told him, 'The doctor thinks it might be German measles.'

'German-*cough*-measles!' he croaked. His frail arm came up in what I immediately recognised as yet another Heil Hitler salute. Then, slowly, he managed to say, with a shallow breath between each word, 'Don't - mention - the - war.'

On his final day, he was in a coma and just lay motionless, breathing very slowly. My mother, brother, sister and I spent the day with him. It was the first time the five of us had been together with no one else present for decades. We talked and joked as we sat on either side of his bed, I've often wondered if he could hear us; it felt like he could.

My mother and I eventually left late that night, leaving my brother and sister to stay with him. I had a young family and needed to relieve my wife of baby care. I was due to return the following morning to take over.

During the journey between the John Radcliffe hospital and my home, about forty-five miles, my dad finally popped his flying boots.

When I got home, Judy told me my sister had just called to say he'd died.

It was like being punched in the stomach, I felt the air leave my body. I flopped down on the knackered old sofa and my kids cuddled up to me. I cried a bit, which fascinated my son, who was then just four years old.

A couple of days later, I was in my writing shed putting the finishing touches to a short speech I was going to read at his funeral. Judy came down from the house with a cup of tea and I read it out to her. I was about halfway through when, once again and to my surprise, I burst into tears. Even as I was crying, I was wondering why this was happening. My dad, who I never really got on with, a man who it seemed had expressed so little interest or care for me, and yet I knew then and can confirm it now, a man I miss every day.

His funeral was funny, though; it would have made him laugh. My dad was very anti-religious – 'a bunch of bloody holier-than-thou sky pilots' would have been his description of a gently spoken vicar – so the service was held at a chapel at the Oxford crematorium. It was packed out; loads of people came to say farewell to Reg, most of them we had never previously met. My dad was clearly a very popular man.

There were lots of old fellows with medals pinned to their suits. One of them was the manager at a local battery hen farm where I'd worked when I was thrown out of school. This man was wearing a beret, had loads of medals on his blazer and sported a big flag which he held throughout the service, standing to attention the whole time.

I read out my speech without blubbing. Just as my father's coffin was wheeled through the curtains at the far end of the chapel, the old soldier holding the flag collapsed. People rushed to his aid and he completely stole the attention away from my dad as he made his final farewell.

He wasn't dead, he'd just fainted, but it was quite dramatic.

As confirmed by many members of the extended family attending, they all agreed Reg would have said something along the lines of, 'Isn't that typical! My big moment and bloody Harry has to steal the limelight.'

I regret not trying harder to mend bridges with my dad when he was alive. I'm sure I could have done more, but if I'm honest,

I doubt he would have opened up and communicated as much as he did in his last hours. What I can say though is he was an incredibly brave man, and he let me remember him without the anger and rejection I'd felt from him for so long. We forgave each other in those last few hours and that has allowed me to carry on without wearing a bitter cloak of resentment for the remainder of my life.

The emotional distance I experienced from my father was something I was determined to avoid when my son was born. I didn't want to be a dad like that, emotionally distant and angry, never revealing my love for my children until I'm on my death-bed.

Oh, how easy that is in theory, and how complex and with such unforeseen consequences in practice. I've been a different kind of dad with my kids but I'm no longer sure I've been a better one.

Three Children, One of Each

The pleasure laundry gives me is difficult to describe, difficult because I am mildly embarrassed by the level of pleasure I experience. It is almost indecent.

Imagine a beautiful sunny day in June, a light breeze and a huge basket of damp washing straight out of the new front-loader.

We used to have an American top-loader. I loved that machine; that baby rocked its way through mountains of family laundry, at least three front-loaders' worth a go. Then it started to rock its way across the floor until it tore its mountings to shreds. Unfixable, relegated to scrap, finished, literally washed out, useless. I don't want to dwell on the symbolism. Sadly missed.

I have to shrug off the fact that I now use a front-loader. It's almost like going from iPhone to Android; it just feels wrong to me. I accept it washes really well and really efficiently and uses less water than the twentieth-century top-loader, but I miss that old industrial muscle.

But whichever machine has done the work, it's the smell of

the resulting laundry that gives me such deep pleasure. I think it's cotton sheets that do the job most effectively.

Freshly drying cotton sheets take me back to one very specific night at the Royal Festival Hall on London's South Bank in the early 1960s. Not an obvious connection, I know. I imagine you were expecting some memory about my mum's apron, her gentle hand on my head as she read me a story, the smell of freshly laundered linen being reassuring, comforting and homely.

No, nothing like that. This memory is about public display, excitement, physical pleasure, mystery and strength, and I suppose inevitably, sex.

It's another one of those memories I feel I can no longer fully trust. Do I have this memory because of the smell? Or do I remember it because I remember the smell having set off the memory in the past, so I am merely remembering the false memory? Has the memory been embroidered to such an extent that the original event is now lost altogether?

Well, I know from family anecdote and historic record that my mother Brenda took me to see Tchaikovsky's *Nutcracker Suite* at the Royal Festival Hall when I was eight years old.

This experience had a very profound impact on me. Not a difficult thing to achieve when my day-to-day life as a child was so humdrum.

Sitting in that vast auditorium next to my mum as the lights went down and the music started was incredibly exciting.

For a start, I had my mother to myself on the trip, a very unusual experience and possibly one of the reasons I remember it so vividly. My brother and sister were absent and I don't know why, I think there may have been another child with us and another mother but I don't recall who.

Here's the question which now intrigues me when I think what my own son was like at the age of eight: what on earth made my mother think taking me to see some classical ballet would be something I'd enjoy? She must have booked the tickets in advance. Did she think even then that I would be 'the one who would like ballet'? And why did she think that? Maybe it was obvious; all I know is it all seemed perfectly natural at the time.

My mother informed me how much I loved it on many occasions afterwards. 'Oh, you adored the ballet. You just sat there good as gold, sweet little lad utterly transfixed.'

I haven't seen *The Nutcracker Suite* since but I've got the music on my phone. It's pretty schmaltzy, isn't it? Not exactly your highbrow ballet pushing the artistic boundaries of current acceptability. I don't know how long it is but I would imagine, having sat through far less demanding fare with my son when he was eight, it's quite a haul.

The ballet struck me in a way I had never experienced before. It was like my dreams: it was the first realisation that other people had dreams like mine.

It was something to do with the innate sensuality of the body, something for which I had no words, other examples or guidance in my family. It would be hard to find two people less in touch with their bodies than my parents. I cannot imagine either of them even knowing what the word sensual meant; they would have had to look it up.

Looking back from the vantage point of maturity, I am

shocked to realise that this skinny little boy with a short back and sides haircut was having such natural sexual fantasies. Literally that: sexual, and in nature.

I remember daydreams of being some sort of semi-naked wild-boy nymph, running through the ancient forest, cavorting on soft moss-covered rocks, stretched and prone with only some kind of chamois leather loincloth for dignity.

Very *Peter Pan*, another play my mother took us to see that also had a long-term influence. The chamois-leather loincloth was essential. It was what Red Indians (1960s speak for Native Americans) wore, and I always wanted to wear one. I knew this from watching the Lone Ranger; his trusty sidekick Tonto was a profoundly erotic figure for me.

Bare-chested warriors with nothing but a bow and arrow and a loincloth.

There was something about the nature of ballet that chimed with me; the shock of seeing others – not kids, these were big grown-ups – having what to me looked like that same pleasure. It was the bodies of the dancers, both the men and women, cavorting about, smelling like newly washed linen that's my strongest memory: really clean people who smelled of freshly washed linen.

I have since pondered if it was the smell of the relatively newly built Royal Festival Hall. It was completed in 1950 and I would have gone there around 1963 or '64 so that doesn't seem likely.

Where would a smell like that come from? It can't have been the ballet dancers themselves as I was too far away to sniff them so that connection remains a mystery.

One particular image has stayed with me: a dancer's back, a woman's, muscular and glistening with sweat, fresh linen sweat. I wanted to be a ballet dancer; I wanted to smell like they did.

Interestingly, in this post-*Billy Elliot* era, I never went to a ballet class and I don't think I even asked if I could, but for years after this trip, every Sunday night I was transported back to that ballet as I climbed into my freshy made childhood bed.

Sunday night was bath night in our very average suburban Northampton household. At this time, very little had changed since the war. Buildings, eating habits, the class system, public transportation, it was the same: dull.

We were a one-bath-a-week family, which now seems mildly disgusting. My present family, being half-Australian, showers or bathes on a daily basis, produces mountains of washing and consumes a hundred times as much water per week as my childhood family did.

The weekly bath was not too deep but very hot, and our beds were changed every Sunday evening ready for the massive weekly wash on Monday, so the smell of clean linen was a pure delight.

There we were, three kids, a barking-mad mother who had been known to wear home-made psychedelic culottes in public, and a deeply repressed, distant, angry and, I now understand, sexually rejected father.

Before I started school, I think I was a relatively happy child, playing in a world of my own, watching my mother bustle around with dusters, laundry baskets or the built-to-last heavyweight Hoover vacuum cleaner as she slogged away keeping house and home together.

One of my favourite pre-school pastimes was dressing up, particularly wearing my mother's dresses and skirts. I must have been allowed to do this, because any step out of line with Brenda could easily result in a rapid and brutal response.

A common occurrence from hearing other people's tales of 1950s childhoods is the 'wait till your father gets home' threat. My mother never had time to use it; she had already thrashed us with whatever was to hand long before my dad even got in the Vauxhall Victor to drive home from the Leicester Permanent Building Society office.

But for some reason, wearing dresses was not seen as a grievous offence. Being an active and (remember the psychedelic culottes) tasteless seamstress, my mother always had offcuts of material available. A brightly printed material bag, housed in a large sewing box, held her collection, which as a pre-school child I would occasionally extract. I would then drape various strips of cloth around myself while I stood in front of her dressing-table mirror. It is now impossible for me to quite imagine what was going through my mind at the time. It was far too early for any obvious sexual overtones; it was just something I felt good about.

What my mother made of this behaviour I can only guess, but it coloured her presentation of me to friends and neighbours.

'I have three children,' she said to Margaret Earl, our soft-spoken neighbour. 'One of each.'

'Oh Brenda, you are so funny,' Margaret responded in mild confusion. I don't remember being offended by this description;

it was repeated many times over the years and was a long-standing family joke but one that seemed to have zero effect on me.

I suppose in those days, if you had a male child who exhibited rather odd behaviour at such a young age, you either tried to beat it out of him or went along with it, and although my mother was not averse to the odd session of violence towards her offspring, she never seemed too worried about my penchant for dressing up like a girl.

When I was around seven years old, I went to a charity children's fancy dress party. Nothing uncommon about that, loads of kids have done the same.

However, I went dressed as the famous nineteenth-century music-hall star Marie Lloyd.

Yes, that's right: Marie Lloyd was a lady, and I was a boy.

Marie Lloyd meant nothing to me then, but I remember my grandmother, who by some accounts started life as a cockney but went a bit posh, singing the famous song to me.

> *My old man said follow the van,*
> *And don't dilly dally on the way,*
> *Off went the cart with me 'ome packed in it,*
> *And I walked behind with me old cock linnet.*

I'm still not sure what a cock linnet is so I looked it up in a dusty old encyclopaedia in my musty old library. Okay, I googled it. A linnet is a small bird in the finch family. There you go.

The whole affair is still a mystery to me. There are moments and events from my early childhood that I can clearly recall as deeply embarrassing, humiliating or belittling, but dressing up as Marie Lloyd is not one of them.

Off I went to the annual League of Pity party in downtown Northampton.

The League of Pity was the children's section of the NSPCC, the National Society for the Prevention of Cruelty to Children, a long-running and fine charity I still support.

My mother was also a keen supporter. She had been a Sunday School teacher in Cheltenham during the early years of the war and remembered the kids who came along to the church hall in winter with no shoes on, the poor kids in an era of even less social security than now.

All through my childhood, we collected money for the charity in these bright-blue moulded cardboard eggs.

Why a blue egg, why 'pity'?

I have no idea now and I certainly didn't then, but the League of Pity party was the gig of the year for me.

I can remember no embarrassment about this event but it's hard not to assume there could have been a certain amount on the part of my mother and particularly my father.

We can look back to the provincial early sixties British Isles and see how rigid people were in their class, race and gender stereotyping, but I think we should give them a break.

A pretty seven-year-old boy who happily goes to a party in a long dress is quite progressive, isn't it?

I remember parading around a large dance floor with all the other children who were sporting a wide variety of fancy dress.

Boys dressed as cowboys, spacemen and soldiers, and girls dressed as bridesmaids, princesses and fairies.

In the centre of the room stood a stern old lady dressed in tweed. I imagine now she would have been a leading light in the League of Pity who was judging us very professionally.

I think I got third prize but I didn't mind: I had a lovely long dress on.

If all this activity was a little bit tough for my mother, it must have been extremely challenging for my fearsomely homophobic father. On one occasion, he discovered me in my parents' ground-floor bedroom trying out my mother's make-up, jewellery and perfume. That episode landed me in some serious trouble. Not so much for the make-up and perfume, more for the self-administered haircut. I had adjusted my early 1960s pudding basin boy's hairstyle with the adept use of my mother's pinking shears.

I think it's fair to say my dad had some issues with homosexuality. He might have referred to them as lily-livered conchies, a reference to conscientious objectors, men who for religious or humanist reasons refused to fight during the Second World War. The implication being that they were a bit fey and 'limp-wristed' and not real men.

An earth-trembling clue to my father's oft-spoken homophobia came many years later when I was walking along the banks of the river Thames with my mum near my parents' home in Oxfordshire.

It was the early 1980s, and I was an independent adult by this time. I had my own car, my own flat and of course my own problems.

I made regular visits to my parental home, relaxing breaks from my slow descent into show business. The path by the Thames at Newbridge was a favourite walk of hers, watching the swans glide past on the muddy water and staring at leisure boats as they chugged along. I had just emerged from another heart-rending romance and was staying there for laundry management and recovery purposes.

'So you've split up with Gill then?'

'Yeah yeah, that's like totally over.'

'Oh dear. She was a nice girl, not one of your regulars, she seemed quite sensible.'

'Thanks, Mum. That's really cheered me up. You should go into relationship counselling.'

'Oh dear, I can't keep up. You've had so many girlfriends.'

'I haven't had that many.'

'Go on. Tell me,' she said, half-resigned. 'How many girl-friends have you slept with?'

'Mum! I can't believe you're asking that!'

As you can see, by this period of her life – she would have been in her early sixties – the subject of sexual activity, when kept at arm's length, was slightly less painful.

'I don't know,' I said eventually. 'I think it's around twenty.'

'Oh goodness, how disgraceful,' she said, facing away from me.

'Well, how many men have you slept with?' I asked.

'One!' she snapped. 'Your father, and that was quite enough, thank you.'

I laughed.

'And how many people has Dad slept with?' I asked, highly amused by the whole subject.

Now she laughed, head thrown back, a slightly manic look in her angry eyes. 'I have no idea, and I don't wish to know about that.'

'Oh wow, we all thought he was having hundreds of affairs,' I said, referring to the many discussions I'd had with my brother and sister on the topic. 'So he must have been.'

I felt I could finally start asking the awkward questions about the mysteries of our family history. I was becoming aware that I had some problems that wouldn't quite leave me. One of them that affects us all is not so much 'where do I come from?' but more 'why do I have to come from here?'

Why was my childhood so stable, clear and straightforward until I was about thirteen years old when it went crazy and unpredictable?

My father lost his job, his permanent job at the Leicester Permanent Building Society.

We've never known why, our father and mother never told us, and now the causes of this disruption have been swept away by the tides of time.

'That must be Dad's big secret though. Was he having an affair when he lost his job?'

'Of course not!'

'Well, what was it then?' I asked in frustration.

'There are certain things I'll take to my grave, my lad,' said my mother haughtily.

'That's so unfair! What happened when Dad lost his job?

It's a total mystery to us. Was it a financial scandal? Did he embezzle millions of pounds?'

'Hardly, look at us now, poor as church mice.'

'Something doesn't add up, Mum. It doesn't make sense.'

'Very little about your father makes sense, my lad. You know that well enough.'

We walked in silence for a short distance and then, unprompted, she said, 'Donkey's years ago, long before we got married, he told me he had once loved another man.'

I stopped in my tracks.

I could not walk another step.

My mother clearly wanted me to know about this. Near zero data, I cannot emphasise enough, barely any information about my parents' personal lives before we were born, or indeed at any time, was revealed to me except this single glowing nugget.

This shining crystal of information opened a door into my father's life that I had never guessed was even remotely there. One, he had actually admitted something to my mother that was so personal and revealing, and two . . .

'You mean Dad is gay?' I shouted.

'Of course not,' snapped my mother, now genuinely angry.

She would often catch me out in this manner; her constant criticism of her husband would suddenly switch to a passionate defence of the same man.

'But what does that mean?' I pleaded. 'He once loved another man, what does that even mean?'

'He was in the Venture Scouts, before the war. I don't know, there was another boy, he never really explained.'

'Bloody hell, my dad is totally gay!' I shouted at a passing swan.

'Ssh,' said my mother. She too had spotted the swan looking at us. It kept near us as if it was listening. My mother lived in a small village, and news travels fast.

My father once loved another man.

In the coded language of the period, does that mean he had sex with another man? Or he just fell in love? Something that was tantamount to insanity in the period just before the Second World War.

I never found out anything more. I knew then, and I was right, that it was not something I could casually bring up in conversation.

There's my dad in the vegetable garden weeding between his brassicas. I've just brought him a cup of tea.

'There you go, Dad. So, yeah, um, Mum tells me you were a bit on the gay side back in the old Venture Scout days, yeah?'

No, that conversation was never going to happen.

I have a photograph of my father as a young man, probably about eighteen years old, sitting with a lot of other slim, young, hard-faced lads, all of them wearing the uniform of the Venture Scouts.

The pack leader, a man in his fifties, sports a toothbrush moustache, very much like Adolf Hitler's. This scrawny-looking fellow is, like all the other younger lads, wearing shorts, his legs are bony.

I just can't believe it's him. Who knows? Only my dad, and I can't ask him. It's not that impossible, the older man seducing an eighteen-year-old isn't unheard of, in fact it's probably quite common. It's the way my father had described it that's intriguing.

It's the sentence my mother used – could that really have been what he actually said?

'I once loved another man.'

Even the act of writing that sentence makes me feel I'm way off the mark. That is not the sort of thing the man I knew, my dad Reg, could possibly have said.

So yes, it would have been impossible to bring up the subject when he was alive and anyway, what good would it have done?

So with a dad who was potentially at least bisexual, or who might have been gay in a more recent period of history, and a mother who at the mere mention of the word sex or indeed any reference to it would shudder and order you to shhhh, the question that used to bother me was this: am I like my dad, always falling in love with women but not being very good at it because I was repressing deeply buried homosexual desires?

I know parents can't make their children gay, in just the same way as a gay teacher isn't going to brainwash his or her pupils into being gay.

It's important to understand my mother's activities in this regard – the Marie Lloyd fancy-dress event etcetera – were specifically focused on me. My brother Peter was a proper boy. He never wore dresses or showed any inclination to do so. He played rugby, he liked cars, he rode motorbikes, he was much bigger than me and much stronger.

My sister was a proper girl, she was pretty with thick golden curls, she loved dresses and dolls and I suppose stereotypically girl things.

This is the question I've found myself asking in later life: which came first, the boy who liked wearing dresses or the mother who encouraged him?

A phrase I once saw scrawled on the wall in a public toilet in the 1970s made me laugh. Scratched into the gloss paint on the cubicle wall was the legend: 'My mother made me a homosexual.' Under which was written in different colour felt tip and contrasting lettering: 'If I give her the wool, can she make me one too?'

I have had several gay male friends whose experiences with their mothers sounded not that dissimilar to mine. My mother was a bright, inquisitive, creative and deeply angry woman. I now think this anger came from unfocused frustration at the strictures of her upbringing and class, and the expectations put on her.

Wife and mother, charity worker, hobby painter, choir member, amateur potter, fairly bad cook. That was about it, that's all she was allowed to do.

She routinely used the word 'livid' to describe her feelings, and she was generally livid about something. As children, we were all wary of her when she was livid.

This is not to dismiss her gentle side, because she was also affectionate and concerned for all her children. I never felt unloved, far from it. I felt a bit overwhelmed by her love and it's this experience that chimed with some gay men I have discussed this with.

I had a very close and complex relationship with my mum: in some ways it was a burden, it fostered guilt and anxiety, it was uncomfortable and made me want to hide or run away.

I suffered many 'apron strings' comments from girlfriends who could sense how close we were.

I can understand in some ways why it happened. My genuine interests in history, reading, writing, art, the theatre all matched my mother's lifelong passions.

We talked a lot when we spent time together. When I visited the family home as an adult she would have long lists prepared for my arrival, handwritten lists of things she wanted to tell me, and I'd have to sit down at the kitchen table with a cup of tea and listen as she worked her way through the list.

I received a handwritten letter from her almost every day from the time I left home in 1972 to when she died in 2001.

That is, dear reader, a lot of letters.

I wrote long letters to her, especially if I was travelling. Probably two or maybe even three a year.

So did they think, when I was a little lad, that I might be the 'other way'? Did they worry about it at all, or am I projecting my early confusion on to them?

There may be a clue to some sort of discussion having taken place between my mother and father because it was shortly after the Marie Lloyd incident that we went on a trip that was very likely a conscious parental attempt at steering me in the right manly direction.

One cold winter's evening my mother took my brother Peter and me to the Royal Tournament at Earls Court in London.

The Royal Tournament was a dramatic display of Britain's remaining post-colonial military might. It was a good move on my parents' part. There were marching soldiers, military music, motorbikes jumping through flaming hoops. Teams of strong marines raced against each other to strip down an old field gun, lash its various components to ropes, swing them across a makeshift bridge, put it back together again and fire three rounds.

But the bit I loved the best were the big Scottish marching bands.

Picture the scene: the huge arena in Earls Court was empty, just wisps of smoke from the last demonstration of British firepower slowly curling towards the cavernous roof.

The commentator, who in my memory was a man called Raymond Baxter who presented *Tomorrow's World* on the BBC, explained that we were about to experience the glory of the Scottish regiment of such and such.

Offstage, and for the first time in my life, I heard those bagpipes start winding up. Even for a wet, middle-of-the-road pacifist like me, that's a pretty evocative sound. The hairs on the back of my little neck stood on end. The rhythm of the snare drums kicked, in and into the arena marched a hundred soldiers, all wearing kilts.

Big tough men with big thick legs, their kilts and sporrans swinging from side to side as they marched.

I loved it. I could not stop thinking about those big brave men in their kilts, the bagpipes, the drums, and the sheer spectacle of their marching.

I have since seen similar Scottish marching bands at the Edinburgh Tattoo when I've been working at the Fringe Festival, my response hasn't changed.

It would have been only days later I stood in the small

kitchen, my mother washing the perpetual dishes of childrearing, when I said, 'Mum, I need a kilt.'

It's not hard to imagine a mother of that era with zero Scottish heritage being asked this by her son and responding negatively, or even with some hostility. Maybe if she were a kindly and empathetic soul, she might squat down to the child's level and gently explain that if he wasn't Scottish and if he continued to want to wear things like kilts, other boys would make fun of him.

None of this happened, she just made me a kilt.

She made it out of a piece of actual tartan she bought especially. This was no half-baked creation made from off-cuts from her sewing box, this was the real thing.

It was sewn together on her old hand-cranked Singer sewing machine, it had a proper waistband, pleats, everything save the sporran.

I was thrilled to bits with it.

It felt so good to wear, and whatever else may have been read into my desire for a kilt, I knew it was nothing to do with wanting to dress like a girl. I wanted to dress like those amazing soldiers with the bagpipes and the drums, I wanted to march proudly, I wanted to be the man at the front of the brigade with the big white stick, head held high.

I can still recall the feeling I had when I first wore my new kilt. I felt proud and very male. It just wasn't a girl-type feeling; soldiers wore kilts for God's sake, I'd seen hundreds of them marching. A kilt was a boy thing.

My father, rugger fanatic, Freemason, member of the local Conservative association, might have had a slightly difficult time with the whole 'Don't worry, it's a male thing for your son to wear a kilt' notion. I don't remember him commenting on my kilt one way or the other, and it's only now I wonder how he dealt with it.

I suppose somewhere I'm still trying to reassure my father that wearing a kilt was an okay thing for his son to do at the age of seven.

Listen: men who wear kilts look very cool. It just helps if you are Scottish, then you can be fierce, proud, hate the English, be treated very well by the French, have a world-class legal and educational system, an incredible landscape of mountains, islands and big skies, have a very progressive attitude to renewable energy but live in an often unspeakably cold part of the world where the population once had the highest sugar intake per head of any country on the planet. They may still, I haven't checked.

So I was a dress-wearing, kilt-adoring, 'sensitive' child. I didn't engage in fighting with other boys, I avoided football as if it were a disease and only went fishing once.

I loved playing with my sister's doll's house and helping her to decorate it, pasting bits of old wallpaper on the walls and used Sellotape to stick bits of cloth over the windows to make curtains.

To balance the image I'm painting here, I did do a bit of tree-climbing and built numerous dens and hideouts in our garden. I rode bikes through muddy puddles and even dug impressive and terrifying tunnels under my father's vegetable patch.

This was after seeing the legendary war film *The Great*

Escape, which I loved. My dad took me and my brother. If there was one thing we could get our father to talk about, it was a general history of the Second World War.

He knew everything about it.

After I'd seen *The Great Escape*, I set about recreating the escape tunnels the allied prisoners dug, although I didn't bother to spread the resulting dirt around the garden using specially adapted trouser pockets.

This tunnelling was enhanced by a biological tunnel-boring machine named Spot, the family Labrador. I devised a cunning method of tunnelling and I'm very proud of this, I think it shows remarkable ingenuity for a ten-year-old.

First, I dug a hole in the ground, not that deep but deep enough for a ten-year-old to jump down into and not be seen.

Then, to one side I started to gouge out a long, narrow bore hole with a garden trowel. I then teased Spot the dog with a fresh bone from the local butcher, I made sure he was fully aware of its crunchy, marrow filled freshness. With Spot watching intently, his tail wagging with delight, I shoved the bone as far down the bore hole as I could reach with my spindly arm.

He'd then shove his massive snout at the hole, inhale deeply and start digging like the crazed beast he was. If there was something to eat anywhere near this powerful pooch, he would stop at nothing to get it. As he was slightly bigger than me, the resulting hole he created was plenty big enough.

This digging system was repeated until the resulting tunnel was terrifyingly long.

Spot did get the bone in the end – I wasn't that cruel, okay?

The hardest part for me was getting the spoil out of the hole and spreading the mass of earth, sand and rock around 'the children's garden' that our mother had put aside for us.

I loved going down this small tunnel. It smelled so special and exciting. Damp earth, roots from the weeds and plants growing overhead dangled from the roof of the tunnel. It was magical and secret. It was also extremely dangerous and made even my mother slightly nervous.

'What if it caves in?' she asked when she finally had a look at the sheer scale of the project.

This hadn't occurred to me. Having a more than capable imagination, I then imagined being crushed by the weight of the earth and rock above me, unable to escape, doomed to die in the damp, dark tunnel.

That put a bit of a crimp on the project but I remember spending hours down there, imagining Nazi soldiers walking above trying to find me.

It did cave in that winter, possibly due to a heavy frost, but thankfully I wasn't in it at the time.

My father noticed that his perfectly level, militarily ordered vegetable patch suddenly dipped along one edge. This was where the tunnel ran and that's when the trouble really started. My parents had no idea of the true extent of my digging, or, to be fair, Spot's digging. The tunnel was about 15 metres long but only maybe 100 centimetres under the surface.

I'm not sure to this day if I was in trouble because of the obvious mortal danger of such childish activity, or the fact that my dad's veggie patch suddenly had a big dip in it.

So, apart from the interest in the military and tunnelling, there were ample signs in my youth that my genuinely nuclear, genuinely middle-class and provincial family had produced yet another gay young man.

By the time I reached my early teens, being gay was the height of fashion. Legalisation of male homosexuality was passed the year I turned twelve and the Gay Liberation Front sounded like a lot more fun than the International Marxist Group or the Workers Revolutionary Party.

So clearly, even with her quip 'I have three children, one of each', my resulting sexuality had nothing to do with my mother's behaviour or decisions.

Clearly there was something in me that was, I suppose, a little unusual. I didn't fit easily into the role defined by my gender. I could argue that the foundation was there for a long life of homosexual bliss, except one vitally important aspect.

There's no polite way of introducing this theory.

It's all about the cock.

I loved the accoutrements of gayness: the dress codes, the mannerisms, the wit, the innate ability to shock the rest of society.

I just wasn't interested in other men's lower parts.

I liked gay men well enough, I enjoyed being with them, they made me laugh. On occasion, they even flattered me and made me feel mildly attractive but I was never interested in taking it further.

I loved girls, I was always falling in love with girls. I was scared of them, confused by them, intrigued by them, and their bodies, their mannerisms, their grace held me spellbound.

It was many years later when Chris Eymard, the man who really was my gay best friend, finally explained it to me in a pithy one-liner. This was during yet another conversation about how a man like me, an occasionally camp and fey man, could be heterosexual.

'Oh, don't worry about it, dear. It's simple: you like cock, but only one, your own.'

It was so simple for him. He was gay and he loved 'the cock' as he referred to it.

Chris was the first and indeed only man I have ever known who I felt understood me completely. He died far too young and I will always miss him. I will explore my relationship with Chris later but he was a truly amazing man. He died of pneumonia, peacefully in his sleep, aged fifty-two. He didn't have AIDS, as many might have assumed, but he did drink more than any other human being I've ever met, and that, apparently, isn't terribly good for you.

But that was the moment, back in the 1980s, that I finally understood I was wholly heterosexual and I've been happy about it ever since.

My mother died on 6 November 2001. I was alone with her when she passed away, sat by her bed holding her hand. It was one of the most peaceful things I've ever experienced. She had, according to Carol, my first girlfriend, who was working as a ward sister at the John Radcliffe Hospital in Oxford, 'cancer of everything'.

She had been unconscious for a couple of days and I'd managed to spend a lot of that by her bedside. I had been reading to her, articles from her beloved *Daily Mail* – why oh why did my mother read that wretched publication? But she did.

I also read her some of the script of *Red Dwarf, The Movie* which I had been given by Doug Naylor, the genius behind the long-running TV series. We had been due to shoot the movie that year and so this script-reading was rather exciting. I wanted to share it with my mum.

When I finished, I put the script down and held her warm hand; she was incredibly peaceful, breathing so slowly it was hard to tell if she'd stopped. I sat back in the low chair beside her bed and I must have nodded off, then something woke me with a start.

I knew, instantly, that she had passed away. Her body, while visually just the same as it had been for the previous couple of days, was empty. She had gone. It was, as I'm sure anyone who's experienced similar will testify, a mysterious and indeed wondrous experience. The body on the bed wasn't my mum; it was just a dormant body.

I rang my brother, and as I explained what had happened, I started crying uncontrollably; however, there was also an element of gratitude that, unlike my dad, she had decided to move on when I was with her.

My brother and sister arrived later that day and spent some time alone with her. Once again her funeral was very popular – there's no other way of describing it. The small village church in Standlake where they lived was packed to the walls, and the wake in Standlake village hall was likewise full of people who clearly adored my mum.

There are still times when I'm working in the garden or out walking in the woods when I'll recall something she said to me, a phrase or silly wordplay that used to amuse her. Or worse, when I see something and want to tell her about it.

Can't do that any more.

From Youthful Vigour to Podiatry

I occasionally visit a podiatrist in a small treatment centre at one side of a public library in Winchcombe, a nearby market town. Although this podiatrist lives in a picturesque Cotswold town, she comes from Manchester and for some reason I find her accent reassuring. She's down to earth, she knows about feet and she's not afraid of them. She just grabs them and wrenches them about in a vigorous manner.

I started to see her when walking became increasingly painful. Her explanation as to why this happened was simple: 'You've got one leg longer than the other and you've been walking too much.'

To discover you're lopsided after almost sixty years is a bit of a surprise. To be fair to my old legs, there's only about a millimetre difference in length.

I'm not loping about with one built-up shoe, but apparently this length discrepancy was what had been causing me trouble. Essentially one foot hits the ground a little sooner and harder than the other.

So, I discovered, I walk too much, so much in fact that the arch on my left foot collapsed.

I'm not going to lie, it didn't look attractive; it looked positively alien. Almost as if you had made a human shin and foot out of plasticine and left it out in the sun. It had kind of sagged and keeled over a bit.

I must do daily exercises to alleviate the damage I've done to my left foot. Stand on the bottom step, relax down so you stretch the calf muscles, then push up on your toes as high and for as long as you can. Repeat until you are bored rigid, every day.

Then I have to stand with a bit of broom handle under my arch, making sure the heel and toe are touching the ground. The pain this causes is so high on the agony scale it's almost pleasurable. When I do those exercises I feel a little bit *Fifty Shades*-ish.

I asked the Mancunian podiatrist how long I'd have to continue with this regime. Stupid of me, I should have known.

'For the rest of your life,' she said flatly as she washed her hands.

When I was in my twenties, I had plenty of accidents, minor scrapes, pulled muscles, strained tendons, all the usual. I'd hobble about for a few days and then I'd be better. My body seemed to repair itself and I didn't pay much attention.

Now, when some bit goes wrong it stays wrong, and you have to accept that you'll spend the rest of your living days 'treating' the complaint.

It would be all too easy to slip into self-pity. When you're young and receive a minor injury, your mates are interested, your mum might be concerned, you may even receive sympathy and emotional support from your girlfriend.

When you're getting on a bit, and particularly in the case of old men's feet, no one wants to know. I fully understand, I don't want to know either.

Old men's feet are hard to love but that's nothing compared to old men's bottoms. What's that about? What is going to happen to my once pert and muscular arse cheeks?

Whenever I see a naked old bloke in the Turkish baths I occasionally frequent, I can't help checking their buttocks. You may put this down to a particularly unusual perversion, but I assure you there is no sexual element in this fascination.

I just don't understand how what was once a naked man's best feature, one which I know some women and indeed men admire, ends up looking like a flat box-shaped lump of dappled flesh with a slit down the middle.

It's not a good look, simple as that.

On occasion, I've nearly put my back out while twisting in front of a mirror trying to see if my arse has turned into one of these sad flat sacks of dappled flesh.

I do still have actual buttock cheeks, but what I like to imagine is a lean toned body is actually a formless slab sagging above what was once a waist. I have no waist, just a straight line from my hip bones to my armpits.

What happened to my shape, to my exquisite da Vinci muscle tone, the beautiful form of the naked male?

Forget it, pal, an overstuffed Rubenesque Greek god lying on a bed of vine leaves with a massive stomach, that's as good as it gets.

But at least I'm clean. I like being clean so much that my wife thinks I wash too much.

She hates the way I wash my hands. 'It looks like you are trying to wash away sin,' she says in a tone that can only come from a lapsed Catholic.

'My main ambition now I'm sixty is not to smell of piss,' was how the comedian Arthur Smith once expressed his attitude to the ageing process. I have since seen a recording of Billy Connolly making the same wish on an old episode of *Parkinson*. I think this is a very fine ambition and one the rest of society should applaud and encourage.

This is mainly down to the fact that over the next twenty years the vast bulk of the population in the UK is going to be a bit old. I just read that every five seconds thirty-two people in the UK turn sixty-five, so surely having the maximum number of us not smelling of piss is a positive move.

It's also not that hard to achieve; a little bit of care while urinating can go a long way in reducing unpleasant odours. It just takes a bit longer and you have to wait, you have to be patient. There is no question: such a run-of-the-mill, everyday activity takes a little longer as the years pass.

My fellow *Red Dwarf* crewman Craig Charles expressed a related concern when he turned fifty. We were both using the gents at Pinewood Studios and he said, 'I never had to push before, Bobby, now I'm in here for ten minutes!'

Of course, we all told him the obvious. 'Get your prostate checked.' I don't know if he has, I must remember to ask him, but if he's like me he will have 'a healthily enlarged prostate' which, I've been assured, is 'nothing to worry about in a man your age'.

This was how a wonderful doctor explained things to me as

he withdrew his finger and discreetly deposited the thin blue glove in the bin.

I've had my prostate prodded a few times. I'm not selfish about it, quite a few different doctors have been there over the years. But the doctor who loved ending every sentence with the phrase 'for a man your age' stays in my memory.

The experience of the blue-gloved finger up the jacksie took place in a reassuringly spotless health centre in suburban Brisbane, Australia.

A full medical was my fifty-fifth birthday present from my very Australian wife.

Her entire family agreed this was just about the best birthday present anyone could receive. I was slightly baffled. As far as I knew I wasn't sick; in fact, at the time I felt in the very bloom of health. My left foot hadn't yet collapsed; my lower back hadn't yet gone ping one morning, leaving me incapacitated for three days. I wasn't overweight; I went running regularly and ate a healthy and varied diet.

Why did she want me to have a medical? Did she know something I didn't?

For those of you who haven't experienced a full medical, especially an Australian full medical, it's not a particularly relaxing experience.

After filling in a form and answering a few basic questions, I was asked to remove my shirt. The operatives attached a great many sticker sensors to my chest, each with a fine wire leading to a small box that was attached to a belt around my waist. I stood on a treadmill, a standard treadmill like they have in a regular gymnasium.

A clear plastic mask was then fitted over my nose and mouth, and a tube went from the mask into a machine that stood to one side.

The operatives started the treadmill and I ran at a comfortable speed for five minutes, although having all the gubbins stuck to my chest and the breathing apparatus strapped to my face was a bit cumbersome.

'Okay, are you ready to begin the test, Robert?' said the charming operative. I thought I'd already done the test but they weren't satisfied.

They adjusted the treadmill so it was on maximum incline. It was seriously steep. In all the times I'd used a treadmill in dozens of gyms around the world I didn't know they went that steep. It felt almost vertical, every step was horrendous and exhausting, within seconds I was wheezing like a retired miner with emphysema.

Before long, I started to lose my vision. I couldn't see anything but red, and when you're running up a hill that can be a little disconcerting.

'Keep going as long as you can, Robert,' came a jovial and calm Australian voice over the sound of pounding feet and rasping breaths.

I soon collapsed in a tangled heap on the floor, ejected by the cruel spinning non-slip mat.

Once I had recovered, I sat down in a sunlit consulting room opposite a charming Australian doctor who was sat behind a desk, looking at my results.

'Okay, Robert, nothing unusual or alarming to report from any of your tests.' He glanced up at me and almost smiled.

'Your blood pressure is slightly below average, which is not a bad thing for a man your age . . .'

I know how old I am! I wanted to shout, but obviously being English I didn't say anything.

'You have a healthily enlarged prostate, nothing to worry about, it happens . . . in a man your age.'

Thank you.

'You did just over nine minutes on the incline running test, that puts you in the top third fitness band . . . for a man your age.'

Suddenly, I was well chuffed. I was the scrawny kid who hated sport, I was the hunchbacked hippy loser who smoked roll-ups and took no exercise other than riding a bike, and I was in the top third fitness band, okay, even for a man my age.

'We had a chap in yesterday, older than you, he was sixty-seven. He did twenty-eight minutes on the same test. I'm just telling you this so you can put your own achievement in context.'

'Thank you,' I said.

Typical, you build a chap up, and just when he's feeling a bit self-confident and smug, you smash him down again.

If what he told me was true, if a sixty-seven-year-old really had run on that torture device for twenty-eight minutes, I was screwed. I knew in my guts that even if I trained every day for a year, went on massive detox diets and focused entirely on my health and fitness, I might have been able to achieve ten minutes, maybe even twelve.

But twenty-eight! Never.

The doctor turned the page on my notes, ran his finger along a line of text and said, 'Now tell me, Robert, I assume you've been on a programme?'

That threw me. I didn't see that one coming.

Some TV shows I've made have been broadcast in Australia, *Red Dwarf* has been on the ABC for many years and *Scrapheap Challenge* was on a cable channel, but he said 'a programme' so I didn't know which one he meant.

'I've been on a few,' I said hesitantly, 'which one do you mean?'

The doctor looked slightly alarmed. 'You've been on a few!' he asked with some surprise. 'Would you like to tell me which ones?'

I listed some of the more popular TV shows I'd appeared on. I didn't want to come over like I was showing off but he stopped me in mid-flow.

'No, Robert, I mean the AA, Alcoholics Anonymous. Commonly referred to as the programme. The twelve steps, have you heard of that?'

'Oh, blimey,' I said. 'Sorry, of course, yeah, yeah, sorry. No, I don't think they'd want me to join.'

There was a short silence. Eventually, the doctor said, 'I see, because I notice there's no trace of alcohol in your blood. Usually, for a man your age, that means you've had to stop drinking because it was a problem for you, hence my question.'

'Oh, right, I understand.'

'Our tests are sensitive enough to discover traces of alcohol that have been consumed in the last two months. You've got nothing.'

I scratched my head. 'I'm sure I drank some wine last year,' I said. 'Not a whole glass, but more than a sip.'

'So you're not a regular drinker?'

'No, I never have been,' I said.

'Well, it might be worth trying,' said the doctor. There was slight admonishment in his tone as if he was telling me to give up smoking.

The tone confused me. Here was a man who clearly put supreme health above all else. You could be depressed, psychotic, riddled with guilt and self-loathing, emotionally repressed and angry, but just so long as you kept slim and fit you'd be fine with this fellow.

Now he was telling me to drink alcohol. 'Just a glass of red wine a day, in the evening, with a meal. From all the research into the area it's clear that it won't do you any harm and it might do you some good. Make an effort, give yourself a glass of red wine every evening.'

After the session was over I sat in the baking sun outside a Queensland cafe and felt wonderful. It was mid-March and it was hot. When you come from the northern hemisphere, that alone is a result.

For the first time in years I knew I didn't have cancer, my prostate was healthily enlarged, my blood pressure was marginally lower than average – not dangerously high as it is with so many men my age.

I was also at the very bottom of the top third fitness band and I had to make an effort and start drinking red wine every day.

This state of bliss lasted at least three days until I was convinced I had skin cancer on one ear and my lower back was giving me spasms. Since that heady peak of fitness, it's been a slow downhill hobble as I rattled through the door of the sixties.

As a young man, fitness wasn't something I ever considered. The whole notion of being fit, of taking part in team sports, was utterly foreign to me. No one I knew or socialised with played football, tennis or went jogging. I couldn't swim until I was thirty-seven and the only exercise I got was from riding a bike.

I did that quite a lot. In fact, I cycled for miles without a second thought.

I ate badly, anything that was available. I tried being a vegetarian, but it didn't last. I tried eating a macrobiotic diet but I couldn't maintain the discipline.

I went to a yoga class once but the teacher very politely asked me to leave. She explained I was distressing the other attendees with my grunting noises.

My wife Judy is a yoga fanatic. Apparently, she's really good at it, although I've never seen evidence of this first-hand. She has never once, in the thirty years we've been together, encouraged me to join her in a yoga class.

'You'll make too much noise. Everything's a drama with you, I couldn't bear listening to the noise.'

Thank you, darling.

I have done some physical fitness classes. In the early eighties, I became a regular attendee at Capoeira classes. For those of you not hip and man-bunned enough to know what Capoeira is, it's a form of Brazilian martial art which looks a bit like dancing and is incredibly difficult to do.

It involves a lot of lunging about and carrying out slow cartwheels and sweeping leg movements against your opponent, although you never make physical contact when you're training.

You must stretch for ages before you begin as every move in Capoeira requires you to put your limbs into positions you never knew they would go.

After each session I could barely walk, and the following day I felt like I'd been run over by a truck, but I kept going because some of the women who attended were jaw-droppingly beautiful and mind-numbingly flexible.

Once again, I made a lot of groaning and complaining noises in these classes but the whole thing was a bit more aggressive and loud so no one seemed to mind.

After my six-month Capoeira fad, I started going to *commedia dell'arte* classes at the Pineapple Dance Studios in Covent Garden.

The ancient and honourable tradition of *commedia dell'arte* is a form of very structured dance and movement that is the bedrock of many stage performers' ability. Charlie Chaplin is often cited as a great example of someone with a *commedia dell'arte* background. I have no idea if that's true but it's a tale many *commedia dell'arte* practitioners like to claim.

Started in Italy in the sixteenth century, it's all a bit twee but I know it had a large influence on my movements and positioning onstage. Not in a clunky, conscious way – it just imbued me with an understanding of how to communicate with an audience, the confident physicality that makes an audience feel relaxed, which is about 55 per cent of a performer's role.

If Nigel Planer ever reads that sentence he will swear I stole it from *I, an Actor*, his brilliant piss-take of self-important thespians and their 'art'. However, I have to live with the embarrassment that I didn't nick it from him and it's a genuine expression of the experience. Yes, it imbued me with an under-standing of how to communicate with an audience.

Oh my Lord, on second reading, the true embarrassment is revealed. I can't deny it, I wrote that without a second thought, I really did think that thought. The alt-right commenter on a *Daily Telegraph* review of a TV show I made who described me as a 'self-obsessed luvvie' was absolutely right. That's me that is.

Whatever, I can't cry over spilled self-aggrandising narcissism. I loved doing *commedia dell'arte* classes and it was one thing I stuck at for a long time.

Yes, some of the young women attending were rather gor-geous, but for the first time in my life I didn't keep going because of them. The teacher was a very petite old man who was charming and patient, particularly with me. He had to be, I had the coordination and physical subtlety of a recently weaned puppy. I was all over the place and would very often lose my balance during a simple little routine and fall on the floor.

It is possible, I suppose, and it has been suggested to me on occasion, that I have mild dyspraxia. When I looked up the complaint many years ago it did all feel rather familiar, poor hand–eye coordination, as in if someone threw a ball at me I would be very unlikely to catch it. I trip on stairs, bang my head on anything remotely near it, lose my balance for no apparent reason, bash my shins on things that everyone else seems able to avoid.

Going to *commedia dell'arte* lessons really helped me focus on my body's movements. I started to fall over less often, I started to have a greater awareness of the space around me, I stopped accidentally bashing into the delightful German woman who stood next to me in the class and didn't want to go for a coffee with me afterwards.

Yes, I did ask, in a fumbling and rather pathetic way, and she declined with style and charm.

Then I met Sonia.

Sonia was from an Italian–French family, which is an invigorating and challenging combination. A searing French intellect and Italian passion do not tend to make for a relaxing life.

At the time we met, she had her hair cut very short. I say very short, it had just started growing back because she had previously been regularly shaving her head. In this post-Sinéad O'Connor world, the sight of a woman with a shaved head is nothing to report, but it was quite shocking in the early 1980s.

Her brutal hairstyle was something to do with a radical theatrical production she'd been directing in Berlin. All the performers, men and women, had shaved their heads.

I never saw the production but it all sounded terribly brave, challenging, gritty, urban and German.

Sonia was a fitness freak, and she actually got me to go to a gym for the first time. She lifted weights and did sit-ups, I couldn't do anything and it all hurt so much I was rapidly overwhelmed by pain and regret.

The day after my first gym session was even worse: I couldn't even get out of bed. Every fibre in my body screamed with pain. Sonia had managed to make me work muscles that had clearly been dormant since birth.

My legs were strong from cycling but that was a curse because Sonia encouraged me do squats with a barbell resting on my shoulders. Yes, I could do the squats but that resulted in me being unable to walk the following day.

It seemed such an odd thing to do, to punish your body for no apparent reason other than to maybe 'look good'. I didn't feel better afterwards, I felt physically sick.

Then Sonia took me to see a film called *Pumping Iron*.

For those of you who haven't benefitted from seeing this groundbreaking documentary, it follows the build-up to an utterly bizarre and nonsensical event: the Mr Universe competition in the USA in the 1970s. The documentary introduced a man called Arnold Schwarzenegger to the world. In the movie Arnold wins the Mr Universe competition for something like the tenth time.

A large section of the film features pumped-up men lifting what looked like train axles with enormous veined arms as they screamed in pain.

It was a complete revelation to me: these men had bodies that were at the same time absurd and unwieldy and yet strangely beautiful.

It must have been a meme at the time: the writer and broadcaster Clive James described Schwarzenegger's body as 'looking like a condom stuffed with walnuts'.

But I was hooked. I wanted to try and do a bit of that. I'd always been the puny, stick-thin kid with spindly arms; I wanted to be pumped-up and butch, butch being an old-fashioned term for 'hench'. Yes, this was long before I realised I'd be better off as a regular bloke. I was trying too hard to become something I'm clearly not and I wasn't very disciplined about it to start with.

However, other stuff happens to your body apart from the pain, you start to get a rush off it. I started going to the gym regularly, I started working out with other men who were three times my size.

Slowly, and much slower than the adverts in the back of American comics tell you, and without supplements or steroids, my body started to fill out a bit.

I started to put on weight for the first time in my adult life. Muscle is very heavy. I didn't have an ounce of fat on me but I gained over four kilos.

The downside was that I felt heavy and I didn't know what to do with my arms when I went to bed. They felt big and awkward. If I lay on one side my arm would be in the way.

Because of the strength of my legs I became an obsessive squatter; that is, I would pull my weight-lifter's belt super tight around my waist, sling a massive barbell over my shoulders and perform squats.

These would be very hard but I was amazed I could do them; however, once again the result was a little shocking. For the first time in my life my inner thighs started to rub together, the bulk of muscle was such that it filled in the gap between my legs.

But I did feel different: I slept well, ate like a horse and had a distressingly increased libido.

On that more delicate topic, it was also around this time I worked on a sitcom script with Ruby Wax. I'd known Ruby for a few years from the comedy circuit but got to know her better when working on *Red Dwarf* with her amazing husband Ed Bye, who directed the first six *Red Dwarf* series.

She once made a slightly pointed comment when I awkwardly revealed that I did 'work out a bit'.

Ruby wasn't impressed. 'The thing guys don't realise is, even when they work out a lot, your muscles might get bigger but your head and dick stay the same size, which means they seem smaller. Does that worry you, Robert?'

To be honest, it didn't worry me because even at the peak of my pumped-upness, due to my previous uber-scrawniness I was barely average.

Then, a couple of years later I met my wife, and my pitiful muscular gain achieved after countless hours in the gym was put firmly into context.

She hates me talking about this but when I met Judy she was built like a regular brick shithouse.

There's no other way of describing her physique. Yes, she was a woman, but a woman with a physique. Judy did not have a mere figure, she was pumped, hench, call it what you will, she had arms most men can only dream about, she had shoulders wider than a door.

The reason for this wasn't some vain, body-building obsession. Judy was a circus gymnast and trained every day. Literally every day, seven days a week. She had to or she couldn't perform at night.

She was in Circus Oz, a wonderful company that's still going strong and performs all over the world; think Cirque du Soleil but funnier, more compassionate, with better music and not as pretentious.

More on Judy's circus days coming later, but once we became a regular item I took up my gym junkie-dom with renewed vigour and, just to make things crystal clear, Judy was never impressed.

I gave up smoking and worked out every day. I used all the nervous energy of a newly reformed non-smoker in the gym. I partnered up with a delightful Anglo-Thai man called Angelo who, like Schwarzenegger, was ridiculously over-muscled. He wasn't very tall and when we met he explained that he was training hard to lose muscle mass and weight because his girlfriend didn't like it.

That explanation says everything we need to know about bodybuilding. Straight men might claim they are doing this to be more attractive to women but there is a tipping point where a male body can become a freak of nature, a terrifying vision of over-muscled, skinned-frog-on-a-dissection-table horror.

I'm not saying Angelo was like that, but his body was impressively over-muscled, and I quite understood his girlfriend's distaste. The reason we worked out together was because he was using what he described as 'light weights' to burn off the extra muscle and reduce the girth of his pumped-up enormity.

If you've worked out as much and as successfully as Angelo and you just stop, all that muscle mass turns to fat.

I could just about lift some of the same weights he used and he encouraged me to push harder, go further, do fifteen or twenty repetitions instead of the seven or eight I might do on my own.

The endless pain the day after a workout faded and my ability to complete absurdly heavy repetitions increased, although I still made rather a lot of noise.

There was one embarrassing day when a very pregnant woman was doing a gentle stretching class in a glassed-off section of the gym I attended in London's Covent Garden.

I was doing squats and lunges with huge weights when my groaning, squealing and wailing was so alarming one of the gym instructors came running in to see if the pregnant woman had gone into labour. She hadn't, and I was asked to keep the noise down.

While visiting my parents during this brief period of muscularity, I helped dig out an old apple tree stump in their front garden. Both my mother and father were openly amazed at the transformation. I had always been teased by them for being such a skinny weakling, a stick insect or, as my mother often repeated, 'Looking like a kid on an Oxfam poster.'

Charming and so sensitive. She did a lot of fundraising for Oxfam, which makes this comment all the more baffling.

As I hauled the deep roots of the old apple tree out of the ground with brute force, my mother took a picture. I still have it and it shows a surprisingly muscular man, head down, heaving a large tree stump out of the soil.

I won't deny I experienced a moment of pride when I saw the picture, but it also depressed me. I think I wanted to be lithe and muscular, more like a ballet dancer than Vin Diesel. The picture shows a big bloke, a sweating, grunting, hefty geezer, not a lithe lethal weapon that women fancy. The best I ever got from Judy was, 'You look okay, I s'pose.'

That period of selfish body worship was all too brief. We had children. The self-indulgence of gym visits was over. The heavy muscles turned to just heavy, my belly expanded and, after making another series of *Red Dwarf* around that time, a few less-kind fans commented that Kryten had clearly been downloading rather too much software.

Now I'm properly old and none of that matters, it's a blessed relief. No one expects me to be hench. I suppose I could go crazy, work out every day and try and get my picture on the front of a muscle magazine with the headline 'Ripped at Sixty, Llewellyn Shows Us How'. But it's not going to happen.

It's another advantage to achieving blokedom. My levels of self-consciousness are now so low that, as anyone who's seen me knows, worrying about how I look is really not an issue.

I still go to the gym but only to get the old ticker up to speed. I still use free weights as it helps maintain my balance and co-ordination, something that needs all the help it can get.

I've just taken the wretched dogs out for yet another long walk and my foot doesn't hurt as much so maybe, even at my age, you can repair yourself a bit.

As long as you do the boring exercises, every day, until you die. Lovely.

Half Man, Half Dog

When I was about eight years old, our mum and dad took us on a family holiday to the Lake District. For overseas readers, the Lake District is a small area of semi-mountainous, very beautiful and wild countryside in the north-west of England, home to the legendary Sellafield nuclear reprocessing plant. Oh yes, and that poet bloke, the daffodil one, William Wordsworth, that's the fellow, he lived there, and Beatrix Potter, the Peter Rabbit woman.

Five of us travelled there in a cramped Vauxhall Victor which, as I have discovered from driving one at a classic car rally in 2003, has incredibly unreliable brakes.

It also didn't have seat belts, but what the hell, it was the 1960s.

We stayed at a bed and breakfast on a farm near Helvellyn, run by Farmer and Mrs Bell.

I really do have an appalling memory for events that took place last week or for names of people I met ten minutes ago, but for some peculiar neurological reason I've never forgotten their names or the events at their farm.

The Bells were charming and kind, the food was amazing but the beds were a bit rough. This was the mid-1960s long before Airbnb reviews. They'd never get away with those beds now, one-star reviews all the way.

The head end of my foldaway camp bed was lower than the foot end, this was due to the sloping floor in the old farmhouse bedroom. I dubbed it the 'blood-rush-to-the-head bed', which for some reason my father found highly amusing.

It was a classic middle-class English 1960s family holiday, lots of long walks through endless rain, lunches in greasy spoon cafes in small towns, making stone dams in rushing mountain streams and what seemed like hours sitting in the car with the rain hammering on the roof as we waited, usually in vain, for it to 'brighten up'.

My mother was always convinced it was going to brighten up. Most of my childhood holiday memories are of sunny days, but not the Lake District, not once on this holiday did it brighten up.

Regardless of the weather my memories of this vacation are happy. I loved being on the farm, even though by today's stand-ards it was as rough as guts and very unreconstructed.

Farmer Bell ran a small dairy herd and I got up early each morning to watch him bring the enormous slow-moving cows into the yard for milking.

I loved watching him work, the smell of the warm cows, the battered milking machinery, the huge churns of milk he rolled out of the door ready to be picked up by the milk truck.

Later in the morning I accompanied him as he herded his sheep on the mountain behind the farm. He had a proper sheepdog who instantly responded to his mysterious whistles and rushed around the sheep keeping them tightly packed together.

Soon after we arrived, Farmer Bell warned my parents that we children should be kept away from his sheepdog bitch because she'd just had a litter of pups. She was very defensive and might bite us.

'She won't let anyone near 'em, not even me,' he said.

He explained that his sheepdogs weren't pets, they weren't allowed in the house as they were working dogs.

Now I have no memory of why, or indeed how I got into the barn where the puppies were, but I know I did.

Under some old farm machinery and general farmyard rubbish was a little nest of delightful collie pups. I crawled underneath the old hay bailers and discarded tractor tyres and curled up with them, listening to them grunting and wriggling against each other. They snuffled around my face in that special sniffy puppy way. These pups were so young their eyes had barely opened but they were warm and smelled delightful.

The mother of the tiny pups was with me and seemed perfectly happy, she wagged her tail and licked my hand, I was never scared of her and my only explanation was she must have been able to tell I was no threat.

Meanwhile, outside the barn and unknown to me there was a bit of a panic. I later discovered that my absence had been noticed and my mum and dad were wandering about in the rain shouting my name.

My brother Peter apparently suggested I'd fallen off a cliff or been eaten by wolves, which, and I don't blame him for this, was probably wishful thinking.

Eventually, Farmer Bell found me. As he opened the barn door the collie mother I was lying next to started growling. I have a very clear memory of him gingerly peering over the rusting farm machinery, seeing me with the pups, shaking his head and saying, 'Well, I'll be damned.'

I got in trouble but it wasn't that serious. Eating with your mouth open could result in a severe scolding from my mother but this incident became a funny family story. Farmer Bell expressed the opinion that I must be half dog as no one else could get near the puppies without being bitten.

The gentle collie bitch in the barn allowed me to experience an emotion I'd never known before. I felt special, different, she had allowed me to do something no other human being was able to do, and for an eight-year-old, that's a confidence-boosting experience.

My relationship with dogs has been long, varied and complicated. I've spent many years living without them and I've been quite happy. I've also looked after five dogs at various times and they have annoyed me and brought joy in almost equal measure.

Spot, the thick-necked and unimaginably stupid but affectionate Labrador that dug an escape tunnel for me was our family dog when I was a child. He lived a long time, ending up blind with no ears and back legs that almost dragged behind him as he shuffled and grunted along.

When I was a full-blown hippy in the early 1970s I was bequeathed a small Lurcher puppy called Cabbage. I have no idea why she was called that but she became a great and reliable hound partner.

I had many adventures with Cabbage, some of them recorded in a previous book, *Thin He Was and Filthy-Haired*, and in many respects she was the most reliable, least difficult dog I've ever owned.

Okay, she got pregnant very young and had six adorable pups, but other than that she was very obedient, extremely clever and very faithful. Until she wasn't.

She ended up living on a farm near Skibbereen in south-west Cork, which she made very clear she preferred to my small apartment in central London and I don't blame her.

When I say she ended up there, she had travelled to Ireland with me, hitch-hiking from London to Swansea. She was a great hitch-hiking companion because posh people thought she looked cute and they'd stop for us. If I'd been on my own I wouldn't have stood a chance.

Then, after the ferry from Swansea to Cork – I can't remember what I did with her on the ferry, I imagine she'd have to have been caged in the car decks – she hitch-hiked with me the eighty or so miles to the house my friends lived in.

She seemed very at home on this remote farm and when it was time for me to return to London, she walked down the long drive to the winding lane with me and stood still as I walked away.

This dog had always walked right by my side, regardless of where I was going, but not this time.

'Aren't you coming?' I asked. She put her head down. 'Are

you staying here?' I walked up to her and for the first time in the four years we'd been together she backed away.

I squatted down, gave her a scratch around the neck and stroked her long, thin head.

The wretched animal then turned away and started to walk slowly back up the dusty drive. I shrugged, stood motionless watching her for a while. At one point she turned around, glanced at me then trotted back up to the house. That was the last time I ever saw her.

A few months later, I heard from the people on the farm that she had settled in and seemed very happy. I knew she wasn't enjoying living in the middle of London so our friendship was a passing thing. Bloody clever animal.

Then came Ruffage. Oh Lord.

This ridiculous cross-breed mutt of extraordinary character arrived in my life a few years later.

I remember naming this bizarre-looking creature. He was the colour of a bowl of porridge with a sprinkling of brown sugar on the top so he looked a bit like roughage. Add to that was his endless and very annoying grunty bark that would judder out of him at any sound he wasn't 100 per cent sure about, this suppressed grunt sounded like a 'ruff.'

Ruffage, for those interested in dogs, was what you would call 'a character canine'.

Even people who had no interest in dogs or who had previously rather disliked them, would, for some inexplicable reason, find Ruffage adorable.

I have no idea what his genetic heritage might have been. He had a full-grown Labrador-sized head, very short legs, a long and ungainly body and an unpleasantly large penis.

I'm not saying this for comic effect. Ruffage was a kit of badly chosen parts, some sort of Labrador slash terrier cross, and so nothing quite fitted together. There was no getting around it: the penis was noticeably monstrous for a dog the size of Ruffage.

It just looked wrong and it was always embarrassing.

Due to the very short stature of his bandy legs, the end of his penis was alarmingly close to the ground as he trotted along and he would elicit distasteful looks from passers-by.

His unpleasant genitals usually came to the fore when a kindly old relative of the family would stroke his enormous head as he sat on their feet.

'Oh, isn't he a darling!' said my Auntie Peggy and she scratched him gently behind one of his enormous ears. He would then become, there's no other way of describing it, aroused.

An already unpleasant protuberance would soon emerge as a vile challenge to civilised society, an impossible-to-not-mention red poker revealing the truth that under the gentle pet exterior of a charming doggy lay a rapacious monster with vomit-inducing cravings.

Oh Lord, he was vile. He'd stand up and do canine thrusting in the middle of the room, 'air-shagging', my girlfriend Lee called it. There was no stopping him: if he wasn't sleeping, eating, urinating or defecating, this dog was air-shagging all the time.

Somehow, and I don't think I can be entirely to blame for this as his owner, he was always getting in trouble, always causing stress. It's not that he wasn't obedient if I was paying attention, far from it.

Ruffage would walk by my heel, sit when told to, he had quite good road sense and was clearly a bright animal. I'd only have to whisper words like 'rabbit' or 'walkies' and he would instantly stand up and wag his tail, and by default his penis, even if he'd been deeply asleep moments before.

His main problem was his abandonment issues. You could not leave Ruffage anywhere, even a couple of minutes in a room alone would send him into paroxysms of anxiety. I'm not sure if I was to blame for this particular neurosis or not, it seemed to come with the dog. Something must have happened to him when he was a tiny pup, who knows? As always in these circumstances, blame the mother. We all do.

Sometime in the late 1970s I was visiting a friend who was the proud owner of a 1960 vintage Riley 1.5. Those of you in the know will recall that this car, while similar to the Wolseley 1500 saloon, had twin SU H4 carburettors.

It's a rare classic car now, and even in 1977 it was seriously cool.

Ruffage was happy enough getting in the back. I put an old blanket on the seats to protect them, I told my friend that this was to stop his claws scratching the leather although I knew it was an attempt to stop his repugnant penile secretions from staining anything they encountered.

We drove to his mother's house to pick something up, his mother had cats and was anxious the little doggy would cause mayhem. She was right: Ruffage loved to chase cats so, very stupidly, I left the wretched cock hound in the car.

This wasn't a stupid decision because he'd suffer from over-heating in a car on a summer's day; it was winter, we left the rear window open a fraction and he seemed calm enough.

After a cup of tea in a nice kitchen with half a dozen cats watching us, we opened the front door to discover Ruffage happily engaged in cleaning his nether regions on the doormat. He was out of the car. Had someone let him out? Did he open the door? It made no sense.

'Fucking hell!' shouted my soon to be ex-friend when he saw his beloved Riley 1.5. The completely intact windscreen was lying on the bonnet, not broken, just not joined to the car. Closer inspection revealed the dashboard was badly scratched and the rubber beading that held the windscreen in place was chewed to bits. He had literally torn out the rubber beading that held the windscreen in place. There were tell-tale scratch marks on the interior paintwork around the door pillars and small bits of chewed-up rubber beading all over the interior.

Then, we assumed because the whole affair was so unlikely, he somehow pushed the large sheet of toughened glass forward and made his escape.

Here's the mystery that would be repeated throughout his long and damaging life. At first, we could find little trace of the rubber beading. If you think about it for a moment, windscreens in cars of this period were held in position by a long strip of moulded rubber beading, one side fitting tightly over the steel bodywork, the other over the shatter proof glass.

Holding this rubber beading in place was a further insert of some form of plastic strip that held the beading and windscreen firmly in place, creating a watertight bond.

If you pull that rubber off an old car you will discover it's quite bulky, indeed quite heavy. Now, we did find many small pieces of chewed rubber in the foot well of the classic Riley, but not enough.

Later inspection of Ruffage's copious droppings revealed the truth. He had eaten it.

Now much as I find a little amusement in describing this creature's genitalia, I think a detailed description of his faecal matter is beyond acceptable manners. Let me just say it didn't actually bounce, at least not at first extrusion, but it's not hard to believe if you were of a mind and balled up the offensive material and threw it at the ground, it might fly back at you. You'd be wearing thick protective gloves of course, I'm not imagining doing this with bare hands, ew.

On another occasion, this time at my girlfriend Lee's parents' house, Ruffage was inadvertently locked in the kitchen. It was a momentary mistake, her parents adored Ruffage. Lee's mother, a formidable American, named him 'Bex Bissel' after the popular push-along carpet cleaner of the period. Ruffage spent much of his waking life sniffing the floor for dropped food products.

Ruffage, bless him, had chewed a massive hole right through their recently installed kitchen door and made his way outside.

Apart from the embarrassment, the anger and expense this caused, the big mystery was where all the wood had gone that once made up a fair-sized chunk of door. It was nowhere to be seen. There were flecks of paint on the kitchen floor but no large chewed bits of timber or splinters.

The following morning when I took this beast from hell for

his morning walkies, I took special care to witness his first movement of the day. I have never seen a machine extrude chipboard, in fact I'm confident that's not how it's made, but that's what came out of Ruffage's unpleasantly oversized rear end.

Tubular chipboard, lots of it.

How can any mammal process wood? Okay, it wasn't mahogany, merely pine, but come on. It makes no sense and I'm happy if you find this observation hard to believe, but I know what I saw and also know I wish I hadn't seen it. It's so utterly gross it's not something you can un-see.

This dog would eat anything. If it was near his mouth and he could chew it, down it would go.

I'm not a bad baker, I don't want to be in the *Great British Bake Off* or any of its increasingly desperate spin-offs, but I can knock out a fairly decent rich fruit cake.

I made one when Ruffage lived with me. I used a Victorian recipe from a dusty copy of Mrs Beeton's cookery book, published in 1901. I found it on the shelves of my friend John's house in a lovely Oxfordshire village called Northmoor.

I had parked our truck, of which more later, in the exquisite walled garden to the rear of the house in the late summer of 1976, the hot one that old farts like me tend to wax lyrical about.

While I was there, I used the Mrs Beeton recipe to the letter. I can't remember the exact list of ingredients now but there were many, including vast slabs of butter and dozens of eggs.

The only extra ingredient, which I'm sure Mrs Beeton would

not have approved of, was a quarter-ounce of very fine Moroccan hashish, crumbled and stirred well into the mix.

It was a dope cake to beat all dope cakes and as anyone with experience of consuming edibles containing condensed extract of the cannabis sativa plant will know, it's very effective.

I can only remember eating one slim slice of this cake and I was smashed out of my pathetic skull for about twenty-four hours. Other young people hanging around John's very relaxed hippy house ate massive slabs and seemed quite chilled about the whole thing, but everyone agreed it was a delicious cake.

With one slice left, I put it on a plate and tucked it onto the top shelf of the little kitchen cabinet in the truck that was our home. A couple of days later I was clearing up, I'd forgotten about the slice of cake on the plate and as I pulled it out, the sizeable lump of cake dropped down, bounced off my shoulder and flew directly into Ruffage's waiting mouth. I shouted at him and grabbed his collar, shoving my fingers into his giant chomping gob to try and scoop the powerful cake from the vile hound's mouth.

I managed to salvage quite a bit. It wasn't that I wanted it back, much too late for that, I was very concerned what this potent psychotropic slab of fruity goodness would do to him.

About half an hour later we discovered that it would do quite a lot.

Ruffage was a very stoned dog.

Now we all know that human beings have a tendency to project human attributes to animals. Instagram, Snapchat and YouTube are littered with examples of 'doggy looks sad' or 'cat looks angry' pictures, but let's be honest, they're dogs and cats and although I accept they experience a variety of emotions, they don't present them in the same way human beings do.

However, Ruffage presented multiple symptoms of being seriously out of his tiny canine skull. He didn't seem distressed, he just lay down in the warm summer grass with his tongue hanging out.

He couldn't seem to move, so for the rest of that day I kept him in the shade and turned him over every now and then. Ruffage became the centre of attention to many young people who were hanging around the house. Much laughter and phrases along the lines of, 'Oh man, that dog is totally zonked,' and, 'Lucky dog, that was some seriously amazing cake, man.'

Later that evening, I lifted his head so his tongue made contact with some cool water I'd put into a shallow bowl. He did some half-hearted lapping and it really looked like he was grinning. I carried him to his bed that night fearing that he would be peeing all over the place. I don't remember anything like that, he was still stoned in the morning, but he could lift his head and eat some doggy biscuits. He loved them. I suppose he had the munchies.

Later the second day he started to drag himself around the garden. His front legs were working but he dragged his rear legs behind him like two strips of damp cloth. He was in a total state and the cause of much mirth among the gathered hippies.

'Hey, come and see Ruffage the Stoner, man. He's hysterical!'

By the end of the second day he had fully recovered and was back to his normal, annoying, eat-anything self.

He lived in London with me for a while. By this time, my long-term girlfriend Lee and I had parted company – my fault again – but anyway, Ruffage was very distressed. He was like the offspring of a divorced couple, he didn't know where he wanted to be, with me or Lee. We had joint custody; she was living in Islington, North London, I was living in Bermondsey, South London.

There would have been many occasions when Ruffage sat in the front seat of my battered Morris Van as I drove him to go and stay with Lee, and an equal number of journeys in the opposite direction.

I've just checked on Google Maps: the journey between the two locations is a distance of 4.2 miles and takes 1 hour 28 minutes to walk.

The reason I've checked is because of Ruffage's most remarkable journey.

I was getting ready to go to bed one night. I took him out for his last minute wee-wee, and he must have done something to annoy me, which wouldn't be unusual. I must have told him off, I can't remember the circumstances, but he sloped off. This wasn't that unusual but I did become a bit worried. I kept going downstairs to the main door of the old warehouse I was living in and whistled. He'd normally come bounding in, tail wagging like crazy, but not this night.

I must have gone to bed but I remember talking to Lee on the phone first thing in the morning.

She rang up to ask why I had left Ruffage on her front step. I said I hadn't and we both slowly realised that he had made this remarkable journey alone, overnight.

He had walked from Abbey Street in Bermondsey, over Tower Bridge, through the city of London, which would require him to cross multiple roads, past the Barbican and the London Museum, up the A1 to Angel, then turn left on Liverpool Road and then presumably along Thornhill Road and left onto Offord Road.

It is so hard to imagine. He had never walked this route with either Lee or myself, some bits of it, maybe. I know he'd walked over Tower Bridge with me, but that was just to St Katharine Docks on the other side of the Thames.

The only explanation must be that as I drove along through the streets of London he was looking out of the window. He must have understood the route and had a very well-developed visual memory.

A few years later, he sadly ate strychnine, a very potent poison that had been put down for foxes in a beautiful copse in rural Essex. To briefly explain why there was poison put down for foxes: it was to kill the foxes so they didn't kill the pheasants that were being raised in the woodlands. This was in order to allow city-dwelling upper-class inbred gun nuts to don tweed and blow them out of the sky. It's a traditional country sport apparently, something that seemed to pass by unnoticed when the hoo-hah about the fox-hunting ban was all the rage.

Probably half a dozen foxes get killed by packs of dogs each year; hunting isn't really about catching foxes, that's just an excuse. Thousands of foxes are shot or killed by road traffic, but that pales into insignificance when compared to the millions of specially bred birds that posh chaps shoot with big guns.

Just saying.

Strychnine is not a pleasant poison and it didn't kill Ruffage straight away. He had violent fits for the remainder of his life that were very distressing to witness. Partly because you

SOME OLD BLOKE

naturally empathise with a creature in torment, but also it has to be said, because in the chaos of the fits Ruffage lost control of his bowels. To be fair, he barely had control of them on a good day, but the poison made everything a lot worse, particularly if it happened in the night on the kitchen floor.

Ruffage passed away peacefully in the Lake District in the mid-1980s.

He was, undoubtedly, a canine legend.

From that day until my daughter was five years old in 2002 I didn't have a dog in my life and after Ruffage, that was a blessed relief. I didn't want another dog, I'd had two children and they were more than enough to fill the void that is human existence.

But my daughter wanted a puppy. We already had a hamster called Vinnie and a budgerigar with numerous names, but she wanted a puppy.

Daisy was a tiny black puppy that had been born in a barn, literally in a barn on a farm outside a village called Snowshill in Gloucestershire. She was the runt of a litter of a ragtag mix of vaguely terrier pups, all of them very sweet.

My daughter took to Daisy immediately and now, sixteen years later, she's still going strong. She's very small, very obedient, easy to look after and doesn't eat or indeed poo that much.

Daisy is an iDog, she needs minimal attention and does what dogs are meant to do. Sleep a lot, walk an amazing amount for a dog her age and size, and not get in the way.

She has run up a healthy amount of vet bills due to various accidents and incidents.

In the past couple of years it must have dawned on my wife

that we were fast approaching the time when both our children would leave home. That time has now come and along with the heartache of your children moving away comes a sense of relief at the lack of minute-by-minute planning and responsibility.

Therefore, it was a surprise to me when complex arrangements were made without my knowledge that would profoundly impinge on this newfound liberation.

My highly intelligent and emotionally mature wife had a bit of an incomprehensible spasm a few years ago. Our daughter hadn't even left home but Judy is wise, and unlike me she plans ahead. Either that or she is barking mad.

I was travelling home on a train when I received a text message from my daughter. It was a picture of her holding a delightful-looking Lurcher puppy. He looked uncannily like a baby kangaroo.

I smiled. I assumed in my naivety that my daughter and wife were visiting someone who had puppies and they took a picture of the cute little fellow. At this point the topic of 'getting another dog' had never been mentioned so I wasn't on alert.

I did notice in the background of the tiny picture on my phone that whoever's house they were in had very similar slatted wooden blinds to the ones we have in our kitchen.

On second viewing the penny dropped: those were our blinds, which meant that this damn dog was already in our house!

When I got home a few hours later, a scrawny, long-nosed stick-hound puppy waddled up to me in the front hall. His tail-wagging was so intense it kept throwing him off balance. He promptly fell over in his gangly-legged excitement, which was described as 'so adorable' by my squealing wife and daughter.

During the excitement, he also urinated on the floor and immediately sat down in the puddle.

So this is Joey, and I want to explain about Joey in as short a time as possible simply because his very existence causes me annoyance.

Joey is a small-brained, lanky, long-snouted, farting stick insect of a Lurcher.

I feel I may need to explain what a Lurcher is to those of you fortunate enough not to have shared a dwelling with one. As far as I understand dog breeds, a Lurcher is an Irish cross-breed, a terrier slash greyhound favoured in days gone by as a poacher's trusty sidekick.

They don't bark, they can run very fast, they are very good at catching rabbits and they walk around with a constant guilty look in their annoying hangdog faces because they are all thieving bastards.

Joey adores me, he puts his long bony head on my lap when I sit at the kitchen table, and looks up at me longing to be loved and accepted. How can I be such a cold-hearted bastard to such a gentle, quiet creature?

Wipe up a lake-sized puddle of liquid dog faeces off your kitchen floor early in the morning, believe me, that'll take the shine off your sentimentality.

The reason, I later discovered, for this appalling mess was the result of him being fed 'a load of grapes because the way he ate them was so cute', according to my daughter, who on other occasions has shown herself to be quite an intelligent young woman.

Grapes are very bad for dogs. Dogs don't eat fruit, though obviously Joey will eat pretty much anything he can get his thieving teeth into.

The wretched hound survived his grape-based diet in case you were worried about it.

Picking up adult-human-sized dog droppings in a plastic bag when out walking with the damned animal can maintain my disdain. How anything so thin can produce such a prodigious faecal mass defies physics.

Having a dog that has to spend weeks with his rear right leg in an enormous yellow, anti-chew bandage because he chased a rabbit through a hedge at thirty-five miles an hour and cut his leg so badly he needed surgery. Five hundred pounds' worth.

He didn't even catch the rabbit.

That's enough about the hound, curse him to the end of time.

It might appear to a casual reader that I don't like dogs, and I want to make it clear that this is not true. It's particularly important that you know this before you read on.

I do like dogs, I'm very comfortable in their company. Even though Joey the Lurcher drives me insane with his needy, sad-eyed, pleading expression, I'm very kind towards him. It's not his fault he entered my life and made a mess on the floor, he's a dog and I don't blame him.

But as I've explained I've always had an affinity with our canine cousins, even when I didn't know how to be a man I could always get along with dogs.

Unless they attack me.

I recount the following tales with no pride, merely shame. I have been in two dogfights in my life. Yes, actual fights, proper, full-on, nasty fights and I have the scars to show for it.

I definitely don't go out looking for fights with dogs. In sixty years, the fact that I've had a mere two full-on confrontations gives this claim credence.

The first one took place in Oxfordshire in the 1970s. I was walking along a public footpath causing no offence to anyone, unless the sight of a scrawny man in his early twenties wearing skin-tight jeans, red steel-toe cap boots, a heavily embroidered black leather jacket and spiky punk hair causes offence.

I was going through my rural punk phase. It didn't last long, please don't judge me.

I was suddenly knocked flat by a powerful force. I lay sprawled onto the grass with the wind knocked out of me. Before I'd had time to think, a large heavily built mongrel dog bounded past me and set on Ruffage.

Before I go on I just want to explain that had I been flattened by a drunk, thick-necked bully-boy human being, I would have run for my life.

I've never had a physical fight with a man. I've been punched, pushed and threatened by men but I've never fought back. Come to think of it, I've never had a physical fight with a woman either, fighting is not what I do.

Unless it's with a dog.

I'm scared of big, violent dangerous men. I'm scared of angry women. I'm clearly not scared of dogs, regardless of their temperament.

As I got to my feet, the ugly sound of a dogfight filled the air as lumps of Ruffage fur went flying in all directions. The reason I'm not describing this very violent struggle is that I truly don't recall much of what happened, the red mist came down. The dizzying haze of blood lust, fury, fearsome anger and heightened awareness that I assume men experience when they engage in hand-to-hand combat on the field of battle.

I was defending my pal, the clear victim of this attack, Ruffage who, like me, didn't do the fighting thing. He was definitely a lover, not a fighter. The confrontation was noisy, bloody and thoroughly unpleasant, but I won.

Strangely, when the owner of this highly aggressive dog turned up he said nothing, he appeared from behind me without drama, a man in late middle-age, respectable and well dressed. He merely put the dog on a lead and walked away.

I stood motionless, watching them leave, I was completely out of breath and could barely see. I did notice the dog was limping, tail hanging low and that made me feel even worse.

I sat down on the grass and tried to calm down. I remember Ruffage, bleeding from the neck, sitting down next to me, his vile penis still on prominent display.

My hands were covered in blood, some mine, some the vicious dog's. My left calf was bleeding and it slowly dawned on me that my back was very wet. I removed my jacket to find it too soaked in blood. The dog had bitten through my leather jacket and punctured a hole in my back. I still have the scar to this day.

I had to go to the doctor and have a tetanus jab; Ruffage had to go to the vet and have five stitches in his neck.

What stayed with me was the visceral experience of fighting, of having no fear in that moment, of having one aim and one aim only: to destroy your opponent. Even if your opponent is a dog.

I had always prided myself on my pacifism, I always knew violence didn't solve problems, merely made them worse. I had imagined being in the trenches and refusing to go over the top, happy to be shot as a coward because this war was stupid. I never wanted to fight, I didn't enjoy seeing other people fight. I hated boxing and hated men who swaggered, strutted and threatened people. I'd seen fights in pubs and watched men getting chesty and jumpy, shouty and thoroughly unpleasant, and I never got involved.

But when that dog attacked me something clicked.

I'm guessing, and thank heavens I've never been put in a position to find out, if my children or Judy were threatened in a similar way Ruffage was that day, I would act with extreme prejudice.

To be fair, Judy is pretty adept at looking after herself, but I remember realising I would happily die to defend my children. So it must be innate and I'm just unlucky that the dog in Oxfordshire turned up when he did.

It shook me up for years. I didn't like that person who was clearly inside me. Where did I learn to be so violent? The simple answer is I didn't, I just knew, we all do, it's in all of us and I don't feel happy or reassured by that.

For all their failings, and they were many, my mother and father weren't particularly violent. My mother wasn't above laying into her kids when times got tough, but it was the 1960s and she never injured her offspring.

Life went on and I forgot about this terrifying confrontation until many years later when my daughter's little terrier Daisy was running around the school playing field with a gaggle of assorted hounds. It was a lovely sight, all the village dogs playing together alongside all the village children, including my son and daughter.

When the dogs were on the far side of the field I could tell a fight had broken out. Daisy, a tiny black terrier, may have been to blame, she's a terrier with size issues and has been known to start some serious scrapping, however the dog she was fighting, I won't name the beast, had a history.

By the time this incident took place I had done five years of weekly therapy, mostly focusing on controlling my anger, not my anger at dogs, just my bog-standard middle-aged father anger. Boring and predictable.

When I got angry at my then teenage son for all the standard annoyances a teenage son produces, there was no change in his behaviour and the atmosphere in the family home was awful.

When I didn't get angry, no matter what happened, there was still no change in my son's behaviour and the atmosphere was a great deal more pleasant. True, we lived in a pigsty with dropped clothes, wet towels, paper, bits of string, skateboards, spray cans and cigarette ends scattered hither and thither but we were generally happier.

It was proof, if ever proof was needed, that getting angry is pointless.

So when I saw this massive dog tearing chunks out of Daisy,

I remained very calm, I walked up to the dog slowly and care-fully, not running towards this vicious hound ready to put the boot in.

By the time I arrived at the scene the big dog had Daisy pinned down and its jaws locked onto her throat, I knelt down beside this already gruesome scene and grabbed hold of the offending dog's collar. As I pulled, I could see that Daisy's throat was already severely injured. I imagine at that moment I knew this was a life-or-death struggle: the big dog was not going to let go.

I discovered if you twist a dog's ears enough they tend to open their jaws; thankfully this worked and the whole event was far less dramatic.

Once I had separated them, the offending dog just shook her-self and went and sat by her owner, who had by that time arrived on the scene.

I then took Daisy to the vet where they joined her back together again with eighteen stitches in her throat, making, according to the vet who kept records, a total of forty-two stitches in her throat she'd had during her long life as a result of similar encounters.

The vet told me she was very lucky. The flesh was torn asun-der, great slabs of skin hanging down and bite injuries within half a millimetre of a major artery, which would have killed her.

I explain all this as breaking up that fight was not easy. I don't know how anyone would have saved the little dog's life in any other way. However, this took place on the playing field outside the primary school my children had attended, although by then they had both left to go to big school.

It would have been a noisy, distressing and unpleasant spectacle for children to witness; it was very upsetting for the numerous parents standing around on this sunny afternoon. However, this violent encounter may be more justifiable simply because my not stopping it would have brought about the demise of two dogs, obviously Daisy, but also the other dog which, if she had killed a dog, would most likely have had to be put down.

So I suppose, on calm reflection, I could claim that I saved both dogs' lives and just to put the whole nasty event in perspective, about a year later I was sitting in the home of the owner of the vile dog and she sat on my foot and put her head on my lap. I stroked her and she wagged her tail. That was a bizarre moment.

The incident with that dog on the playing field kept me awake at night. Was there a really violent man inside me that civilisation and the law just about kept in check, but under the right circumstances I could turn into a murdering psychopath? I mean I didn't merely tweak that dog's ears, I really twisted the fuck out of them, I wrenched that dog's ears with all my strength until it howled in agony.

With the right provocation, might I do the same to a human being?

There are ample examples of men, and let's be realistic here, 99 per cent of people who are more than willing to do hideously violent things are men. I have always liked to think I'm not like that, but those encounters with dogs really shook me up. I had to admit that I am capable of violence when pushed into a corner. I suppose we all are.

I wrote a book in 1994 called *Punchbag*, which dealt with violence between men and women, inspired by the work of the 'Full Impact Self Defence' movement, whose classes I witnessed in America. This is a system that teaches women how to defend themselves in the event of a violent sexual assault. It wasn't some carefully choreographed fight scene from a superhero movie, it was an ugly struggle.

A group of around ten women would be taught a few very basic moves by a female instructor during a morning's class. After lunch, a man in fully padded body armour would enter the room and 'attack' them.

The women could fight back for real, not pull their punches and kicks, they could lay into the man as hard as they could, knowing he would not be seriously injured.

This system of self-defence for women is not new, it started back in the 1970s and over a million women in America have done the course. My wife did it and it was one of the single most disturbing things I've ever had to watch. She can fight, really nastily, and since I witnessed her landing a punch I've always been wary of her abilities.

The padded assailant, that's the term used to describe the men in the body suits, who fought with Judy was a lovely man called Elliot. In normal life, a gentle, slightly hippyish musician from San Francisco. After Judy's graduation fight Elliot took me to one side.

'Judy's good, you're a lucky guy. She's an amazing lady, but you take care, she hits real hard.'

I tried the suit on when I spent time with the men who take part in this incredible training and got punched in the stomach by one of the male padded assailants who had a black belt in Jiu Jitsu. I literally took off, such was the force of the blow. It hurt, but I didn't have to go to hospital, which I undoubtedly would have had I not been wearing the bizarre protective get-up.

I won't go into the detail of these classes now. If you want you might be able to find a copy of *Punchbag* in a second-hand shop or on Amazon.

What it showed me is that anyone is capable of violence, it's part of our natural make-up and although I find it hideous and disturbing, I've had to accept that it is part of who I am.

Thankfully, it's not something I indulge in. I have never attacked anyone, and now I'm far too old for such antics.

Unless your dog goes for me, in which case all bets are off.

Right, I'm going to tie a plastic bag around Joey's injured leg so his second anti-chew bandage doesn't get wet and take the demented hound for yet another walk in the English rain.

Oh, the joy they bring.

Postscript

Since writing this chapter I have had to rethink my relationship with Joey the Lurcher.

One Sunday afternoon in February, I took him for one of his favourite walks early in the morning. We were under beautifully clear sky as he ran around excited, sniffed leaves and engaged in normal dog activities.

Later that afternoon, Judy took him out in the car for

another walk, incident-free, walking with other dog owners in the village who all adore Joey.

When she came home, she opened the car door. Joey was in the back, and before she could put the lead on him, he bolted. He had, it turned out, seen a cat in our garden and like any sight hound, he pelted after it.

He ran through our hedge, which is a very thick and thorny affair, and out onto the lane that passes our house.

He was knocked down by a car and died a few moments later.

I squatted down next to his still warm body with my wife and we both cried and wailed. He was a beautiful dog, not obedient, not sensible, but incredibly affectionate and always entertaining.

I spent the afternoon digging a hole in the garden to bury him, occasionally breaking down in tears. I kept asking myself why I was crying so much, he'd always driven me mad, he'd always been looking at me longingly, resting his long head on my lap, staring at me and wagging his tail.

I was sobbing uncontrollably when I said to Judy, 'I didn't want this to happen.'

When my daughter Holly came back from Bristol where she now lives, we gently lowered him into the hole on top of his disgraceful old bed.

We covered him up and said our goodbyes.

For all his many faults and annoyances, he was much loved in the six years we had him.

RIP, Jo Jo.

Postscript Two

Daisy the much-loved terrier passed away two weeks after Joey's untimely demise. She was coming up to seventeen years old; she was incontinent, blind and deaf towards the end but still very fit. I took her out for a three-mile walk on her final day and she seemed fine but overnight she deteriorated and was eventually put down by the vet the following morning.

I had to dig another grave in the garden, and we've just finished putting a little flower bed on both canine resting places to mark their passing.

We are now dogless, and for all the joy they brought us, it's kind of a relief not having to clear up after them.

Leather, Thread and Tears

I'll make your shoes and make them well,
They'll surely last for years.
I'll make your shoes and make them well,
Of leather, thread and tears.
 — 'The Shoemaker's Lament', author unknown

I have flat feet. I know I've talked about it already and I know it's nothing to be ashamed of but they are a bit weird.

If I get out of an Australian swimming pool on a blisteringly hot day and walk across dry concrete, I leave weird-looking wet footprints. I was never aware of the unusual trail I leave until my lovely supportive wife, who has healthy high arches and can swim like a dolphin, pointed it out.

'Your footprints are sick,' she said with a look of genuine disgust. 'You've got no arches, you've got penguin feet.'

I smiled lovingly, knowing she wouldn't be able to say such a thing to someone she didn't feel safe with.

I have since pondered this carefully and realised this isn't the case: Judy feels safe with everyone, which means she really does think I have sick penguin feet.

I've had flat feet all my life. I had to walk barefoot across parquet floors in doctors' surgeries when I was very young; specialists watched me carefully and rubbed their chins.

I have learned that if you have what are known medically as 'rigid' flat feet, then you do tend to walk more like a penguin and back in the First World War era, you couldn't join the army. I don't have rigid flat feet, I have flexible flat feet, which means I could have joined the army and gone into battle and been shot, bayonetted or blown to bits.

Not something I was pleased to discover.

My feet are very sensitive and I have suffered because of it. I have some kind of spatial awareness problem below the knee that results in my shins and particularly my toes being at very high risk of minor injury on a daily basis. When my children were young I took to wearing stout, steel-capped boots. Not when I was out and about, I wore them indoors. I would arrive back home in soft walking shoes, then sit down and chat with my excited brood as I strapped on my massive steelies.

This is because of the intense pain I experienced if I trod on a lonely piece of hard plastic left out as part of a game.

The result of grinding a discarded plastic building brick into the sensitive sole of my flat arch came to be known in the family as the 'Lego Hop', an ungainly dance routine with accompanying soundtrack of muffled wailing and rapid breaths.

This is an apparently amusing dance to observe but a very painful experience for the hopper as the nerves send alarming signals up the legs and to the already regretful brain of the participant. Should have had my boots on.

However, although my feet have been a major cause of concern for most of my life, I don't think this had anything to do with the fact that I became a shoemaker when I was nineteen.

It's such a ridiculous thing to become. I am much the same age as Bill Gates and Steve Jobs. While they were tinkering with computer code, reaching for the future, seeing what could become of the still nascent personal computer revolution in the early 1970s, I was looking back to a time when people made things by hand, not machine. When people spent time making things that would last.

I can't quite trace the roots of this desire. I suppose it's partly being brought up in a country with a long and complex history, surrounded by very old things. It's partly due to my mother's obsession with stately homes, castles and museums, things I was taken to on a regular basis as a boy. This must have affected my view of the world. New, modern and mass-produced was bad; old and handmade was good.

I have read of the lives of Bill Gates and Steve Jobs and although there are a lot of similarities – the desire to change the world, the need to live differently from our parents – the huge difference was that they were obsessed with computers, machines that not only held no interest for me but which I would positively have despised.

Computers were used by governments and the military, banks and big corporations. I had no vision of computers in my future. I had a vision of a utopian low-tech economy where everyone grew their own food and travelled by foot or bicycle.

So, in 1975, when Bill and Steve saw the first signs of a

computer screen with a graphical user interface, the sort of thing we are all used to now, I started making shoes.

I worked as a rough-hewn medieval-style leather bag maker and I wasn't looking for a job when I was offered one. I used to travel to London once a month to buy leather fittings at an establishment called Berbo Buckles situated just off the Tottenham Court Road, these lumpy brass buckles, dome-headed rivets and D rings would be used on the highly embellished medieval bags I produced and sold at pop festivals in the summer and to one or two hipster boutiques in Oxford and Bath the rest of the year.

It was after one of these buckle-acquisition trips that I noticed an old man sitting at a low workbench with a half-finished shoe in his lap. This was on Tottenham Street, the building is still there, now an office supply shop but at the time I spotted this man, early in 1975, the area was still full of artisans producing anything from shoes to hats to gloves and suits. Small workshops with one or two people working in them, often Eastern European Jews or Greek Cypriots who had fled their countries for a variety of understandable reasons.

The front door of the building was open so I walked in as only a nineteen-year-old would, went down the dusty old stairs and into the room.

'Hello, I just saw you from the street. My name's Robert and I make shoes too,' I said, lifting my foot to display the pair of crudely fashioned medieval boots I was wearing.

The man smiled. 'You make those?' he said, and I wasn't sure if he was about to burst out laughing or congratulate me.

'Yes, I'm a leather worker. I work in a commune in Bath.'

The man looked at me like I was crazy, which really, when all's said and done, wasn't so cruelly judgemental.

'You make shoes yourself?' he said with what I took to be a thick Greek accent.

'Yes, they're called Goof Boots. They're like, the radical alternative to platform soles.'

'Good shoes,' said the man. He smiled at me kindly. 'Very good.'

I heard someone coming down the stairs behind me, turned and saw a smartly dressed man with a neatly trimmed beard.

'Morning, Stavros,' he said, completely ignoring me.

'Morning, Mr Schweiger. This man make his own shoes.'

Mr Schweiger raised his thick eyebrows and finally acknowledged me. 'Oh, where do you work?' he said with a kind smile.

'In a commune in Bath.'

'A commune. Goodness me,' he said slowly. He looked down at what constituted my boots and remained silent for a moment.

I feel I should describe Goof Boots a little. I had devised them on my own after I took apart a pair of discarded suede desert boots to see how they were made.

I had also read how, during the Vietnam war, the Khmer Rouge had used old tyres from destroyed American cars and trucks to put stout soles on their combat sandals.

I worked out that I could use old car tyres to put very hard-wearing soles on my fabulous Goof Boots.

I think a hippy friend in Bath had come up with the name because when you walked around in my semi-ridiculous footwear you looked a bit like the cartoon character Goofy.

I had no understanding or technology to make shoes that

fitted anyone in a conventional sense so I just made a leather bag that surrounded your foot, a slab of old car tyre on the sole, laces around the ankle to sort of hold them in place.

I think basic would describe them well.

I couldn't tell if Mr Schweiger was impressed or alarmed. Probably, he was a bit of both.

Stavros kindly intervened.

'Mr Schweiger, this boy need learn to make good shoe.'

'Does he indeed, Stavros? Well, we do need an apprentice.'

I had a pub lunch with Mr Schweiger, which he very kindly paid for, and a week later I arrived at their other, main shop for my first day of training as an apprentice shoemaker.

The Victorian vintage sign above the window stated 'James Taylor and Son, Bespoke and Orthopaedic Shoemakers.'

The shop on Paddington Street is still there to this day and they still make bespoke and orthopaedic shoes. A bespoke shoe, like a bespoke suit, is made to measure. They only make it for you, it won't fit anyone else, it is bespoken for. Posh and rich people like that sort of thing.

Up to the point I entered James Taylor and Son that bright May morning I had been living in a wonderful communal house in Bath, earning an almost decent living as a fully fledged, independent leather worker.

However, I wasn't happy, I felt I was merely pandering to wasteful consumerism, making what were essentially fashion accessories, bags, belts and wristbands. Hippy trinkets, worthless nonsense. It was bourgeois and wasteful, I felt I should be making something people actually need.

I had a dream of running a collective shoe factory, employing hundreds of men and women who all shared in the success of the company, not like in pre-Stalin Russia but in a revolutionary new way of running a business. I wasn't that interested in being a 'craftsperson', that too was bourgeois, I wanted to be a revolutionary collective industrialist and challenge the world.

So, you know, perfectly realistic ambitions.

It's possible the reality of learning how to make shoes by hand using traditions and tools that were hundreds of years old may have taken the initial shine off this ambition. I knew I needed to understand these traditions in order to challenge them, and the people I worked with at James Taylors were fascinating.

Frankie, Stephan and Mr Becker.

Frankie and Mr Becker (I never learned his first name) were Jews; Frankie Polish and Mr Becker German. Stephan was a Czech communist, probably an unfortunate choice if you were a young man in Czechoslovakia in 1939. They met in a concentration camp in Poland where their Nazi guards had a real thing about high-quality boots. Because they were all highly skilled shoemakers, they, along with a couple of tailors, were put in a separate shed and allowed to work, eat and sleep there.

They were also not murdered, which was a big plus for them.

They survived the war making and mending jackboots for Nazi soldiers. They each had a number tattooed on their left forearm which, due to the fact it was very warm in the workshop and they had their sleeves rolled up, were plain to see.

I didn't learn this straight away, of course. On my first morning, I entered a small basement beneath the shop with Mr Schweiger.

It was an almost magical sight, the walls were covered in wooden shapes, thousands of them. The space was cramped and chaotic, small benches with powerful lamps pointing down on piles of tools and glue pots, bits of leather and what looked like small candles.

Mr Schweiger introduced me.

'This is our new apprentice, Robert. He's already very skilled at making bags but he wants to learn how to make shoes.'

That was it. Mr Schweiger scuttled back upstairs to the shop and I stood looking at these three old men. No one said anything for a while.

Eventually Frankie motioned to me. 'Come sit here, Robert, I show how to make shoe.'

I sat down at an empty bench next to him but continued to stare at the walls. I knew enough about shoe making to know the wooden things on the wall were called lasts, and there were literally thousands of them covering every spare inch of wall. Every customer James Taylor had ever sold shoes to had a pair of lasts made for them and they'd been making shoes for hundreds of years.

Frankie was an old man in 1975 but still worked long hours at his bench, his enormously strong hands working the leather of a pair of posh brogues.

One by one, these old men explained how to do the various stages of making a shoe, stretching the leather over the last in a very particular way to ensure the shoe was flexible where it needed to be and rigid where it supported the foot.

The first time I tried to stitch the thick leather sole to the welt of a shoe – that's the bit that sticks out around the base of old fashioned shoes – Frankie gave me slow instructions in very basic English.

'Push awl through, slowly slowly,' he said. Just to briefly explain again, an awl is a curved metal spike, thin, very sharp and attached to a wooden handle, you use it to make a hole in the thick leather sole through which you pass the thread. I then stitched the sole using hand-twisted linen thread covered in tar and beeswax, which in turn was wound onto a pig's bristle which acted as a needle.

When I said this was shoe-making using traditional methods, I wasn't joking, this is how shoes were made in the 1700s and it's still going on to this day.

After stitching away for about an hour, Frankie took the shoe from me and looked at it, then said something in Polish and it made Stephan laugh. Stephan translated for me.

'Frankie say stitches look like dog pissing in snow.'

I nodded, I could see from the way Frankie was shaking his balding old head that I had a long way to go.

I found working at James Taylors strangely relaxing. I had been self-employed for the previous two and a half years, and having a very regular daily routine helped me calm down a bit. The contrast between my life outside the little basement work-shop and the daily lessons I was getting from these three old men was very pronounced. I was living in a variety of squats in North London, including, for one short period, a primal ther-apy community.

It's hard, in fact it is genuinely beyond me to try and explain what the hell a primal therapy community was, but in 1975 it really wasn't so unusual in the circles I mixed in. If you looked in the classified adverts at the back of a copy of *Time Out* during this period there would be half a dozen primal therapists advertising their screaming services.

A dilapidated house next to the North London line in Islington was home to about twelve women and one man, a very neurotic New Yorker called Jerry. He was a primal therapist who had studied with Arthur Janov, the father of Primal Therapy and the man who wrote the bestselling book *The Primal Scream.*

There was one room in the house completely padded with old mattresses, floor and walls covered, lots of cushions, no windows, even the door had a scabby old mattress strapped to it.

Nearly every evening we'd all gather in the room and have a screaming session. Well, I didn't, I just sat and watched in open-mouthed awe and occasional terror.

Jerry would be doing most of the screaming. He dribbled a lot as he spoke, well, spat a lot, mostly about his father and mother. His sister, who also lived there, was a very startling-looking young woman. Okay, she was gorgeous and I fancied her but nothing came of it.

After this noisy night, I'd get on my bike early each morning before any of the screamers awoke and cycle the few miles to Marylebone High Street, lock my bike to a lamp post outside the shop and step into the basement to make shoes for rich people. I think that was a fairly extreme contrast.

After a few weeks, my self-awareness remained unchanged but my skill at making shoes started to improve. I learned how to build heels on shoes using layers of thick leather, how to sharpen my knife, I mean really sharpen it, because a shoe-maker's knife has to be very sharp. My fingers became hardened and stronger, I learned how to stretch the upper, the bit of a shoe you see when you wear them, over the last and stretch it in the right direction, holding it in place with thin nails.

I learned how to sew a welt onto the shoe, incredibly difficult to start with but slowly I got the hang of it.

One day Frankie gave me a pair of lasting pliers, like a regular pair of pliers but with longer handles and a small hammer built into it. This was the tool you used to stretch the leather upper over the last and then tap in thin nails which held everything in place until you sewed it.

'I had these all through war,' he said. 'Very good tool.'

'Thank you, Frankie. I'll look after them.'

I did.

I still have these pliers, they were made in Berlin in 1907.

As I was sitting with these three quiet men in the basement I started to hear them tell their story, how they had come to England in 1948 when they had been treated for all the diseases they'd picked up in the camps.

I can't recall the way I got them to talk about life in the camps, but they did, not in any great detail but snippets would come out.

'Camp very bad,' was about all Frankie would ever say.

'Frankie lost family,' said Stephan. 'Everyone gone.'

'Everyone gone,' confirmed Frankie quietly.

'I lost some of my family too,' said Mr Becker.

'Your family rich, go to America,' said Frankie.

Stephan nodded. 'Many leave for England, or America, but

many not have hope. I was in Prague, making shoes. Germans come and arrest me and sent me to camp. There I meet Frankie.'

'Stephan good shoemaker,' said Frankie. 'Soldiers like boots, we make good boots, we get food.'

That was about it really. I was fascinated to hear their stories but I had to be very patient. If I asked a direct question they would just shake their heads and stay silent.

I spent six months in that basement and by the end of it I was turning out half-decent shoes. Nothing like the quality these old men could produce, but just about passable.

I was paid £25 a week, which felt like a fortune. For younger readers, I'll point out that in the sandwich shop across the street from James Taylor and Sons you could buy a sandwich for 12p.

The area of London around Marylebone High Street was new to me at the time. It was a discreet but clearly wealthy area, even more so today, and just around from the shoe shop were the offices of Apple. Not the computer company, the record label owned by the Beatles.

I was sitting in bright sunshine outside the pub one lunchtime when a dark green convertible Rolls-Royce pulled up at the corner. Sitting behind the wheel was Paul McCartney, beside him sat his wife Linda. I imagine a long-haired hippy teenager sitting outside a pub staring at them so openly may have caught their attention, indeed, Linda smiled at me. Paul gave a discreet wave as they pulled into the high street and roared off up the road. I must have been in their presence for maybe twelve seconds but it had a huge impact on my worldview.

I don't remember seeing anyone famous before that. It was a strange experience because both those people were so iconic, especially in the mid-seventies. I knew they were just people but that brief exposure to their incredibly different existence left me a little slumped. I went back into the basement and sewed shoes feeling rather forlorn. The Beatles were such a cultural phenomenon, I was also a big fan of Wings, if anything I preferred Wings to the Beatles. Sacrilege, I know, but I was very young when the Beatles appeared on the world stage.

So I carried on making shoes but occasionally fantasising about the glamorous, wealthy and exciting lives that Paul and Linda must be living.

One day, Mr Schweiger suggested I learn a bit about pattern cutting so I started working on the ground floor of the shop, in a small workshop behind the public area. Here I met Mr Carpenter and Mr Wilson, two very English chaps who were pattern cutters and closers. Those jobs describe the art of cutting the leather that makes the upper of the shoe and sewing it together on a treadle-powered leather sewing machine. This is very fine and precise work with many strictly adhered-to traditions.

Unlike Frankie, Stephan and Mr Becker in the basement, neither of these men ever let me anywhere near their tools and didn't want to teach me anything.

However, Mr Carpenter, a flamboyant gay man, was very entertaining. He not only cut the leather and sewed the parts together to make the uppers, he also dealt with a lot of the more cranky customers. Mr Carpenter was a people person, that's how he described himself, adding, 'Particularly if those people are guardsmen.'

I think I learned more about cruising and picking up lorry drivers in toilets than I did about making uppers for shoes from Mr Carpenter but he was great fun to work next to.

He was very much from the Kenneth Williams school of gayness, dressed very smartly, outwardly straight but very open with me about his shenanigans.

However, just being in their company and watching them work taught me a lot. I tried copying what they were doing and stayed in the workshop after they'd left. I'd then try using their much-coveted sewing machines, practising stitching bits of leather together.

Mr Carpenter would measure a customer's feet in order to build a last for them, I never saw this happen as I wasn't allowed into the public part of the shop.

'You'd frighten them off,' said Mr Carpenter, always immaculately dressed. 'You look like the wild man of Borneo, darling.'

He would then use those measurements to make a single last, rasping bits of wood off where the last was too big and adding carefully shaped pieces of leather to build it up where it was too small.

This single last was then sent off to the last turner, who, using this single last as a model would attach it to a special lathe which would turn two new ones out of beech wood, one left one right, obviously.

I learned about this as I was often sent off with a bag full of single lasts to deliver them to the last-turner's workshop, now a private house on Gosfield Street.

Mr Carpenter shaped and smoothed these lasts, worked out the design of the uppers with a pencil, cut a pattern to fit that design, sewed all the various parts together and handed it all over to Frankie, Stephan or Mr Becker who would complete the process.

I really did work all this out by observation rather than instruction. I found if I kept Mr Carpenter chatting about his evening shenanigans he'd let me watch what he was doing.

My official role at the time was repairing shoes. James Taylors only repaired shoes they'd made and another very old and grumpy man showed me how to do this.

I have no idea who the old grumpy fellow was, he was the only person who worked there whose name I can't remember. There's a clue: if you're old and grumpy a nineteen-year-old won't remember your name when you're dead and gone.

So I felt quite confident that I could now make a pair of shoes, and it wasn't long after seeing Paul McCartney that I decided I had learned enough. I was becoming increasingly restless and didn't want to live in London. I dreamed of living in some little fishing village in Wales or Ireland, making shoes in a little shop, being my own boss and not having to keep to set hours.

One day I rang Mr Schweiger from a call box near the squat I was living in. 'I can't come in today,' I said. 'I'm too depressed.'

'Well, we all get depressed, Robert,' said Mr Schweiger. 'I suspect Frankie and Stephan and Mr Becker have more reasons to be depressed than you and they manage to come in every day. Try and buck up and we'll see you later.'

I left the company a month later and set off on my travels.

About two years after I worked at James Taylors I met a man around my age who was wearing the most amazing pair of boots I'd ever seen. He had been an apprentice at John Lobb's, the really posh shoemakers, and was obviously a great deal more gifted at making shoes than I was. I was really impressed with his heavy black pull-on boots. His name was David Lobb, he was distantly related to the Lobb family who founded what is probably the most famous and illustrious boot-making company in England.

John Lobb's shop is on St James Street just around the corner from Buckingham Palace. They are the Royal Bootmakers. They have made shoes for just about every posh person you've ever heard of, and famous people, and infamous people, and even, now I think about it, fictional people.

In the James Bond books by Ian Fleming, Agent 007 always wore shoes made by Lobb.

I'd learned about the John Lobb company when I worked at James Taylors and had been told in no uncertain terms by the very unhelpful Mr Wilson that I'd have no chance working there, as they only employ the best.

A few months after meeting David I was working for John Lobb, so screw you Mr Wilson.

David and I started working together fairly swiftly, initially as out-workers for John Lobb and James Taylors, but before long we started getting our own customers. By 1979 we had set up a company called Bermondsey Bootmakers in an old warehouse on Abbey Street in Bermondsey, living and working in the same rather spacious building.

Before long we had other employees working for us. We had hundreds of pairs of lasts, a couple of sewing machines, large cutting tables, multiple work benches, Radio 1 blaring away and copious amounts of coffee and cigarettes to keep us working.

We did earn a half-decent living but we worked ridiculously long hours and, apparently, I talked too much. It was towards the end of my time at Bermondsey Bootmakers that I started performing and after a relatively brief and thankfully painless transitionary period, I stopped making shoes.

I've still got all my tools and the first pair of shoes I made for myself in 1978. I can't wear them any more, my feet have spread too wide and if I'm honest, they were always a little tight. I made the lasts myself. At a glance and to the average Joe, they might look like very posh shoes but a close inspection would reveal all the tiny mistakes I made and botched over.

Thankfully a cheering audience indicated to me that I wasn't cut out to make shoes, I was destined for the far shallower and less useful existence of showing off onstage and screen.

Peculiar Travel Suggestions Are Dancing Lessons from God

The solitary house on the hill overlooking the City of Bath was more than just a derelict dump, it was possibly quite dangerous.

There were major cracks in the walls, not uncommon for houses of that vintage. What many tourists don't appreciate as they walk around Bath's exquisite streets is that most of the Georgian houses were built by speculators in the eighteenth century and they did a pretty shoddy job behind the impressive facades.

I ended up in this semi-derelict dump after fleeing from London with two delightful hippy friends, Gerald and Nadine.

How we ended up in this house, a squat on a quiet street high above the Georgian city, is now lost in the mists of unrecorded history. I've no idea whose house it was. I assume it belonged to the council and they would have to demolish it or spend a fortune making it safe, either way it was empty and we moved in.

I was happy there. I felt I had escaped from the terror of London, which in the mid-seventies was a fairly terrifying city to live in.

One morning as I cycled to work through the centre of London, I felt the deadening impact of a shockwave from a bomb that blew a shop to oblivion on the Tottenham Court Road. The street had been cordoned off and for the first time I can remember I realised that police officers get scared too. The policeman standing behind the cordon making sure no one went through looked terrified, poor bloke. And rightly so – it was at the height of the IRA bombing campaign and everything felt dangerous.

During the time I'd been living in London learning how to make shoes, I met a young woman called Lee. She wasn't one of the many women I instantly fell in love with as soon as I met them, what I'm trying to imply here is that among the dozens of women I fancied, longed for and was rejected by during my time in London, Lee wasn't one of them. I suppose I came to think of her, to quote Arnold Judas Rimmer, 'As someone I met.'

Lee had been a regular visitor to the squat I was living in while I was making shoes for James Taylor. This squat had a never-ending supply of hot water so many people came around to use our bath. We had endless heat and light courtesy of Her Majesty who owned the property we had purloined, sorry, liberated from the oppressive ruling class. This is how I remember the situation, the Royal Estate owned massive slabs of property all over the country but particularly in central London, during this period in London the massive redevelopment of the city was just getting underway. This meant hundreds of properties were standing empty, waiting to be knocked down. Add to this the standard UK housing crisis and a medieval law about squatters' rights, and hey ho, a very nice little four-bedroom apartment right next to Regent's Park.

So, our bathroom was busy. I knew even then that many women valued cleanliness slightly more than the grubby, long-haired men they hung around with. Lee was one of these clean women and I remember making her a cup of tea one day while she was waiting her turn in the bathroom and discovering she was from Manchester, but that was about it.

How she found me in the tumble-down house on the hill overlooking Bath I have no idea, but find me she did. I feel the need to explain to young people who might be reading this that we had no phones, no email, texts, WhatsApp, Facebook Messenger. The clever people who developed these systems had yet to be born. We had handwritten letters that we posted in envelopes with stamps on. And of course there was the 'Hippy Grapevine', which for Bath, at the time, was the Hat and Feather pub in Walcot.

So Lee arrived out of the blue, and Nadine could sense immediately what was going on but I was utterly oblivious.

People just showed up because, well, because they did. My reasoning at the time, to quote Kurt Vonnegut, which I did all the time, was this: 'Peculiar travel suggestions are dancing lessons from God.'

That's what I thought Lee did, she accepted a peculiar travel suggestion from somewhere and just showed up. Actually, it turned out she had just dropped out of university in London, and had come to Bath with a rather soppy guitarist boyfriend who had a gig at the Hat and Feather. She rather casually dumped him and was a bit adrift so thought she would look up a hippy friend from London and find somewhere to crash.

I did recognise her as she walked into the dusty front room where I was making shoes. She smiled, put her bag down and I made her a cup of tea.

Lee was very bright and full of ideas that I liked very much. She and I talked earnestly about the very basic human need: shelter. That's how basic we had become. We didn't talk about owning a property or mortgage interest rates, we were discussing notions of moss-covered hovels, the benefits of caves, the very essential need that human creatures have for shelter, for safety, nesting and breeding.

Lee had been studying architecture at University College London. She was highly academically gifted and ferociously bright, well read and intelligent. She had also dropped out of her course and wanted to experience hands-on shelter building.

We both felt the same about the endless hassle of squatting and how it had worn us down. Lee had lived in another squat in London nearby the one I'd been in but had to move out when they started to knock it down.

I had very high ideals about shelter. I wanted to live in a yurt, or a moss-covered den like a hobbit. I wanted to be free of the trappings of mortgage and rent and the hassle of home ownership, but I wanted somewhere secure to live.

None of this seemed in the least bit contradictory to me

I had comprehensively rejected all notions of property ownership, getting a proper job, living within 'the system' as I would have referred to it.

I was determined not to compromise myself just to fit in with mainstream society. It was clear to me that mainstream society was dysfunctional and in terminal decline. A common theme of the mid-seventies was the imminent collapse of the capitalist status quo, the oil crisis had temporarily spun the world out of control, or so it seemed. I had cycled past mile-long queues of cars waiting to buy a meagre ration of petrol. It seemed so absurd, so hopeless. The secure suburban post-war world I had grown up in had ended, this was the decline of Western civilisation and power. The final tatty end of empire where the pomp and bigotry of the British ruling class was under severe pressure. It was over, the people were fed up, the revolution was inevitable.

The fact that the following thirty years would see an incredible explosion of free market global capitalism and the total collapse of alternative economic models would have seemed the least likely scenario to me, and indeed many others.

To my nineteen-year-old mind, the clever, well-informed people like my peers, the urban peasants, the freaks, gays, weirdos, commune-dwelling hippies and alternative technology nerds were busy creating something new.

That was the term I loved and longed for. We were building an 'alternative society', not trying to change the existing power base from the inside, but creating an alternative, less wasteful, more humane and sensitive system that put people and the environment first, not crushed them under the need for profit and endless, pointless economic growth.

Lee seemed to be of a similar mindset and we talked about this kind of thing for hours.

I told her about a man called Rod who I'd recently met at

another squat in Bath. Rod had a lorry that he used to move the timber he needed to convert people's houses. He had helped build extensions on communes in Wales, Devon and Cornwall. He knew lots of very cool alternative society people. Rod was a carpenter, I was a shoemaker, it was all potentially very bucolic, the foundations of an alternative society.

Okay, apart from the IRA bombing campaign, world poverty, Watergate, the oil crisis, Vietnam, nuclear tests, Margaret Thatcher becoming Tory leader, more nuclear tests and a horrific accident at Moorgate Tube station that killed 41 people, apart from all that, it was all rosy in my little world.

When Rod's truck wasn't being used to shift timber, he used it as a home from home when he was on a building site. It had a bed and a wood-burning stove, cosy seats, a fold-down table and a wooden stable door on the back.

I walked down the hill with Lee and we went to see Rod and sat in his truck as he made us a cup of tea on a gas stove built into a unit Rod had constructed from salvaged timber. I could see Lee really liked it. He told us he wanted to sell it, I asked him how much, and he said £150.

I had £11 in a building society savings account my father had opened for me. I had £3 in my pocket. Lee said she would pay for it and three nights later we were living in our truck.

It truly was as simple as that. I don't remember asking Lee where the money came from, stuff just happened. Lee had a little money and a driving licence, and was ready for a bit of adventure, I was full of crazy ideas, so we made good travel partners.

I want to point out right now that at this stage in the proceedings

Lee and I were not lovers. Not in the least, not even casually, as was the fashion at the time. We managed to sleep perfectly happily together in a very narrow bed in the back of a three-and-a-half ton converted furniture truck on a quiet side street in Bath with no trouble at all.

The truck had a petrol engine, a naturally aspirated 3.5 litre straight six. I knew that much, it also looked very clean for such an old engine, in fact, it looked immaculate. There was a removable cover in the cab between the driver and passenger seats, you could lift off this cover to inspect the engine. It glimmered like a museum exhibit, it was spotless.

Making it perform like an internal combustion engine should do, for example, make a noise like an engine and create motive power, was not quite so simple.

This 1963 vintage BMC FG K40 had an engine that was incredibly difficult to start. It never got any easier and for the two and a half years we lived in the truck that wretched spotless engine never started without a struggle.

Once it was running it was incredibly reliable. We drove thousands of miles in it using petrol at the rate of nine miles to the gallon, at a top speed of 60mph (with a fair wind and some skilful double-declutching).

After leaving home at sixteen and roughing it all over the place, never feeling at home anywhere, always feeling nervous about the following day, where I would end up, how I would pay the bills, whether I would end up on the street, that all disappeared the moment I settled into this metal box on wheels.

If someone didn't like us, didn't want us to park in any particular location, we'd move on.

It fitted my nineteen-year-old worldview perfectly. This was shelter and freedom of movement; this was home, anywhere. It made me feel incredibly confident and free.

We spent a week with the truck parked in the same place Rod had left it. Lee did have a driving licence, I didn't. Sure, I'd driven go-karts but that doesn't really help when you sit behind the wheel of a three-and-a-half-ton truck with no power steering.

After much discussion about where we might go, we decided to pack up and head off out of town. Lee sat behind the massive steering wheel and turned the key. The engine turned over, sounding like a metal bin of spanners being hit with rocks. Nothing, no way was this machine going to start. Before long the engine was turning slower and slower and no hint of it firing.

Thankfully, as often seemed to happen in Bath around this period, a long-haired hippy walked past. It was someone I knew. His name was Simon Chippendale, I still know him, he's a lovely fellow with an incredible grasp of engineering and mechanics and a passion for bees.

For those not familiar with Bath it is a Georgian City in the West of England built on top of a Roman City and nestled in the folds of seven hills. Some of those hills are very steep, the truck was parked at the top of one of those hills.

Simon sat behind the wheel with confidence and enthusiasm.

'I'll soon have this lovely old beast purring like a kitten,' he said confidently. Simon had a degree in engineering from Cambridge University, he'd lived in California, he was a grade-one dude. Simon released the hand brake and the truck started to gently roll forward down the hill.

He managed to turn left down a terrifyingly steep side street and let the speed build up, he was going to bump start this truck if it was the last thing he did. It was very close to the last thing any of us did as the road was absurdly steep and narrow while the truck was very heavy and wide.

The gearbox made agonising grating noises as he fought to engage second gear and consequently bump start the lazy engine.

Thankfully, he managed to do it. The truck lurched violently as he released the clutch, the engine burst into life and the brakes just about saved us from going right through a late Georgian railway worker's cottage at the bottom of the hill.

We sat for a while recovering, Simon revving the engine to 'warm her up'. He climbed out and waved us goodbye as Lee took the controls.

The first twenty miles were not relaxing for either of us. The biggest vehicle Lee had driven up to that point was her mother's Mini Countryman.

We drove on, I gave directions and Lee fought with impressive strength and commitment to keep the lorry moving, negotiating narrow lanes and complex junctions without stalling.

Top speed in this lump of 1960s engineering was 60mph (95kph) on a flat road. If we faced a hill it would slow to a crawl. We regularly created a long tail of mildly annoyed motorists behind us on busy A roads.

A few hours later we arrived in Oxford and parked in a place called Port Meadow, a beautiful expanse of floodplain very near the centre of the city.

We called in on a few friends in Oxford, spent the night there and then headed into London.

Lee wanted to pick up her remaining stuff from a squat some of her university friends lived in.

It wasn't fun spending a night in London, the lock on the wooden door at the back of the truck was about as secure as a pair of old pants and the streets felt a little bit wild, so I was very grateful the following day when we headed out of town.

How we scraped along for the next few months is hard to recall, we lived very frugally. I sold a few pairs of shoes, I still have an order book I used at the time to record the name, address and type of shoe that various individuals we met commissioned me to make. Flicking through it, I can see I was quite busy but my income was very low.

The truck smelled of tobacco, oak tanned leather, sandalwood incense, burnt toast and paraffin, until we obtained a Tilly Lamp.

We drove up and down the country, stopping at friends' houses, filling up our water system, using bathing and laundry facilities where we could, sleeping together in a cramped bed and talking incessantly, laughing hysterically and, for my part, feeling safer than I'd felt in years.

We ended up at Lee's parents' house in Manchester over the Christmas and New Year of 1975–76.

Lee's childhood home was a comfortably large house in a smart suburb of south Manchester, it was warm and friendly and her parents were kind and generous and didn't seem to immediately judge me. I felt welcomed and accepted by the large extended family that had gathered together for the festive period.

Lee's mother was a perceptive and inquisitive American woman who clearly loved her youngest daughter. Lee's father was a professor at the Manchester Medical School, a surgeon of Swedish origin although he'd been born in London.

Her three elder sisters and their husbands and children were also in attendance, along with numerous guests, some of them academics in the medical field who taught with the professor.

He was a jovial old man, just retiring when I first met him. Red-faced and clearly in his cups, he was very affectionate but slightly distant as all men of his generation seemed to be.

Lee and I slept in a large bed in an enormous bedroom. It was so luxurious, a big double bed with clean sheets. It was glorious to eat wonderful food, then sit by the fire with Lee's sisters and drink whisky as we talked, maybe wander off to have a deep bath before bed.

I was very happy. I really felt I'd moved on from the chaos and grime of my life over the previous few years.

During the few days we stayed there, the truck parked next to the spacious garage in the garden, we stripped everything out of the grubby interior we called home.

We washed everything, painted parts of the wooden interior and found storage areas for all the kitchen items given to us by Lee's mother.

I slowly became aware of the family's anxiety about Lee. They were a very academic family, all the daughters had been to university and all had graduated.

It mattered to them that Lee, their youngest, had dropped out of university and suddenly turned up just before Christmas in an old truck with some scrawny long-haired boyfriend.

Except I wasn't her boyfriend, not in any sense I understood the term. I was just a friend.

That almost changed one night as we lay next to each other, busily discussing our relationship. This wasn't some embarrassing adolescent muttering, we both had considerable experience with the opposite sex, but we agreed that for the time being, we were both happy to remain celibate. It was rather relaxing not to be expected to do anything as complicated and awkward as to have sex.

I experienced some guilt on Christmas eve when Lee's mother suggested I ring my mother and tell her where I was. This hadn't occurred to me and as soon as she suggested it I felt awful. This was the first Christmas I hadn't spent with my own family, even during the years where I was a stoned-out emaciated street hippy, somehow I had always made it home to experience the Yuletide family get together.

I didn't even hate being there. Although I had to endure ample negative comments on my life choices there was always a lot of noise and laughter in my old family home.

I rang my mother, my father answered. 'I'll get your mother,' he said and I heard him put the phone down. He didn't ask me where I was or what I was doing. That was normal.

The conversation with my mother was brief, pained and awkward. She was clearly upset. I could tell by the way she said, 'It's fine, darling, you have a lovely time, and Happy Christmas.'

My mother cut the conversation short. 'It's expensive to make a long-distance call,' said my mother, as calling from Manchester to Oxfordshire was then. Everything was always too expensive for my parents and I was now experiencing a family where things like making phone calls and buying food were not considered an extravagance.

The sheer luxury, the size of the house, the smell of wood polish and clean linen, the stimulating conversations and the food, oh Lord, the food that Christmas was amazing and different to anything I'd previously experienced. The mixture of the Swedish culinary influence and American Christmas tradition gave their family household a special magical quality I've never forgotten.

I'd only ever known a slightly down-at-heel old English Christmas dinner, a bit of chicken with all the trimmings, crackers with paper hats and a very good Christmas pudding – my mother was brilliant at making rich, stodgy puddings.

My father would open a celebratory bottle of Liebfraumilch, a very sweet German white wine. He would always put on a German accent as he poured it and then perform an abrupt 'Heil Hitler' salute before he tasted it. This was again, just in case you're worried, for comic effect.

I first tasted something that could be described as fine wine at Lee's parents' house. I didn't even know this stuff existed before that Christmas. We had turkey, ham that didn't come in slices but a massive lump you had to carve bits off.

I assume the reason these events have stayed with me so vividly is that I had been hungry for the previous three years. I could never quite afford enough food. I had lived such a low-impact, hand-to-mouth existence that food had always been very basic and 90 per cent vegetarian.

I couldn't afford to eat out because in the 1970s eating out was either a posh expensive restaurant and they would never have let me in, or a greasy spoon cafe where everything was fried in lard. That was it.

At this stage in my life, fruit was an orange, an apple or a banana. I'd never seen a mango, didn't know what a real pineapple looked like, or a peach. They all came in tins. In the summer, I could pick strawberries and raspberries; I'd grown up eating rhubarb, which I loved, but the exotic food, the fruits, the amazing bread that was supplied in abundance at Lee's family Christmas was a revelation to me.

With a fresh-smelling truck, clean clothes and copious amounts of food we set off. After the obligatory stress of getting the truck started, we drove from Manchester to the Lake District where Lee's parents had an old cottage.

It got even better! The cottage was a dream come true for me, a small stone building tucked into a steep wooded hillside with a stream, or beck, running through the garden.

I distinctly remember the cold clarity of the air, standing in the garden when we arrived and breathing deep lungfuls of the most delicious, fresh, cool air I'd ever experienced.

We had gone there to earn money. Lee's parents were paying us to redecorate the building that had just been extended and renovated ready for their retirement. Both these amazing people lived well into their nineties in this beautiful spot.

We painted walls, hung wallpaper, walked five miles through the dark to the local pub, slept in separate rooms, talked, planned, dreamed and ate nice food.

I was happy; I could really feel my life had turned a corner.

When Lee's parents came to visit one weekend, I learned more about their lives from Lee's mother, the powerful matriarch of the family.

I've always been an early riser and got up one morning with a plan to walk in the nearby woodlands alone. The countryside around the cottage was glorious and wild, very unlike Northamptonshire and Oxfordshire where I'd grown up.

I crept down the stairs holding my hand-made boots, lace up, over ankle Derby cut with heavy double layer oak bark soles and steel quarter tips on the heels.

As I opened the door to the kitchen I was slightly taken aback by the sight of Lee's mother sitting by the Aga cooker in her dressing gown.

'Good morning, Robert.' Her Boston accent was softened by thirty years of living in England. 'Would you like a cup of tea?'

I was a little flustered. This was the first time I'd been alone with her. She smiled kindly at me, but I somehow knew I was in for a grilling.

I now understand this moment. When I meet my children's friends or lovers I'm bursting with questions. I've learned to go easy, to take time, not to ask too many things, but I always want to find out more about them.

Clearly, Lee's mother had been biding her time. Who was this strange young man her daughter was living with, in a truck, when she should be studying at university?

She grilled me about my parents, my education, the fact that I had been expelled from school was noted, did I have a criminal record? I was honest with her: I did have a criminal past, although I wasn't sure I had the actual record to go with it.

Essentially, I had let a very amusing friend give me a lift in a very expensive car when I was seventeen, and the car, strictly speaking, didn't belong to him.

(The details of this sorry chapter in my life are explained in a previous book, *Thin He Was and Filthy-Haired*.)

She asked what my father did in the war. I explained as best I could and mentioned he had been an RAF navigator and pilot.

The topic of the war lingered and I was told the story of how Lee's parents had met. He was a field surgeon with the British Army, trying to save the lives of injured soldiers in forward operating theatres.

She was an American Army nurse who had landed on the Normandy beaches a few days after D-Day after they had cleared most of the bodies, but with masses of badly injured boys to care for, she had clearly seen carnage and horror on a scale I cannot begin to imagine.

They met during the war and worked in various allied medical units across Europe. Forced apart then reunited, they married secretly in London. It was an incredible story with far more detail than I'm giving here, I don't feel it's right for me to recount those details in case my memory has embroidered them beyond the facts, but it's fair to state that they'd both helped a great many people to either survive or die a little less painfully.

When I recounted this event to Lee later that day she seemed delighted. I had survived the famous inquisition; it seemed I was being accepted into this extraordinary family.

As some may remember and others may have heard, what was ahead of us in 1976 was the hottest, driest year on record in the British Isles.

It didn't rain a drop from early April until mid-September. This has never happened since and if it did, we'd all be in serious trouble.

The ground was so dry it cracked open, it damaged buildings, the country resembled Australia in a midsummer drought. The fields were dusty brown, the reservoirs were muddy puddles, there were water shortages, standpipes in the street and endless long, hot summer days.

It was brilliant.

We eventually wound our way back south, took a long jaunt through Wales where we dropped in on the odd commune or friend's cottage to deliver shoes or get new orders for elfin slip-ons with Celtic rune designs on the vamp, and chunky work boots with contrasting colourful additions around the lacing and toe caps.

We'd park in woodland, or farmyards, at the end of tree-covered lanes, it was idyllic.

We stayed near friends from Oxford who were living in a row of cottages in the village of Fyfield not far from my parents' house.

It was here that we met a puppy belonging to a delightful organic, vegetarian hippy family, a puppy who would become the legendary Ruffage.

Lee instantly adored him. He sat on her foot and had an erection within thirty seconds of meeting her. So now we were two post-urban peasants and a dog living in a truck. But we had suntans and relatively clean clothes and occasionally enough money to buy decent food.

It was during this period of bucolic bliss that one sunny

afternoon, as Ruffage lay panting in the shade of the tree we were parked under, we closed the rear door and Lee and I made love for the first time.

Now the term 'make love' can be cheesy and a bit embarrassing but I chose it carefully. This was a very long, slow courtship at a time when such things didn't happen among our peers.

I'm ashamed to admit that I did occasionally have sex with women whose names I never knew. In those days, it just happened. I'm not saying it was regular occurrence, possibly three or four times in my life. All the other women I had sex with I knew very well, but the fact that it was so incredibly casual and inconsequential is now hard to comprehend.

I have since learned how common this casual sexual behaviour was from an American academic I met in the late 1990s who had just completed her contemporary history doctorate. Her theory was that I lived through a period she had dubbed the 'Triple P-A' decade.

That is, Post Pill Pre-Aids.

From the late 1960s to the late 1970s, according to her thesis, people could have sex without restraint, gay, straight, it didn't matter. The woman wouldn't get pregnant because of the Pill, and the biggest risk was a slightly embarrassing STD that was curable.

So yes, on that delicious summer afternoon Lee and I made love. It was wonderful, it was gentle and slow, and I didn't feel depressed afterwards.

We went back to Wales to deliver shoes and get paid, we spent one night parked right next to Lake Bala, where a proper Welsh farmer let us stay, 'as long as it's only one night' he said in Welsh, with his young daughter translating for us.

This setting was nothing short of ludicrously bucolic. Lee stripped off naked and swam in the lake; I paddled as I couldn't swim, Ruffage had a swim, immediately went back into the truck and shook himself, soaking everything.

We had no plan, no ultimate goal, we tried to find somewhere peaceful to park up for a couple of days and that was good enough.

We eventually wound our way back to Bath, possibly with the vague intention of joining up with a convoy of similar trucks and buses and heading to a festival we'd heard about in Devon. I thought I might be able to sell a lot of elfin shoes decorated with tassels and bells.

Elfin gear was massive in the mid-to-late seventies, just before bin liners, safety pins and mohawk haircuts.

The day we arrived in Bath we soon discovered everyone we knew was working on a film. There was much excitement about this as people we knew, people who survived on unemployment benefit and super low-paid work, were suddenly cash rich.

We strolled through the centre of the city to an area blocked off from traffic, a street crammed with big trucks and generator sets rumbling away in ex-military vehicles.

We met some friends dressed up as eighteenth-century peasants, although it was hard to tell the difference from their normal attire, they kind of dressed like that anyway.

We learned that the film was *Joseph Andrews*, based on a Henry Fielding novel. *Tom Jones,* the previous film by the same production company and director, had been a massive commercial success.

The director, who I saw at a distance but never met, was Tony Richardson, who was then married to Vanessa Redgrave, so this was no small budget affair. This was a big movie with proper cameras on cranes, famous people in the cast and a massive crew.

The British love long-dress dramas, always have, always will. This was one of those. Horses and carriages, dirty peasants, lecherous vicars, posh old ladies with big hair and sexy young men in loose-fitting white shirts, which they generally take off at some point to chop wood or scythe grass.

I can't recall the details but it soon became apparent we could use our truck to move equipment if we wanted.

We were introduced to one of the men with money. I now understand he would have been a line producer tasked with making sure the logistics of a big film crew ran smoothly. At the time, I had no idea how a film production operated, which may have been an advantage. Total innocence can get you a long way. Never pretend you know something you don't, be naive even if it's embarrassing, that's the way you learn. I must have understood that back in the summer of 1976, although I'm certain I never consciously made the connection.

The production of *Joseph Andrews* was mobile, there were many locations in the script and they had to supply food, somewhere for the crew to stay and the right kit to get the job done.

As far as I understood it at the time, the man with the money was a tough-looking hippy bloke a good bit older than me with a Land Rover and access to a lot of cash. I think he may have been ex-military and I'm fairly confident he had firearms, although I never saw him brandishing them.

The filming in Bath was complete the day we arrived, but following orders from the tough-looking hippy in the Land Rover we had been allowed within the barrier where the crew were located.

Somehow we had ended up being part of the crew. No interviews, no forms to fill in. We had a truck, they needed to move stuff, get on with it.

I helped load boxes of thick wires and connectors into the back of our truck while Lee sat in the cab studying a map we'd been given. Next came a couple of huge arc lights and the stands and rigging that went with them and I was handed £50 in cash to pay for petrol and supper and we set off for the Cotswolds, the next location for the film.

I sat in the passenger seat and showed Lee the money. I had never held that much money in my life, I had never had anything like £50 in my possession at one time.

She smiled and started the truck. For once it started first time and she gingerly reversed out of the crew compound and into the busy streets of Bath.

We drove across the Cotswold escarpment to a village called Bourton-on-the-Hill just outside Moreton-in-the-Marsh. If you are ever in the area there is a magnificent tithe barn in the village, it's occasionally open to the public and is a truly spectacular building.

This barn was the location for the next scene the cast and crew were going to shoot.

Once we arrived in the courtyard in front of this massive

medieval building, it must have become apparent to people higher up in the chain of command in the production that we lived in the truck.

'Can you stay here the night, bit of added security?' said a man with a big walkie-talkie. We discovered that the cast and crew were staying in various hotels and bed and breakfasts in the area. Clearly, we didn't need accommodation so we agreed to spend the night next to a row of massive furniture trucks full of equipment and props. We were paid another £50 for our services.

Late that night by the light of our paraffin lamp I counted out money. After filling the truck with petrol and buying food, wine, toilet roll, tobacco and dog food, I had £68. The most money I'd ever had in my life, the most money I'd ever seen up to that point. I slept with it rolled up under my pillow.

Ruffage had very little difficulty living with a film crew. In a field on the opposite side of the road from the tithe barn was the catering tent. We went over early in the morning and stood in line, now with security passes around our necks.

We ate very well but not as well as Ruffage. He stood by each chair in the big tent full of extras in eighteenth-century costume and wagged his tail. Before long someone would notice him and hold out a bit of ham or bacon for him. He wolfed it in seconds then nudged their leg for more. As people cleared their plates, quite a few of them put bits of pie or leftover meat on the grass for him.

He ate so much he could barely walk. We found him later that evening lying on his back, legs in the air, his massive swollen stomach almost making his unpleasant penis seem an appropriate size.

He followed us back to the truck, grunting with each step. I had to help him up the steps, his stubby little legs couldn't manage the extra weight. If you are a dog lover or a vet, yes, I'm aware that Labradors, whose genetic heritage clearly resided in Ruffage, will literally eat themselves to death. We did keep an eye on him and he did shed the enormous weight gain later.

After filming took place in the massive tithe barn, the location changed to Chastleton House, an Elizabethan mansion not far from Chipping Norton. Once again this magnificent house now owned by the National Trust is open to the public, it's worth a visit if you're passing. This time the crew trucks, cast caravans and catering department were located in a beautiful meadow alongside the house.

Somehow, probably because I was happy to do it, I became head of toilets. I dug a big pit in the far corner of the field into which I tipped the contents of the 'Sanilavs,' the portable toilets that were in all the caravans used by the cast. It was a big cast, there were lots of caravans and lots of Sanilavs, I was busy.

I can proudly boast that I have buried the droppings of many very famous actors from that era and I was happy to do it. By this time we were earning more than £150 a week (to put that into context, £150 in 1976 was the equivalent of more than £750 today) and we didn't have to buy anything: not food, petrol or dog food. Nothing. The production even gave me the shovel to dig the hole and I've still got it to this day in my shed.

By this stage Lee had done a bit of work as an extra in the film, a background artist, dressed up in peasant clothes with Ruffage sporting a makeshift rope lead the props department cobbled together. Someone, I'm sure it wasn't Tony Richardson the director, but someone noticed Ruffage the dog. They must have decided he looked suitably peasant-like and suggested an actor with a speaking role playing a yokel hold the lead.

Suddenly, Ruffage was in the cast. He did four days filming, was thankfully fairly well-behaved and earned some serious dog-acting fees: £10 a day. That's the equivalent of £50 in today's money. For Ruffage, the grossest dog in canine history. Ker-ching.

While we were parked in this unspeakably beautiful meadow next to Chastleton House we met a few members of the cast. One of them, a delightful old actor called Michael Hordern, peered into the back of the truck and commented how homely it was. Lee invited him in for a cup of tea and he accepted.

He sat with us for an afternoon wearing full eighteenth-century costume telling stories of his career. I later discovered how famous he was, my mother 'utterly adored' Michael Hordern, he was in hundreds of films, look him up, you'll see.

We eventually met the star of the movie, the man playing Joseph Andrews. A young and very handsome actor called Peter Firth. Some of you may know him from his role as Sir Harry Pearce in the TV series *Spooks*, the grumpy old bald bloke who runs MI6. Yes, him.

Back then he was a slim young man with glorious golden curls.

He became a regular visitor to our little home, swooping in wearing a loose shirt and breeches, swearing about how shit it was making this film.

It is possible that during these visits a small amount of marijuana was smoked and on one hot, hazy day my toilet cleaning rota was a little delayed.

During lunch that day I was criticised by a large and angry woman because I hadn't emptied Beryl Reid's Sanilav.

I felt guilty. Here I was, eating amazing food for free, getting paid more money than I'd ever imagined and I was so stoned I'd forgotten to do my job.

I rushed to her caravan immediately and carried the bucket as discreetly as possible through the crowds of extras, the hundreds of parked cars and rows of caravans and trucks.

I believe Ms Reid was waiting impatiently outside her caravan, I never spoke to her but I was very aware who this *grande dame* of stage and screen was. She was slightly terrifying, constantly surrounded by a crowd of fawning and very camp men who wore gold watches, weird city shoes and had brightly coloured jumpers slung over their shoulders with the arms loosely knotted at the front. Their hair was long, but not overly long, not hippy long, more Bee Gees' long, very coiffured and flouncy.

I clearly didn't register in their world as anything other than low-life toilet scum and I can distinctly remember not being even mildly offended by this.

After filming at Chastleton House was complete, we packed up and travelled all of five miles up the road to the Market Place in Stow-on-the-Wold. Here we parked behind high stone walls in the grounds of a run-down stately home. The site is now a Tesco supermarket.

Peter Firth rented a beautifully converted double-decker bus that was parked in the garden.

It was fairly apparent that Lee found this handsome young actor very attractive but I don't remember feeling jealous, I found him very attractive too, so I quite understood, plus he didn't seem that interested in anything as mundane as sex.

It was so hot every day, we got used to it with barely a comment. Every morning I woke up to crystal clear skies and hot sun. 1976 was very unlike your average British summer. One evening when Peter returned from filming and I'd buried the last Sanilav full of blue toxic liquid and high-end faecal matter, we walked down a quiet lane that leads away from Stow-on-the-Wold.

I can recall what I was wearing and it causes some embarrassment now. Baggy blue striped dungarees and red leather clogs. That was it.

I was very tanned and scrawny with thick long hair almost reaching my arse. In 1976 I was a full-blown, died-in-the-wool, truck-dwelling hippy dude.

Lee would have been wearing a thin cotton dress with no bra, something that annoyed my mother, although it's important to point out my mother wasn't on the walk with us.

As we strolled along the lane somewhat slightly stoned, Ruffage jumped up a bank ahead of us and we heard a splash. As we got closer we realised he'd jumped into an old horse watering trough partly obscured by the overgrown hedge that surrounded it.

This Roman-era, large stone water trough was being fed by a spring which even in that hot, dry summer was still producing copious amounts of freezing cold water.

Peter, clearly not a man ashamed of his body, immediately stripped off and plunged into the freezing cold stone bath. Lee, due to her Scandinavian heritage and also not ashamed of her physique did likewise, but it took me a little longer as I wasn't in the least bit confident about my body. But it was a very hot day so I eventually followed.

It was freezing, I made a lot of noise and could only stay in the water for about five seconds. Lee got out next, stood on the path with her thin summer dress, now completely transparent and plastered to her in classic wet T-shirt fashion, in broad daylight and barely fifty metres outside a classic Cotswold market town.

Digging her prized single lens reflex camera out of her droopy shoulder bag she took a picture of myself and Peter sitting on the edge of this stone bath full of icy water.

I no longer have a copy of this picture but I remember it well, a black-and-white photograph of two naked young men sitting in the evening sun. There are no revealing glimpses of anything untoward, it was all very tasteful. The water trough is still there if you're interested, it's down a narrow path called Well Lane, just on the northern edge of Stow-on-the-Wold.

One of the main reasons I remember this brief moment is the sobering recollection of penis size differentiation. I'm far too old now to have concerns about this dull topic but the icy-cold plunge I'd just taken had a dramatic effect on my twenty-year-old manhood. Imagine a tiny button mushroom poking out of neatly mown grass. Yep, you've got it, enough said.

Peter hauled himself out of the water and sat next to me. Glancing down at my button mushroom, he laughed. Not in a cruel way and for some reason I wasn't offended.

When I followed suit and glanced down at Peter's meat and two veg, no such shrinkage was apparent, my goodness no.

Why is biology so unfair?

After about six weeks working with the *Joseph Andrews* film crew, we decided to move on. I assume the production were working in a studio for the remainder of the shoot and didn't need the road crew any more. No more Sanilavs to empty, no more free food, no more wads of cash from an old ammunition box in the back of a Land Rover. No more spliffs with handsome well-endowed actors.

On the plus side, the fact that we left the production probably extended Ruffage's life by a few years. By this point he was almost spherical, a massively overweight waddling balloon of a dog, grunting and panting just walking along the road.

We also had about £300 in cash (the equivalent of £1500 today), which we deposited in Lee's bank account.

We headed south from the Cotswolds and ended up on Dartmoor for the night. We parked in a very remote spot but the evening was delightful, we ate wonderful food we could finally afford and the sun was shining, the sky blue and cloudless.

There were numerous evenings like this when we lived in the truck, evenings where, for the first time in my twenty years, I experienced genuine, deep relaxation. I felt very fulfilled, happy, calm and at one with myself. I was looking after myself, reliant on no one, I had zero anxiety about where I was going to live or what I was going to eat. I had worked hard, fixed things that were broken, polished things until they shone, everything was tidied and put away in its proper place and I'd sit down, roll a cigarette, pat Ruffage on his enormous head and truly relax.

The following day we drove to Her Majesties Prison, Dartmoor, a fairly forbidding place in a wind-blown and sparsely inhabited corner of the British Isles.

It was here we visited an old friend who was serving a prison sentence for the theft of a couple of tons of lead from a church roof.

This was Pirate Paul, a legend from my misspent Oxford youth. Anyone who saw the stage play *Jerusalem* by Jez Butterworth will remember the character of Rooster Byron, played brilliantly by Mark Rylance. When I saw the play a few years back, I was transported back to those days. It was as if Mr Butterworth knew Pirate Paul as well as I did, but could obviously write about him with far greater skill.

Paul was a scallywag, a ne'er-do-well, a thieving wheeler dealer, a midnight rambler, a completely untrustworthy scoundrel and I adored him.

Maybe, and I feel cruel for even suggesting this, but maybe Paul wasn't the sharpest knife in the petty criminal drawer. He'd pinched the lead off the roof of a chapel in the middle of Oxford. Simple job, ladder up the side of the building, crowbar to ease the lead up, peel it off the roof, roll it up, chuck it down to the ground, take it down the scrapyard, get a few quid and go to the pub. Job done.

The only downside was that the chapel happened to be next door to where he lived. I understood the reasoning, but had I been there at the time I might have suggested caution. But for Pirate Paul it was easy pickings.

Sadly for Paul, the police arrived to find his entrance hall piled up with rolls of freshly peeled lead and when all the other minor and petty offences he'd committed were taken into consideration he got three years in the slammer.

For reasons that now escape me, he'd been transferred from Oxford prison to Dartmoor, which meant he was getting very few, if any, visits from people he knew. He was delighted to see us when we'd finally gone through all the ancient historic cart gates and entered the visitors' area.

We'd had to leave Ruffage outside, so we tied him to a stout post in the car park, having learned by then if we left him in the truck he'd simply destroy the thing, chew his way through the wooden door and for the following few days deposit a trail of vile chipboard tubes along the highways and byways.

We spent an hour with Paul. He hugged Lee for a little too long, explaining that it was the first time he'd hugged a woman in years. In his normal day-to-day life outside prison I think it's fair to say Paul hugged a lot of women.

When we had used up all our visiting time and after multiple, prolonged hugs for both of us, we left through the main gate while being scolded by some fairly terrifying prison guards. Ruffage had been barking non-stop and had set off all the guard dogs, the noise was deafening.

'Get that fucking mutt away from here, pronto,' said a very large guard as we scurried towards the now frantic Ruffage. We unleashed him and legged it as fast as we could.

The contrast between Dartmoor and where we ended up that evening could not have been more pronounced. We drove down off the moor to what Lee had described as a farm just to the east of Plymouth on the South Devon coast. It belonged to the parents of a girl she'd been at school with, and we would be attending her twenty-first birthday party.

When we finally found this farm, it was obvious from the first glimpse that this was no run-down hovel with a rusting shed full of pigs behind it. This was a magnificent fourteen-bedroom Georgian country house, the sort of place BBC location scouts would beg to use in yet another Jane Austen long-dress adaptation.

The girl who was turning twenty-one was a sturdy, horsey, jolly hockey-sticks type. She greeted us warmly and admired the truck. I have zero recall of her name but it would have been posh. Jocelyn, Cressida, Ophelia, something along those lines.

She said she'd guide us to where we could park up and climbed aboard the truck. Lee drove down a long lane between high hedges and onto a wide field. It was only as we reached the brow of the small hill in the centre that we realised this field overlooked the sea. It was the most magnificent spot. We were parked on the top of an amazing promontory with the sea on three sides far below.

Out of all the places we stopped, this one was possibly the most spectacular. We were so privileged to be allowed to stay there. This wasn't a crowded camp site near a Devon beach, this was a field on a massive private estate with a private beach down a steep track to one side.

The party that followed was more extravagant than anything I'd attended to that date.

I believe the father of the young woman who turned twenty-one was something in the Tory party, the guests at this event were a social group I didn't tend to hang out with. Large numbers of slightly fey young men who clearly styled themselves after characters in E.M. Forster novels. The young women were loud, sturdy and very horsey, so I can't imagine how a skinny long-haired hippy would have blended in, but blend I did.

We stayed for a week, hosting several evenings with the younger people from the party and family who came up the hill to relax and smoke dope, probably not something they could have done in the formal gardens that surrounded the main house.

Not long after leaving the idyllic retreat we transported around twenty very odorous hippies from a dismal hill encampment in Devon to Stonehenge Festival with two tipis tied onto the roof.

Yes, there were hippies who lived in tipis full-time back in the 1970s.

Transporting tipis is no easy task, I'm not sure how long the truck was, maybe five metres, but the poles were around eleven metres long.

As we drove along we could see the enormous, bouncing wooden poles overhanging above us with a dirty T-shirt tied to the far end. There was the same ridiculous overhang out of the back. I don't want to consider what would have happened if the half-baked knots and rotting rope we tied them on with had failed.

The journey was fairly arduous with a truckload of hippy mothers, their fly-specked and crying babies, some incredibly droopy men and a large collection of scabby dogs. Not to mention one person on acid, a diabetic junkie and a box full of cats and kittens. Ruffage was not well pleased with all these travelling companions.

However it was quite entertaining. Squatted on the floor of the truck's cab as we trundled along was a figurehead of the extreme hippy movement, a man called Sid Rawle. It was hard to understand what Sid said due to his habit of smoking copious amounts of marijuana using a device known as a chillum.

This is essentially a hollow wooden or clay tube with marijuana tamped in at the thick end. The amount of marijuana Sid stuffed in these stinking pipes was huge, it was a little like smoking a small bonfire.

The fact that Sid Rawle lived to his mid-sixties is impressive. Back in 1976 his voice sounded like he was speaking through a soot-choked chimney, horse, dry and rasping.

Sid was a bit of a legend in hippy circles, he was thrust into the limelight in the late sixties when a huge group of hippies and students squatted in a 100-room mansion at 144 Piccadilly in London. Sid became their spokesman as the police moved in and evicted them. He later formed some sort of commune on an island off the coast of Ireland owned by John Lennon, so, you know, the stories were good, what we could understand anyway.

It was a massive relief to unload the poles from the roof when we finally arrived at Stonehenge that evening. I opened the back door and a long line of drooping hippies slowly emerged.

The smell in the back was, as my mother might describe, a bit 'goaty'.

We didn't stay at the festival, which was illegal and I could sense that bad stuff was about to kick off. We scarpered pretty quickly and left the area.

I wasn't a terribly good hippie. I didn't really like being stoned or drunk and I found these people to be fairly annoying. I wasn't one for the more drippy faux spiritual aspects of hippiedom, although to be fair to Sid Rawle, he spent his life organising gatherings and arguing for a more equal distribution of wealth and land in particular.

Sadly, he was the sort of person it was all too easy for the powerful to dismiss as a scraggy-haired nutter, but I would argue his core beliefs were benign and humane.

Eventually, after two and a half years pottering and many more adventures around the country, the truck ended up in the playground of a disused school in the village of North Leigh, Oxfordshire.

I moved out and started living in a building again, Lee went to London to do an apprenticeship as a shoemaker with John Lobb and Company. It was a very sad moment. I loved living in the truck, it was a very special time for me. On the odd occasion I would climb inside to find something on a winter afternoon, the interior now bare and cold, I found it very hard to accept we really had moved out.

I eventually sold the truck for £300 to a photographer from Taunton who wanted to use it as a mobile darkroom and studio.

What I learned during my life in a truck was very formative for the rest of my life. I became able to properly look after myself, I learned how to be tidy, how to fix engines, how to change tyres, how to light fires, cook, clean and save a tiny bit of money.

All fairly useful skills. Lee and I lived together in London for a short while but then drifted apart. The Truck Adventure was no longer keeping us together. But we have stayed friends all these years since. She soon became happily married to a film-maker and now has two grown children.

To this day, I will occasionally be driving through some obscure village in Wiltshire, a lay-by in Herefordshire, a lake in North Wales and suddenly remember I've been there before. We'd spent a few deliriously happy and peaceful nights living in a metal box parked at that spot, a small camp fire, a very fat dog with a large penis, some half-finished leather elfin shoes and a cup of tea.

Who Will Sing and Dance for You?

During the summer of 1981 there were numerous riots in England. The reasons behind this seemingly spontaneous explosion of rage on the streets were many and complex, but heavy-handed policing certainly didn't help. This was the dawning of the age of Thatcherism, not a happy time, but looking back from the present day, blimey, they'd hardly started.

When I say they, I mean the seismic shift in global politics that destroyed, very effectively, the previous thirty years of policies which struggled, mostly in vain, to make British society a little less economically unbalanced.

Thatcher in the UK and Reagan in the US were the first signs of the brutal retrenchment that led to Brexit and Trump.

There, I've said it, cards on the table. I'm not keen on either.

Anyway, back in the early 1980s in Brixton, Bristol, Liverpool and many other cities there were large-scale incidents involving hundreds of people and millions of pounds' worth of damage.

The TV coverage was comprehensive, the newspapers full of lurid tales and images of streets on fire.

The mini-riot that took place at the junction of Dalston Lane and Kingsland Road in East London was, by the standards of the day fairly contained. Plenty of police vans had rocks and bins thrown at them, there was a lot of shouting and a few windows got smashed but no buildings got burnt out and no one, as far as I recall, died.

While these shenanigans were going on in the street, in a room above the bar of the Crown and Castle pub on the corner where the riot broke out, four men stepped onto a makeshift stage.

I was one of them.

We wore suits and ties, but all the suits were baggy and ill-fitting, bought from charity shops. The ties were wide and loud, bright colours, we all wore brown Doctor Martens lace-up shoes and our hair was cut short, although mine stuck up on the top of my head without the aid of gel.

This was the first performance of what would become The Joeys, although at this time we didn't have a name for the group.

It was the first professional performance I ever gave. We each earned ten pounds and the memory of this night is for ever burned into my brain.

It was genuinely terrifying.

Well, it was terrifying for me. My fellow performers were seasoned professionals. Even as a child, I had never performed onstage, other than being the page boy to one of the wise men in a primary school nativity play, which it's fair to describe as a minor role.

I had never, in contrast to many performers, been desperate to get on a stage and show off. It's not that I wasn't a loud

mouth, it's not that I was introverted, shy and shunned attention, but the notion of performing onstage had never occurred
to me.

I didn't long to be an actor, it didn't interest me. When I
worked as a part of the production crew on the *Joseph Andrews*
film I had no desire to be in the film and I wasn't obsessed with
the lives of actors or their careers.

I always wanted to be a writer but didn't know how to do it,
and meeting Bernie and Graham suddenly gave me an outlet.

I can't remember any other details about the day of that performance. I know that at the time I was making shoes in a
warehouse next to Tower Bridge, I had a Morris Minor van,
and I know we drove to Dalston in it and it survived the riots.

I know I was feeling nauseous and thinking of ways to pull
out of the evening's arrangements. Bernie and Graham had
done this kind of thing many times before but I never had.

We entered the pub, which appeared to me to be full of
grumpy old blokes. I worried that this would be our audience.
We went upstairs and got changed in the empty kitchen at the
back of the room where we were going to perform. It smelled of
cooking oil and everything was covered in a thick layer of
grease.

Graham had a running order of the bits we were going to
perform. I remember looking at that and through the terror I
was experiencing, nothing made sense.

I suppose we must have rehearsed the show in the days
before, presumably in Bernie's apartment on Queensway in
West London, but I have zero recollection of that, I can only
remember that night.

Then Barbara, the woman who organised the event turned up. She informed us the crowds were building. She worked with Graham in some social work capacity but was very committed to organising political theatre events in her spare time.

'You ready?' she asked, I wasn't but I knew we had to go through with it. We entered the room.

It was packed. I knew a lot of the people in the audience which gives me the impression that I must have told everyone I knew to come along to see the show.

We climbed onto the small stage at one end of the room. The crowd fell silent and Graham introduced us, I cannot imagine what we looked like or how we came across. I was so nervous and felt totally inadequate, I distinctly remember thinking that it would all be over soon and I could go home.

No one recorded this event as there wasn't the technology available to do so. I know I had written a three-part sketch about a Second World War bomber crew who were flying over Dusseldorf late at night looking for an open kebab shop. This included some discussion about homophobia and a lot of slapstick.

What I will never forget was an incredible and life-changing revelation. Something I'd never experienced before.

Many weeks before this night I'd sat alone feverishly typing scripts on my mum's old manual typewriter, then, as we stood on that tiny stage delivering the words I'd written, people in the audience were laughing.

Not a polite giggle, more massive guffawing: they loved it.

That was the most intense feeling and it stayed with me: something I'd written made people laugh.

I know we sang songs, which went down very well. Graham had written those, brilliant lyrics and great accompaniment from the man on the piano whose name I can't remember.

Finally, we got to the last song. We did it with gusto. When it finished, Graham and Bernie said, 'Thank you very much and goodnight!' and the crowd roared their approval. I remember standing between them onstage looking out at the packed, noisy crowd clapping and cheering. Happy, delighted faces, it felt surreal.

I then noticed that Bernie and Graham were bowing like proper actors at the end of a play, so I did likewise.

It was only later that night, back at the Bermondsey warehouse I lived in, that my friends recalled the moment with much laughter, they said that at the end of the show, I looked like a rabbit in the headlights. Standing staring at the audience with my mouth open while Bernie and Graham bowed like professionals.

My strongest memory of this experience was the elation I felt when we'd finished. We returned to the greasy kitchen to change, gabbling and laughing, congratulating each other on the success of the show. I was dizzy with excitement. I'd never experienced anything like it, it was a high, a boost, a feeling of rocket-like acceleration into another realm.

I was instantly hooked and I have often reflected since that night that if, for whatever reason, the show had been a bit of a damp squib, if it had been merely 'okay' and 'not too bad for a first outing', I would never have strayed onto a stage again.

But it was deemed a rip-roaring success by everyone I spoke to who saw it.

So my life changed at that point. Over the following weeks, not only did Bernie come up with a name for the group, The Joeys, but we got booked to play other venues.

It was around this time that the cultural phenomena of 'alternative cabaret' and 'alternative comedy' was the hip new thing. People like Rik Mayall, Ade Edmondson, Nigel Planer and Peter Richardson, Alexei Sayle, Dawn French and Jennifer Saunders were appearing regularly at the Comedy Store and Comic Strip in Soho, venues The Joeys never appeared in.

Looking back, we did somehow exist outside what had already become the established anti-establishment alternative comedy scene. Many well-known TV faces for the following decades started their performing careers at those venues, but we had different plans.

A motivating force behind what we were doing was that we were overtly political. Bernie and Graham, unlike me, were very well-informed in the intricacies of left-wing politics. Graham lived in a flat in Kennington with two other left-wing activists, quiet men who looked at me askance. I was convinced they thought I was a capitalist sleeper agent, possibly a Thatcherite fellow-travelling Tory scum-bag. I wasn't anything of the sort, but I was also not very good at being a proper, hardcore leftie. I had always been self-employed. At the time The Joeys started, I ran a business that employed people, I even had a business bank account.

Graham and Bernie's critiques of the rampaging free-market philosophy touted by Margaret Thatcher were obviously prime material for us. We genuinely had something to kick against, a powerful populist right-wing government with an enormous majority in Parliament and an opposition in tatters.

We talked about the impact hard-hitting political theatre could have. I felt in my bones it would be minimal, but I never voiced those concerns. I was learning so much so fast I didn't want to mess it up.

After a handful of shows with the pianist whose name I can't remember, I know he was a lot older than the rest of us and he smoked a pipe and wore a flat cap, anyway, he didn't really want to do it any more and left us. Through the various contacts we had between us we met Nigel. He was an industrial-design graduate who could play the piano beautifully and had a small recording studio. He was perfect, although he had a beard. Unlike today, back in the early 1980s beards were not cool, at least we didn't think they were, but Nigel didn't wear a flat cap or smoke a pipe and was a very creative and very skilful musician.

So from that point on, we were four: Bernie, Nigel, Graham and Rob. The Joeys.

It took six months for me to transition from hunch-backed shoemaker into full-time performer; the business I had been a partner in, Bermondsey Bootmakers, continued quite happily without me.

For the first year we toured around London, playing two or three venues a week. We opened a joint account with the Co-op bank, which would occasionally have as much as two hundred pounds in it. Quite how we survived is beyond me now, we earned an absolute pittance.

Up to this point in my life, I had seen quite a few Shakespeare plays with my mum, been to a couple of pantomimes as a kid, watched a couple of school plays, but in comparison to your average drama student or run-of-the-mill actor my experience was tragically limited.

During that first year of my life with The Joeys, if I wasn't onstage, I was watching someone else who was. I went to see everything, diving into my new life with gusto. In the daytime I went to dance, mime and *commedia dell'arte* classes. When I wasn't doing that I was writing sketches, crudely rhyming song lyrics (never my strong point), and comedy monologues.

Graham wrote brilliant lyrics as I've already mentioned, including what would become our opening song for many years. It had a jazzy, up-tempo feel to it, strongly influenced by Joe Jackson's 1981 album, *Jumpin' Jive*.

Who will sing and dance for you,
Make you glad when you feel blue,
Do you know who you're talking to
We're the J-O-E-Y Joeys.

When it comes to politics we're correct,
Our ideological lines connect,
Sexism and racism we reject
We're the J-O-E-Y Joeys.

We're Bernie and Nigel and Graham and Rob,
And most of us have a daytime job,

We've social skills as you can tell,
And we're terribly polite 'cos we was brought up
well.

We write our act collectively
Work in communal harmony
And plagiarise outrageously
We're the J-O-E-Y Joeys.

Now Nigel on Piano plays a real cool lick
And Bernie wears suits and is really slick
Robert is worried where his life will go
And Graham's a closet skinhead that's why he's
slow.

You may not think that we are stars
'Cos we still do gigs in pubs and bars
That's why we also sell used cars
We're the J-O-E-Y Joeys.

A Skiddle-ee dee bop
A Skiddle-ee dee bop
Skiddle-ee dee bop de bop de bop

Well you may think our act is trash
Loud and silly and boring and brash
But we don't care 'cos we've got your cash
We're the J-O-E-Y Joeys

We're social climbers through and through,
and even though we may be nice to you
When we get famous if we should meet,
We'll walk right by you on the street.

So who will sing and dance for you,
Make you glad when you feel blue,
Do you know who you're talking to
We're the J-O-E-Y Joeys.

We sang that song literally hundreds of times and I always loved doing it.

There are lines in the song that expressed our concern that success might affect us, might make us feel self-important, something we frowned upon; we did not want to believe we were special. This was our job, we were just comedy workers.

There are lines in the song that captured what we were trying to do, in particular 'sexism and racism we reject'.

Much of our discussions, sketches and songs were around the subject of feminism and the male response to it, not a reaction, a response. We accepted that all men were sexist but the idea behind The Joeys was that we were trying not to be.

It's a fairly hazy political concept, I grant you, but we were very serious about it. We often received complicated criticism about our stance, some of it justified, some of it baffling. It was a minefield to wander through, terms like 'feminist men' and 'right-on trendies' were bandied about, although we always refuted them.

A very memorable heckle we once heard came just as the audience applause died down at the end of a show. We heard a woman's voice shout from the back of the theatre, with some anger, 'Men still rule the world!'

This devastatingly accurate appraisal of the gender war was then followed by a clearly very male shout of, 'Yeah.'

I can't remember who the woman was, I know she was Australian but I can't recall who she was. I remember who the man was though and it makes me smile to recall it. His name is Michael Morris, who went on to co-found and run Artangel, an organisation that develops and promotes big artistic installations and events all over the world.

He's a lovely bloke. I've seen many of the events and exhibitions he's helped produce. We've discussed this moment a couple of times and I just thought it encapsulated the contortions men go through who consider such things as sexism, patriarchy and male cultural hegemony.

Although they were both right of course, it was the male 'yeah' that fascinated us. It became a catchphrase within the group. We'd be loading up my battered old van and someone would shout, 'Men still rule the world!' to which the response would always be a guttural, male, 'Yeah!'

It encapsulated the impossible position men are in when 'being supportive' of feminism. How on earth do you do it without perpetuating the very thing you are trying to undermine? Patriarchy, big word, massive, five-thousand-year-long tradition, a tradition that is currently being reinforced all over the world. Bearded nut-jobs in fundamentalist religious subsects, hideous tanned white old men strutting about like tatty cockerels. Oh yes, patriarchy is alive and well. Men did then and do still rule the world, The Joeys' keen analysis of this culture did little or nothing to diminish it, but the heckle stayed with us.

We were the living embodiment of the contradiction that all men who think women get a raw deal are in. By merely breathing, you are in many ways part of the problem.

I don't remember hearing the term 'politically correct' being used during this period, even though the notion was alluded to in our opening song. It may have been around but as we all know, the whole imaginary concept of 'being PC' was cooked up by right-wing male journalists to denigrate attempts at shifting cultural attitudes.

You didn't know that? Well, it's true and you know now.

There you go, that was the sort of thing we'd say at the time. So yes, we were a left-wing, anti-sexist, anti-racist men's comedy group and strangely enough, contrary to how that might sound, I think we were quite funny.

Our audiences laughed, a lot.

Sometime in early 1982 we started a regular Saturday night slot at the Covent Garden Community Centre, a building that is now probably a branch of Fat Face or a Belgo restaurant.

A young student from Manchester University drama department became a regular warm-up man for us. He produced prodigious amounts of new material each week, delivering his monologues at breakneck speed.

His name was Ben Elton, and he went on to be quite successful. Okay, he went on to be a huge, gut-churning success. Just about everything Ben wrote was a success: fronting the hit TV show *Saturday Night Live*, co-writing *The Young Ones*, co-writing *Blackadder* with Richard Curtis, writing the book of the stage musical *We Will Rock You* and penning dozens of best-selling books.

As The Joeys' popularity grew entirely by word of mouth, we started filling bigger and bigger venues, packed upstairs rooms in pubs all over London, and not long after, around the country. It was during this heady period I met Sarah, who was a member of a long-standing feminist theatre group called Cunning Stunts.

They were very funny, surreal and very unlike the slick, besuited Joeys. I'd seen them perform a few times and really enjoyed their bizarre take on the world.

Sarah and I had a bit of a romance. It was never very serious; well, looking back, I'm sure I behaved like a total dick. She was a wonderful, talented and very intelligent woman and I was a bit of a twat. I'm saying this because it's possible I didn't take our dalliance very seriously, but she may have done.

The Stunts had a venue booked at the Edinburgh Fringe Festival but they didn't want to risk paying for the venue with their own show and possibly losing money. If I remember correctly, the group were approaching the end of their run, some key members had left and it felt like they had this one last gig to do before they went their separate ways.

Sarah played the trombone, an instrument I discovered was painfully loud when you were in a small room. All of the Stunts were musicians and did not follow the supposed female tradition of trying to look attractive to men.

They were quirky, original and at that time, very popular. It was Sarah who suggested they split the Edinburgh venue and running costs with The Joeys. Three weeks in a bar called Buster Brown's near Waverley train station at the Edinburgh Fringe Festival in 1982.

I had heard of the Edinburgh Fringe Festival but I'd never been to it. I'd only been to the city of Edinburgh once with my mum and dad when I was a kid. We went to watch the Edinburgh Military Tattoo, you remember, bagpipes, drums, marching, men in kilts. I loved it, obviously.

The Stunts had booked a two-bedroom flat next to a bakery in Edinburgh, and so when August came around, Bernie and Nigel and Graham and Rob caught the night train to Edinburgh. We had so little money I cannot now imagine how we coped, I do remember getting on the train in London, steamy with summer heat, and getting off in Edinburgh feeling like I was being cut in half by bitter cold wind.

We found the flat, it was tiny. There were six members of Cunning Stunts in two rooms and three Joeys in a very cramped bedroom. Sarah and I slept on a mattress in the entrance hall.

I'd never been a student but I imagined that's what it would have been like, however I wasn't eighteen, I was twenty-six and had my own flat in London. I remember finding the accommodation arrangements quite tough to start with, but thankfully the Stunts and The Joeys got on very well together.

The woman who had organised the whole thing was called Jeanette Winterson, literary-minded readers will recognise the name. She has since become a very successful author, *Oranges are not the Only Fruit* being one of her early successes. She had booked everything and arranged the venue and transport for the Cunning Stunts.

We all traipsed off to Buster Brown's for the first performance. It was becoming clear to us that the Edinburgh Fringe was quite a big affair, I had no notion of how many shows were on until I read the Fringe Brochure. It was as thick as an old-fashioned telephone directory and our event was on about page 132, a tiny bit of type at the bottom of a very busy page. No one was going to see that.

The venue wasn't so much a bar as a seedy old disco. It had a tiny stage and weird lights, not like a theatre or even a decent room above a pub, it was a pokey dive with hideous decor.

Our hearts sank, but we made the best of it we could.

I went out to the street with our single poster, a screen-printed A1 sheet of thin paper. We all loved the poster, designed by a lovely bloke called Derek who married Lee, the woman I'd lived with in the truck.

However we could only afford to print very few of them and as I recall we only had one left. I stuck it onto the board outside the venue with Blu-tack, worrying that someone might pinch it.

When it was time for the Cunning Stunts to start the performance, there were four people in the audience.

Literally four.

We had always joked that we would never do a show if there were the same number of people onstage as there were in the audience. We'd been very lucky, it had never happened, but as we stared out from behind the makeshift curtains at the back of the little stage, there really were only four people sitting at the back. Rows and rows of empty fold-up seats in front of them.

Just before the Stunts started their show, one lone audience member arrived, which raised the total to five. We knew we had to do the show.

We did do the show, the five people watching clapped enthusiastically when we'd finished and as we were leaving I asked Jeanette what the takings were like. We'd grossed £25 and the rental for the space was, I recall, £50 a night so things were not looking good.

We took down our one poster and traipsed back to the tiny apartment and drowned our sorrows.

The following night there were fifty people in the audience. We didn't know how they'd heard about the show, we only had one poster and we didn't have any leaflets like all the student theatre groups did. The audience just appeared. Thankfully, that evening's performance went really well again.

On the third night it was sold out, packed to the rafters and we got a blazingly positive review from a man called Jack Tinker in, of all newspapers, the *Daily Mail*.

From then on there were huge queues outside the venue each night, dozens of people hoping to get returns or no-show tickets.

This was the year that saw the first Perrier Award, a comedy award that many people you've heard of have won. We weren't even nominated, in fact we didn't know about it until long after the festival had finished, but that year Hugh Laurie, Emma Thompson and Stephen Fry won it. They were with the Cambridge Footlights, the very opposite end of the spectrum to The Joeys, or so we liked to think at the time.

On returning to London, The Joeys went from strength to strength. We had shows booked up for months in advance. We were earning our living from showing off. It was such a massive change in my life. Up to that point, I'd always scraped a living by making things and selling them but now I was earning a crust from doing something I really loved.

In the few years before the founding of The Joeys I'd become friends with a remarkable New Yorker called Michael. He was a huge, as in very tall, loud, New York Jew. He discussed his Jewishness at great length and in a very loud voice. He'd say phrases like, 'I'm Jewish, whaddaya expect!' or, 'Don't ask me, I'm a Jew.'

Michael was an architecture student who had dropped out of college and become, as he described it, a 'fag interior decorator'.

His false modesty didn't suit him. He was an incredibly successful furniture maker and property developer who tragically died of a heart attack at a very tender age. I still miss him now thirty years later.

At the time he had a big yellow VW transporter van that he used to shift the furniture he'd made and he was fascinated by The Joeys.

'Goddamn leftie hypocrites, I love you guys!' he'd bawl at us at the end of a performance.

Towards the end of that year, we got a booking to do shows in Amsterdam, Michael drove us there in his big yellow van. The back was lined with old mattresses and all our bags.

We had a week-long run at the Melkweg, at the time a legendary hippy hang-out just off the Leidseplein near the centre of that beautiful city. Melkweg means Milky Way in Dutch, the building had once been a dairy and the Oude Zaal (Old Hall) was a brilliant venue. Packed out every night with amazingly cool-looking Dutch hipsters who got all the English jokes and were a brilliant audience.

I'd never been to Amsterdam before. It felt incredibly romantic and special. We spent long nights drinking in clubs, having late breakfasts at the American Hotel, cycling bikes around the streets and, of course, because it was still cool to do so, smoking lots of cigarettes. We could have smoked dope but interestingly none of us did. I can't remember making a decision about it or even discussing it, it was just something we had all done in our earlier life and had moved on from.

Everyone smoked in Amsterdam and inspired by this I created a character called Helly Hhupter, a cool Dutch interior decorator who only ever entertained the rest of The Joeys, I don't think I ever performed as Helly onstage.

He talked about indoor gardening, riding cool bikes, having lots of sex while listening to Janis Joplin and smoking thousands of cigarettes. I think we decided it might be a little bit offensive to present Helly to a Dutch audience. More recently, when I've been in the Netherlands and I've paraded my early 1980s Dutch accent, no one seems to mind, but then again they were probably being ridiculously tolerant of the old British bloke who they truthfully found deeply offensive and ignorant. Dutch people are so nice.

I was loving my new life. It felt like it all changed in a couple of weeks although in reality it was over a year. It felt as though one moment I was hunched over a shoemaker's bench, the next I was drinking Dutch lager in a really cool club surrounded by incredibly tall and very beautiful women. And tall and very handsome men, and everyone was smoking.

I could not quite believe that I was allowed to earn a living dicking around onstage.

Then, just as it was really getting good, at the end of that year everything went a bit miserable.

Graham, a brilliant lyricist and poet, a fantastic, funny performer with a wonderful sense of humour, brilliant timing and confidence, a wordsmith of outstanding ability decided he wanted to do mime.

I was devastated; he wanted to leave The Joeys because, as he patiently tried to explain to me, he didn't feel comfortable with the public face of the group, essentially if I remember correctly, four men who were 'opposed to sexism'.

It's not that Graham was a massive sexist and he couldn't keep up the pretence, if anything he was the wisest member of the original group regarding sexual politics. However he'd met a young woman who did mime and they went off and mimed together.

No doubt they had intense discussions about the minefield of sexual politics we were inhabiting and I think Graham felt politically exposed. I'm guessing, I never really knew.

So it was just Bernie and Nigel and Rob, until we met Chris.

If we were looking for someone a bit like Graham to fill the gap, we could not have found anyone less plausible. Chris was gay, funny, bitchy, brilliant, troubled, gentle, conflicted, incredibly talented and occasionally terrifying.

He had trained as a classical ballet dancer, he studied 'the dance', as he referred to it jokingly, at the Royal Ballet School, first at White Lodge in Richmond Park and later at the Royal Opera House in Covent Garden.

And he could sing. Boy, could he sing. And tap dance, and leap about and do those pirouette things that ballet dancers can do.

He was, in many ways, the most unlikely replacement, and yet it worked. Chris gelled in a way I don't think we could ever have imagined. Instead of fizzling out, this new Joeys line-up exploded onto stages all over the country. We could fill any theatre we were booked into. Looking back I have no idea how. We didn't appear on television, so the only explanation I have is that our reputation was 95 per cent word-of-mouth and 5 per cent great reviews in magazines and newspapers.

We found a manager, a lovely man called David Jones, who was a brilliantly efficient producer. He always had a big book with him, and when we sat around talking about what we wanted to do, he would write in it in really big writing, taking notes and not forgetting anything. David booked huge tours for us, all over the UK and some in the Netherlands.

In 1983, Bernie kept a record of how many shows we performed. We were onstage 287 times that year, which gives the impression that we had very few days off.

Chris very generously bought an old Land Rover and we spent a day making very uncomfortable seats in the back out of old wooden pallets and a bit of foam padding. We'd load the Land Rover with Nigel's electric piano, tape machines, props, banners, costumes and general baggage.

We actually had costumes. We ditched the double-breasted suits and wide boy colourful ties and with Bernie's sartorial eye came up with a new look. We all wore the same blue shirts, high-waisted baggy corduroy trousers, red braces, red ties and brown Doc Marten shoes.

We worked hard writing new material all the time, rehearsing, touring, travelling, joking and living in each other's pockets. We were almost like a band, the fact that only one of us was a musician was the only difference. The interpersonal relationships and tensions were just like every story I've heard of bands on the road.

The pressure on this small group as we became more successful was intense. We had to talk about every booking, we had to discuss the implications of playing in various venues. When we were asked to perform to the sixth-form pupils in a private school in Dorset, the discussions went on for hours. We eventually decided to turn it down even though the fee was generous.

We didn't earn that much money even when we were filling big venues but it was the first time I managed to save anything. Up to this point I'd always earned just about enough to last a week. As The Joeys' success increased, I was sometimes earning a couple of hundred pounds a week, which felt like a fortune.

At the time I was sharing a small basement flat in Islington with a wonderful Anglo-French architect called Christophe. We are still very good friends. I'd return from a gig late at night, Christophe would be up painting or working on the plans of a building and he'd put the kettle on, light up a couple of untipped Camel cigarettes, hand one to me and say, 'So, how did the show go, Robert?'

'Yeah, pretty amazing actually, like nine hundred people, we stormed it, yeah.'

He would then pull out a big calculator and do some mock calculations.

'So, maybe three hundred people, that's quite good.'

He was annoyingly accurate in his reappraisal of the actual number of people who came to see us. He knew me well, he knew I very occasionally had a tendency to exaggerate just a tiny little bit.

'Yeah, might have been three fifty to four hundred.'

'Three hundred,' said Christophe with a gentle smile.

We did so many shows in so many community centres, theatres and town halls they have all blurred together, however one very memorable night stayed with me. It was when I realised that this little band of brothers was bigger than the sum of its parts.

We were doing a Sunday evening concert at the Royal Exchange Theatre in Manchester.

We'd heard that it was sold out before we arrived, which, I can honestly claim, was not that unusual.

We were getting ready in the dressing rooms when our manager David entered. 'You just have to go outside, you have to see this.'

I went down a few flights of stairs and out of the stage door at the rear of the building onto the street. There was a long row of people outside the venue, I walked past them and not one of them gave me a second look.

I turned the corner and saw the queue extended the full length of the next street, I walked to the far end, around to the entrance to this magnificent venue and the queue continued. This wasn't people who'd got tickets, they were already inside, this was people queuing in the hope they might get in due to no-shows.

These people were waiting to see a comedy group that had never been on TV. We didn't have an album, we just did gigs.

It really was an extraordinary night.

The Royal Exchange Theatre is a massive spherical steel framework built inside an even bigger hall, once a trading exchange for cotton, if memory serves. I had been there once before with Lee's parents back in the 1970s where we saw a production of *The Country Wife*, a restoration comedy written in 1675 by William Wycherley. The production starred an incredible but at that point unknown actor who blazed on the stage, his name was Gary Oldman.

So this, in my mind at least, was a legendary performance space: onstage you are effectively at the bottom of a giant fish bowl with people all around you, mostly above.

I don't know what happened that night or quite why the show was such a success, but I remember it as being a truly amazing event. We loved performing and the audience loved the show.

One audience member stays in my memory, a woman who had to be in her eighties was sitting on a cushion on the floor at the front of the stage. The theatre staff had managed to cram in an extra handful of people and this woman was clearly sitting with her family members. She laughed and clapped with enormous enthusiasm and I've often wondered what this experience was like for her. She had clearly been born around the turn of the twentieth century, would have grown up in a brutally rigid ultra-conservative society where woman didn't have the right to vote. Maybe we represented something about the changes she'd lived through, her joy and exuberance a sign that we were saying something relevant.

We also did a one-off performance at a place called Findhorn that stays in the memory. Findhorn is a spiritual community and eco-village near Inverness in Scotland. We were doing a tour of Scotland and I knew very little about the place before we arrived. It is now a very well-established community with amazing buildings and impressive renewable energy installations but back in the mid-1980s, other than the lovely hall we performed in, it was mostly caravans and sheds on sand dunes near the end of a military runway.

The show was a sell-out, a brilliant audience and we had a wonderful reception. When we were clearing up and getting changed after the show, our road manager came into the dressing room and whispered that the audience were all still in the hall. They were all holding hands and blessing the room because we had used some 'bad language'.

It's not that The Joeys were particularly sweary. In comparison to stand-up comics of the time and even more so today, we were like a bunch of vicars. But the hall was, we learned, a spiritual space and the residents of Findhorn thought it necessary to kind of re-consecrate the building after we'd 'defiled' it.

I thought this was quite cute but my fellow Joeys were amusingly derisive about the smug middle-class hippies who were doing the blessing.

That said, we were all quite happy to benefit from the generosity of the same smug middle-class hippies when we spent that night in a wonderful house that the community loaned us. It was a huge place that had once been the home of a very wealthy Scottish distillery family.

Bernie got amusingly drunk and was hysterically funny. He made me laugh so much I could not breathe. I remember kneeling on all fours in a huge old kitchen trying to get my breath back, I can't remember what he was doing other than being strangled by an aggressive mop he found in a cupboard.

Chris also got rather drunk and was less funny.

And here was a problem that haunted the group.

Chris was an alcoholic, a proper one.

I'd known plenty of people who maybe drank too much, got morose, got a bit shouty and fell asleep, but they were just occasional heavy drinkers.

I didn't know what the word alcoholic meant until I met Chris. Over the next few years he went through the slow descent all addicts go through, the endless denial, the time-consuming morning re-build, the exquisite period between lunch and early evening where he would be such an absolute delight to spend time with and then as the evening wore on, I'd leg it to avoid the coming horror.

It was not long after this that Bernie, who could be very stern and incredibly politically knowledgeable, stopped drinking. I loved Bernie when he was a bit sozzled and when he was sober, which was most of the time; he would analyse everything and constantly catch me out when I revealed how hopelessly politically ill-informed I was.

This was a curse I was very aware of at the time. The Joey who was funny and creative when drunk and a bit dry and caustic when sober stopped drinking, and the Joey who was amazing, funny and creative when sober and a nightmare when drunk, drank even more.

Chris, I can say hand on heart, was the most emotionally wise man I've ever met. His insights into the human condition were moving and supportive, never critical. He understood human failings, he understood love, compassion, cruelty and forgiveness in a way no other man I've ever met has understood. When he was drunk, which was every night, he became a nasty, bad tempered and aggressive bully who would take enormous offence at the slightest thing.

Chris's long-term boyfriend Michael was nothing short of a saint and supported Chris through this nightmare with calm, non-judgemental love.

They had been together for many years when I met them, Michael was also a dancer but of a slightly different variety. He was a male stripper in a gay bar in Soho. Some older readers may remember a story of a staunchly anti-gay Conservative MP who had been arrested for 'an act of gross indecency' in the establishment Michael worked in and claimed he was drunk and stumbled into the place by accident.

Michael knew him as a rather unpleasant regular customer, but of course the MP was happily married and probably got away with it due to his expensive lawyers, I truly don't recall.

But Michael was an extraordinary man, a gentle East Ender who sounded like a bit of a diamond geezer but was a charmer, and through Chris and Michael I discovered an amazing theatrical group called Bloolips.

Six very camp gay men who wore frocks onstage, which of course sounds like a drag act. But they were 'radical drag'. They were very insistent that this wasn't drag, it was men in frocks. Bloolips were sidesplittingly funny, presenting half-baked stories which I suppose you could have called a play, every scene packed with gags, throwaway songs and casually camp dance routines. It was obvious that they had so much fun doing it, it was infectious, uplifting and inspiring.

Seeing Bloolips helped me enjoy performing a little more. In the early years, I was always so nervous and tense, longing for the show to be over so I could go home and be alone. I'm really not cut out for the sort of life most people in show business embrace with gusto. I'm not good at staying up late, I get very ill if I drink too much and I'm very good at getting up early. That's a terrible affliction if you're a performer. It's always drink loads, late to bed, very late to rise. But Bloolips showed me that you could really enjoy your time onstage, I just needed the confidence, the acceptance that people had come to see us and wanted to enjoy themselves. They weren't coming to have a miserable time and hate us.

I think it took me around two years of constantly appearing onstage to work this out.

As I've said, being in The Joeys for five years was very like being in a band. We started small, gradually got more successful, played bigger and bigger venues where we felt more and more pressure to produce new material. The only difference between The Joeys and, oh, I'll pick a well-known band out of the ether, the Rolling Stones was, they made a huge amount of money because they could sell records.

We didn't have anything to sell except what we did onstage so we were always close to broke.

When we did finally get asked to appear on television, the medium just didn't sit well with us. We always felt emotionally as well as financially ripped off by the production companies or broadcasters that hired us.

There are some clips on YouTube from some of these TV shows, including a strange interview by Joan Bakewell for BBC's Newsnight programme which I find embarrassing to watch now.

But the television industry had noticed us, in one specific incident which was fairly disruptive, they noticed me.

We were performing at the National Theatre. I'll start with that sentence because it sounds rather grand, but it's true, we really did do a few shows at the National Theatre on London's iconic South Bank.

Okay, it was outside on the terrace, they weren't going to let scum like us perform on the hallowed stages indoors. We performed in the early evening during the summer but we got huge crowds. It was part of some long-forgotten cultural 'bring the streets to the National Theatre' event, but we got paid so it was all good.

It was after one of these performances that a young BBC producer approached me to see if I was interested in being in a new TV comedy drama.

I later learned that he was talking about *Video Stars*, an equally long-forgotten show that was written by an American man called Howard Schuman. I'd actually heard of him because during the 1970s he'd written an amazingly successful drama series called *Rock Follies* which even though I didn't have a TV,

I had seen. It was water cooler TV; everyone of my generation watched *Rock Follies*.

One day soon after meeting the man in the melee after the show at the National Theatre, I went to see the producer, director and Mr Schuman at the old BBC Television Centre in White City. I'd never been there before and I found it hugely alien and intimidating. I explained to them that I felt I was in a very difficult position, that I was part of a group and we always did everything together and anyway I didn't want to be an actor.

They seemed to find this amusing and told me not to worry about it; they were looking for someone 'with your special energy, Robert'. I never knew I had any special energy, this was the first time anyone had said anything like that.

I read out some of the script for them with as much of my special energy as I could muster, which wasn't much because I was so nervous, but I told Howard Schuman I really liked the script, which I kind of did.

In some ways the story was an attempt at trying to recreate the success of *Rock Follies*, which was about the lives and struggles of an all-woman super group, like Abba without the blokes.

Video Stars was about the lives and struggles of some crazy young people who, somehow, I don't remember the plot details, got hold of broadcasting equipment and launched their own TV channel, like crazy anarchist kids with camera equipment. Of course, the big bad corporations hunted them down, or something.

They weren't offering me a walk on, or a bit part, they wanted me to be Teddy Whazz, the lead role. Teddy Whazz, a crazy kid with mad hair, just being crazy on TV. A bit like any number of crazy kids with 80 million subscribers on YouTube today.

The script had hundreds of lines for Teddy. How was I supposed to remember all those?

Anyway, long story short, after lots of anxiety and soul-searching I said no, and Tim Curry ended up playing the part. You know, Tim Curry, a proper actor.

I remember watching it on Bernie's nine-inch black-and-white portable TV and feeling immensely relieved I hadn't done it.

Four years after we first caught the train up to the Edinburgh Fringe Festival, we travelled up again, this time in our own touring Land Rover.

That year we appeared in a large venue called the Assembly Rooms on George Street. The shows were all sold out before we started; we were on the 'must-see list' with loads of posters and masses of publicity in every newspaper and magazine.

We had also been hired to link a Channel 4 programme about the festival. It was called *Edinburgh Inside Out* and includes my first, very cack-handed attempts to interview people in front of a camera.

Our researcher on this show, the man who arranged everything and booked the acts we were going to feature, was a scrawny young lad called Jonathan Ross. He was a powerhouse of energy and enthusiasm, always had his eye on the main chance and was brilliant at fixing things. He went on to be quite successful too, apparently.

We used bits of material and characters from past shows to link various parts of the programme together.

I used to play a character called Scrumpy the Clown. He was based on a few people I'd met when I lived in the truck, cider-damaged nutters from Devon and Somerset, wild men with three teeth and no shoes who stumbled about in a haze of dope smoke and body odour.

Scrumpy was a very drunk mime artist who was constantly swigging out of a stoneware jug full of brain-breaking scrumpy, although of course in my case it was just apple juice.

I resurrected Scrumpy to present links on the programme, this time in costume, a filthy striped T-shirt, cack-handed make-up and a pair of highly unflattering black leggings with holes in topped off with a massive pair of boots.

The little section ended with Scrumpy lying on a busy pavement with his ass hanging out of his mime artist's tights. Still grinning, dribbling and mumbling.

The programme was broadcast on Channel 4 soon afterwards and of course my mother saw it; she'd told all her friends to watch – her son, the odd one, was on the television.

Here's her review when she called me the following day.

'Saw that dreadful programme from Edinburgh, what a shame, such a waste, you, lying on the street with your bottom out. Does your generation really think that's amusing? I didn't need to see that, my lad. I saw that quite enough when you were in nappies, such a shame.'

Thanks, Mum.

Doing all this filming during the day followed by a show every night was, as you may be able to guess, quite tiring. I don't remember much about the rest of the festival, the parties, the endless discussions about comedy and politics we had in various bars around the busy city.

The strains were beginning to show in the group. Bernie would be a little bit irascible, I was regularly accused of bullying by everyone in The Joeys, and Chris would get so drunk after the show I can't actually remember what happened; I generally ran off and hid in my bed.

It was the first time in five years that we didn't get on really well. One of the biggest joys of that period for me was the camaraderie, the closeness of the group, the mutual support, the security we got from working so closely together.

This experience in Edinburgh that year was the first time it didn't feel quite the same.

I know I flew back to London from Edinburgh when we'd finished, looking at the beautiful city as we climbed into the sky and thinking, 'I like this life.'

I would have been twenty-eight years old. During my entire adult life to that point I'd had near zero money, I never went on holiday, I rode everywhere on a bike, I had no savings, I didn't own property because I could barely pay the rent.

I'd always managed to scrape by, but I think it was during this year that I became aware that I'd been very lucky.

Somehow the chemistry of these four men onstage resonated with people. The huge audiences we attracted clearly liked what they saw, maybe because of the political climate of the period, the make-up of the group, the fact that we could perform to a pretty high standard, I'm not sure. Anyway, it worked.

It was very clearly three straight men and one gay man working together without any of the tragic old reactions.

183

In rehearsals and endless discussions, we talked through all the issues we faced both internally and externally regarding sexism, homophobia and racism.

We wrestled with the obvious contradictions and hypocrisies we all lived with and I certainly learned an enormous amount about the politics of gender, the endless difficulties of seeing the repugnant attitudes of some men and being in some way linked with those attitudes simply by dint of gender and skin colour.

During this period, there was much talk of a Canadian and US tour; our manager David had spoken to numerous producers and venue owners who were very keen to book us. We knew many international bookers had seen us in Edinburgh that year and David started planning a tour while we were appearing at the Bloomsbury Theatre in London.

We had pre-show meetings in the dressing rooms at the Bloomsbury, a London theatre we loved to work in. We did regular two- or three-week runs there for four years. The American tour sounded so glamorous and exciting. I'd never been to the United States or Canada, I'd never flown on a long-haul flight, I'd never been outside Europe. We were due to appear at theatre festivals in Washington DC, Seattle, San Francisco, Vancouver, Montreal and maybe even New York.

This was big time, this was why we were all doing it. Wasn't it?

Bring on the existential crisis: what was it all about?

The Joeys had taken over all our lives, it was our identity, we were all 'Bernie from The Joeys', or 'Robert from The Joeys'.

I don't remember worrying about this personally; I was having an amazing time but I think Bernie was having problems with it. It did take up our entire lives, we had worked so hard and for so long, we'd performed thousands of shows by this time and we were still scraping along just about making a living.

People we'd met during this period, Ben Elton, Rik Mayall, Ade Edmondson, Nigel Planer, Dawn French and Jennifer Saunders, had all gone on to start careers in television; we'd met Stephen Fry and Hugh Laurie when they were still students. I remember wondering how they knew how to work on television so early in their careers.

It was only later that I realised that the people they'd been at university with had gone on to run the television industry. I never attended any university, so I didn't know anyone like that.

However, the strength of the group made all these pointless comparisons disappear. We had a very strong identity and a very determined work ethic. We were always introducing new material into the show, new songs, new monologues and double acts. This was one of the beauties of the structure we worked in and I admit I only really understood it after it was all over.

We would always start with a song, well rehearsed and a reliable crowd pleaser. It would be loud and rousing with a couple of gags, then we'd do a few tried and trusted sketches or monologues, after which we might try something completely new. Some of these new bits worked wonderfully and were soon incorporated into the regular running order. Some of them were utterly hopeless, not funny, not interesting and barking mad. We discreetly binned them and moved on.

The reason we'd risk such potentially dud material is we knew the next bit was a hit so we'd get away with it.

What this did for me was supply an amazing structure to try out new material; I was always writing things and seriously, I'm not saying this out of some false modesty, 90 per cent of it was dire. Unfocused nonsense, a vague idea with no tangible heart or meaning.

It was rubbish. But the bits that did work, well, that was what spurred me on to write more.

I produced literally boxloads of densely written sketches and monologues, and the vast majority, thankfully, never saw the light of day.

It was during the final season of shows at the Bloomsbury Theatre that things got really bad. Bernie and I, who had always been incredibly close and who had for all intents and purposes formed The Joeys in the first place, fell out.

I'm certainly not going to point the finger of blame all these many years later; I'm only going to point to the intense feeling of regret. If only we could have finished the group on a high, agreeing we all needed a break and go our separate ways.

The American tour was cancelled, everything fell apart.

It was incredibly depressing, I'm sure it was for all of us. I was completely at a loss as to what to do next.

Chris and I spent hours talking things over and eventually decided to try and carry on in some new form.

We went on to do a show to fulfil some of the bookings The Joeys had lined up. We just about got away with it but there was never the success we experienced with The Joeys.

During this period, Chris and I wrote a sitcom idea for Channel 4. It got commissioned. We made six episodes and I'm genuinely sad to report it was pretty terrible. It's worth mentioning the contrast between the energy and explosive joy of live, unfettered performance and the pitfalls of trying to transfer that to the small screen.

We recorded this series in a closed set, no audience. If we'd had an audience we'd have known after the first recording that it wasn't very funny.

Chris and I wrote, produced and performed in *The Corner-house* for Channel 4. It was originally called *The Last Straw* and was set in a corner cafe run by an old gay man, played by Chris, who had a young straight waiter, played by me.

Well, it was a brave attempt to challenge orthodoxies; it had its heart in the right place, but it wasn't remotely funny. You see, it was a clever reversal of stereotypes but it went further, our plumber was a woman, my best friend was black and my girlfriend was Scottish. Radical.

I can't describe it any further, it's too painful.

Each episode had a theme of my character screwing up in some way, and Chris's character finally throwing down a tea towel and saying, 'That's the last straw,' at which point the plunky plunk piano music would announce the end credits.

Yes, that bad.

At the same time, our ex-researcher pal Jonathan Ross had managed to get his first chat show commissioned by Channel 4; this was called *The Last Resort*.

The men in suits at the channel decided they couldn't have two shows with the word 'Last' in the title so we had to change ours to *The Cornerhouse*. Yeah, you see, Jonathan didn't have to change his, he was more important and more talented and more popular and we weren't in the slightest way bitter about that.

At the height of The Joeys' success there were two other groups we worked with many times who had equal success. An amazing music group called Pookiesnakenburger, and a wonderfully clever and funny theatre group called Cliffhanger. We'd all pack out venues at the Edinburgh Fringe, TV executives would come along to those performances and a year later we were all busy making our first TV series.

We made *The CornerHouse*; Pookiesnakenburger made a six-part series on a variety of musical themes with vague stories attached and Cliffhanger made a series of one-off comedy dramas.

They were all broadcast, they all started well as regards to audience figures then rapidly dropped into obscurity.

Many years later when I met up with various members of the Pookies and the Cliffies, as they were known in the trade, we argued as to which of these early attempts at TV was the most abysmal. We each claimed the one we made was worse, was the least funny, interesting or memorable.

I was determined *The Cornerhouse* took the biscuit for being the most toe-curlingly appalling, but members of the Pookies reminded me of how bad their series was and the Cliffies did likewise.

To put the talent of some of these people into perspective, leading members of the Pookies went on to form *Stomp*, the amazing live percussion stage show that millions of people around the world have seen in very long-running and incredibly successful shows.

Robin Driscoll from Cliffhanger went on to work with Rowan Atkinson on the Mr Bean TV shows and movies. He's a brilliantly funny comedian and made an absolute mint from working on Mr Bean and he still owes me ten quid.

The incredible joy I experienced at the end of a blistering Joeys performance has only ever been recreated on nights in a TV studio working on *Red Dwarf*. There are more than a few similarities from my perspective between working in The Joeys and working on *Red Dwarf*.

The big difference is we don't write *Red Dwarf*, we just do the showing-off bit, which I have to say is a great relief.

So I owe more or less everything that's happened to me to those five formative years touring the country as one quarter of a now-forgotten theatrical phenomenon.

The Joeys, let me assure you younger readers, were massive. A box office record-breaking fringe supergroup of hyper-talented performers.

I can say that now. At the time I'd probably have said, 'Yes, we're doing okay, but we need some new material.'

Three Eggs on a Chopstick

She walked onstage in a tattered black tutu, heavy boots, a mop of unruly hair and a dollop of lippy (Australian for lipstick) on her generous mouth. She shouted the word 'egg!' at no one in particular and a small parachute fell from the ceiling high above her which she seemed to catch without looking.

In a tiny harness beneath the parachute was an egg.

She shouted, 'Egg!' again and a small, yellow, remote control model Jeep drove out from the wings; in the driver's seat was another egg. She picked up the second egg and again shouted, 'Egg!' Someone unseen at the back of the auditorium threw an egg in her direction, which again she caught with ease. She pulled a small stick from somewhere in her frock and shouted, 'Chopstick!'

She then proceeded to balance the chopstick on her nose, and, one by one, all three eggs on top of the chopstick. At the last moment she stood in front of the silent crowd and spread her arms wide, three eggs, one on top of the other, on a chopstick, balanced on her nose.

The crowd went bananas, they stood and cheered, they

clapped and whistled as she maintained the ludicrous balance for an impossible length of time.

Finally, she leaned forward and the eggs fell separately to the ground, breaking in a mess on the stage. Real eggs, no glue, no string. She caught the chopstick and tossed it in the air, again catching it with such nonchalant ease that the audience even applauded that. She offered the crowd a brief smile and stomped off the stage.

This took place during a performance by Circus Oz in the Assembly Rooms main theatre at the Edinburgh Festival in 1987. I will never forget it. I was mesmerised and enchanted. I suppose, in a shallow way, I was in love.

The rest of the show was equally brilliant: incredible feats of gymnastics and acrobatics, amazing music, and staggering feats of strength, particularly from the young woman who balanced the eggs on a chopstick.

I went to see the show several times because I was working in the same venue, doing fairly sub-standard comedy routines that weren't really going anywhere.

After one of the Circus Oz sell-out performances I hung out in what was dubbed 'the star bar'. I had a pass that allowed me access, I was an Edinburgh old timer by this point, I'd performed at every Fringe Festival for the previous six years and knew the ropes.

In the star bar that night was a gaggle of performers from the Circus who'd just come offstage and were relaxing away from their huge audience. Circus men in weird tights and baggy yellow shirts, women in weird tights with big red lace-up boots and spangled tops. These were Circus gypsies, a type of performer who up until I saw Circus Oz I had little interest in, but these people were different.

I casually moved through the crowds with my orange and soda and stood near them. They were so dishevelled-looking, so confident of their incredible physical prowess. They were all muscular and tall, and I'm talking about the women here: they were built like commandoes, they had arm muscles that wouldn't shame Jean-Claude Van Damme. I noticed the woman with the thick mop of dark hair and the full lips, the one who balanced the eggs. She was sitting at a big table with a crowd of other Circus people, all of them turning their backs to the rest of the noisy room.

I 'casually' moved near her, plucked up my courage and said, 'I really enjoyed your show, I loved the egg balancing, it's amazing, really really amazing, you're amazing, I really loved the show.'

I said that all in one breath, very quickly, and it's possible my voice went quite high a couple of times as I blurted it out.

The mop-haired woman slowly turned from her friends and looked up at me. She was chewing gum. Her eyes moved up and down my scrawny frame, she made a slightly pained smile, said nothing and turned back to her mates.

That was it. I moved away.

I managed to wangle my way into the Circus Oz show every night from then on but I gave up on trying to talk to the egg-balancing woman. On the last night of the festival I did a final performance at a huge benefit for the Nicaragua Solidarity Campaign, an organisation I'd been involved with for some time.

It was held in the Usher Hall in Edinburgh, a venue with 2,200 seats and every one of them full.

The short period I stood in the wings waiting to go on is a very clear, sharp memory. Proper stage terror.

I had to follow a man called Robbie Coltrane. Lucky me.

Robbie is a larger-than-life figure, he's brash, confident, funny and, of course, very Scottish.

I was feeling about as nervous, unfunny and insecure as anyone who has ever stood on a stage in front of 2,200 people, in Scotland, following Robbie Coltrane.

I don't like to crow, but ladies and gentlemen, I stormed it that night. I literally rocked the house.

For whatever reason, the crowd loved me. I forgot all about the woman with the eggs, and for that one night I thought I was king of the hill.

From that moment on, I had more gig offers than I could actually perform. I returned to London and became a full-time stand-up comic.

But I was a guilt-ridden, hypocritical member of the urban media elite so this was a phenomenon that I worried about a great deal. I had performed at the concert to help raise money for a really important cause. At the time, the Sandinista National Liberation Front were a popular socialist revolutionary group in Nicaragua. They had ousted the previous American-backed dictator Somoza and started rebuilding the country.

Their near neighbour, the United States, didn't like having a socialist government in their backyard so started arming the Contras, a fanatical combination of right-wing and criminal elements formed into a ragtag military group backed by the CIA, and at the time of the concert the Contras were wreaking havoc.

So that's why I did it. I was theoretically supporting a fledgling socialist state but then it had also re-launched my performing career. I had been in the doldrums for months, I had resorted to being a cycle courier and part-time shoemaker. I had to pay the rent.

That one appearance changed everything.

Later that year I did a gig with Eddie Izzard at the Basingstoke Arts Centre. I was a mildly posh-sounding, middle-class white bloke who did slightly quirky, self-deprecating jokes and some silly voices and walks. Some people laughed politely.

Eddie was at that time a mildly posh-sounding, middle-class white bloke who did even more obscure, quirky non-jokes, rambling stories and mumbled side thoughts and everybody loved him. He stormed it in Basingstoke.

The next time I saw him onstage was at the Secret Policeman's Ball, by then a very well-established benefit concert to raise funds for Amnesty International.

Eddie, who wasn't that well known at the time, came onto the stage in a flamboyant glittery coat, high heels and loads of make-up. I seem to remember him talking about wolves running through the park and a pile of spiders ringing his front doorbell. Anyway, the audience loved him, he was the star of the night.

He's done okay since then apparently.

I didn't quite have that sudden rocket ship to fame and success, more of a damp string of fire crackers, some of which occasionally made a polite bang, but I was happy. I knew I wasn't really cut out for stand-up comedy.

Stand-up comedy is a very competitive art form and although I'm quite a competitive person, I can also acknowledge a simple truth: I wasn't terribly good at it.

When I watched people like Jack Dee, Lee Evans, Jeremy Hardy, Jo Brand or Omid Djalili perform, I could sense that they were simply better at it than I ever would be.

That said, I survived. I managed to earn a living doing it, touring around the clubs, bars and pubs of the increasingly well-established and business-like comedy circuit.

It was during this period that I wrote a play, *Mammon, Robot Born of Woman*, which was inspired by seeing the movie *RoboCop*. I have written about this at length in *The Man in the Rubber Mask*, so I won't drone on about it here. I managed to book a space in the Assembly Rooms at the Edinburgh Festival in 1988.

I was going back to Edinburgh with a new play, something I'd wanted to do for years.

A few months before the 1988 Edinburgh Festival I received a copy of the Assembly Rooms programme, noticing at once that my haphazard and amateur attempt at promoting the show had backfired and there was an utterly inappropriate listing for it.

I had to fill out the description of the show long before I'd written it, a barely formed science-fiction idea about a woman engineer who creates a lifelike robot as a surrogate RoboYuppie to trade for her on the stock market. The what? How is that even interesting? It makes no sense!

I did notice that right after the shabby listing for my show there was a performance by three comics, one of whom was a woman called Judy Pascoe, an Australian who'd just won the Melbourne Comedy award for her show, *The Last Great Adventure*.

So, come early August we started the show, which I performed with an amazing American woman called Deborah John Wilson. I'd met Deborah during The Joeys era, we'd even been her 'white-boy' backing singers at a couple of gigs.

I'm going to do some second-cousin-style name-dropping here: Deborah's brother is an actor called Yaphet Kotto. If you don't recognise the name, google him. An amazing screen presence and one of the cast in the original *Alien* movie. Deborah could project a similar force onstage. She was also very funny and an amazing singer.

Deborah and I shared a pleasant little flat on a quiet Edinburgh street and worked all day, rewriting scenes and changing moments. We were both very focused on making this fledgling show work.

Suffice it to say it was quite successful.

Okay, it was sold out from the second day, even posh TV people couldn't get a ticket. It led to me being in *Red Dwarf* and it was nominated, I repeat nominated, for a Perrier Award, which was won that year by the often understated but brilliant comedian Jeremy Hardy.

Every day as I was packing away props and cleaning up the theatre after another performance of *Mammon*, this woman called Judy Pascoe arrived.

Judy was tall and strong with big 1980s curly hair, and very unlike the woman who balanced the eggs on a chopstick on her nose I'd admired the previous year. It wasn't long before I discovered she was one and the same person.

And her new show was wonderful.

She had left Circus Oz shortly after I'd seen her, and she'd left her boyfriend too, who was also in the Circus, and struck out on her own. She'd performed *The Last Great Adventure* at the Melbourne comedy festival that year and she had won a prize, which was a ticket to the UK and a stage at the Edinburgh Festival.

That stage was the same one I was using. There are literally thousands of stages and venues at the Edinburgh Festival every year. And it wasn't just that she was using the same stage but she was also using it immediately after my show.

There are so many shows performed at the Edinburgh Festival that they run immediately after each other. The turnaround is frantic, you have just a few minutes to prepare when you arrive and to clear out when you're done.

I saw Judy's show more than once, it was wonderfully funny and very Australian, with quite a lot of material about her mother. She still performed a few tricks, one of them the classic pull-the-tablecloth-away-from-under-a-load-of-crockery, which she did with panache every performance.

A romance blossomed, which was the last thing I wanted. In previous years, romances at the Edinburgh Fringe were always a disaster. I had promised myself that this year would be different: I wouldn't get involved with anyone.

After two weeks seeing Judy every day I had to admit to myself this promise wasn't going to hold.

We started to hang out together. Initially, Judy lived in a flat about half a mile from mine in London. She was very focused on her stand-up routine, a rewrite of the show she did in Edinburgh with more gags.

She was a brilliant stand-up, and at the time there were very few women comics working the circuit so she got a lot of work.

I spent the occasional evening driving her from gig to gig, standing right at the back where she couldn't see me.

'I can't do it if you're at the front gawking at me,' she said lovingly. I like to think it was lovingly.

We even did gigs together, but only three times. Once in Edinburgh, but not during the festival. That one worked, we both went down very well, the crowd liked both of us.

Then in Sheffield, where I may as well have stood onstage and apologised for thirty minutes, that would have been funnier than my so-called material. It was dreadful, no one laughed once. They didn't even bother clapping when I finished. I bombed, I died, I crashed, use any metaphor you like. I was dreadful, and I was fairly depressed when I went back to the green room where Judy was waiting.

'Tough crowd,' I said.

As soon as Judy walked onstage they loved her, whoops and cheers and much laughter. She stormed it and she was very happy afterwards.

'Great crowd,' she said as she wiped off her make-up.

Simon, the man who'd organised the event said to me afterwards, 'They came to see Judy and they had to sit through your thing. I felt a bit sorry for them.'

Lovely.

Then there was Brighton. Strangely, I find this more uncomfortable to recall. Judy went on first and did her opening routine, which always worked. I'd seen it work dozens of times. But this time: nothing. The place was packed, but the crowd just sat and watched. Nothing.

She struggled on, but it wasn't working and it's the most horrible thing to watch. Someone you love and admire having a really tough time and there's nothing you can do about it.

I went on immediately after her and for whatever chemical or electrical reason, I have no other explanation, this was one of the very few truly spectacular gigs I ever performed as a stand-up comic.

I didn't even stick to my material, which was never that good anyway. I can't remember much but I do recall talking about Salman Rushdie working in my local chip shop. Mr Rushdie was in hiding at the time after receiving plausible death threats from Islamic fundamentalist nutters because he wrote a book, *The Satanic Verses*, which they didn't like, not that they'd read it, but they were told not to like it by even more fundamentalist nutters.

Anyway, I stormed it. I slayed them, I loved it.

After that gig, we drove from Brighton to Lyme Regis, me driving, Judy sleeping in the back. It wasn't our most chatty journey but we got through it.

But that was in the early heady days of romance. We had a lot more to get through in the following thirty years.

It's very hard not to be slushy and romantic about the strange series of events that brought us together. Okay, I'll modify that a bit: it's very hard for *me* not to be slushy and romantic about it. Judy has no problem not being slushy and romantic about it; she can appreciate the romance but she holds it in context of thirty years of struggle and compromise, raising two children and building a home for them.

She would have forgotten about any slushy romance as she focused on her children's education, unlike my attitude to school, which was more along the lines of, 'It'll be over soon, don't worry about it.'

We have been through a lot together, much of it heart-breaking and depressing. We have misunderstood one another for years at a time, cried, screamed, slammed doors, sulked and bitched at each other, but somehow, we've come through it.

Not that unusual, in fact a fairly common experience, but due to the immense number of relationship break-ups, particularly in show business, I consider it a bit of an achievement.

The cast of *Red Dwarf* is something of an anomaly. If you were to take any four TV actors of our generation I don't think you'd be surprised to discover that one or two of them had left wives and children and started a new family.

All four of the *Red Dwarf* cast – Danny John-Jules, Chris Barrie, Craig Charles and myself – have been with the same women and the same kids for twenty to thirty years. So has the *Red Dwarf* writer/producer/creator Doug Naylor, so has the long-time director Ed Bye.

I'm not reading anything into this at all. It's just an observation, but one I'm mildly proud to be part of.

Judy and I have reached a state of tolerable equilibrium. We lead fairly separate lives professionally, but very close lives emotionally. We spend as much time together as our busy lives permit and I cherish those periods.

When she is away, I miss her, when I'm away, I miss her, when we are together I feel whole.

Breeding

'Sir, I want to talk about my penis.'

This was one of the most resonant lines I ever delivered on *Red Dwarf*.

It was in the episode 'DNA' from series four, when Kryten, the character I play in the long-running sitcom, is 'transmogrified' into a human being. If you haven't seen it, don't worry about it, but it is quite funny apparently.

After being a mechanoid for 3 million years with, as Lister put it so succinctly, 'nothing down there except plastic underpants and a trade mark', Kryten is made human and has to start dealing with his new-found genitalia, an appendage he is less than impressed by.

'Is that the best design they could come up with? The last turkey in the shop look. Are you seriously telling me Perry Como sang "Memories are Made of This" with one of those stashed in his slacks!'

I don't really want to talk about my penis at all. It's very boring, what I want to explore is the contrast between lust and breeding.

Drink, drugs and gambling are often seen as diversionary

activities that people use to avoid facing the ultimate pointlessness of human existence. Oh well, there's religion too. I suppose I should add that to the list, although that is a little unfair.

Along with the list of drink, drugs, gambling and religion I'd like to add a fifth, and I have a very specific experience that reinforces this addition.

I smoked some dope in Bath in 1974. That statement alone does not make me stand out as unusual, but for whatever reason – psychological, chemical, societal – I got a bit scared, a bit paranoid, and I had a minor panic attack.

While under the influence, the only thing I could imagine in the jumble of alarming thoughts that calmed me down was the fantasy of looking at pornography. Not falling in love or having sex, no, this was very specific: acquiring and looking at pornography.

Looking at pornography felt, for reasons now beyond my grasp, to be a safe place for me to be.

You see, I'm a lightweight when it comes to alcohol. For me there is a hair's breadth between being a bit tipsy and being seriously ill for a couple of days.

I got bored of smoking dope around the age of twenty. I tried LSD once (it was amazing, never again), cocaine a couple of times (really annoying, never again), and that's about it.

I find gambling the most obscure of the human vices. I have, through work, been to Las Vegas many times and I have never wanted to gamble a dime.

But if I walked past an 'adult' book store in London, Paris, New York or Berlin in the 1970s and 1980s, I was drawn inside with a compunction that equates to an alcoholic passing a pub.

I could not resist going to have a look. Now, it's important to point out that I was often in a long-term, generally happy sexual relationship at the time. I wasn't a lonely isolated man with no social contact, I was a gregarious member of a wide social circle.

However, if you are a heterosexual man and you are friends and even lovers with women who are virulently upset by the very notion of pornography, this interest is doubly problematic and that indeed, may be the other spur to my unhealthy obsession.

It was so deeply wrong, so secret and hidden that it became even more exciting and dangerous.

I hid my interest in pornography more than any other activity I've ever had. I was so shamed by it and yet so driven by it.

There is an important distinction here; I need to define what I mean by pornography as it's very specific to the period.

In the 1970s and 1980s, before the internet and more relaxed regulation, the pornography I was seeing was exclusively images of young women with either very few, or no clothes on at all. It wasn't graphic representations of shagging, there were no men in the pictures and, without question, no erections.

I don't think I saw an image of an erection before 1985. I didn't know you could take a picture of one.

I have argued, and this may have some validity, that exposure to pornography of this nature wasn't very helpful to an emerging male sexuality. As far as I understood it, purely from the images I'd seen, sex was a naked woman.

It didn't involve me in any way. It was about looking, you could argue 'possessing', albeit from a distance, a sexually compliant woman. A naked woman who was in a position of sexual availability which, from my now wide experience, isn't really a very central part of sexual relations between men and women.

Basically, when I was confronted with a sexual partner as a young man I didn't know what to do.

Not unusually, it was all very awkward but I eventually got the hang of it.

Today, for a young man exposed to the torrent of available pornography on the internet, I cannot imagine the psychological impact. I worry it may not be benign.

I have also argued that it may be more healthy: young men may have more idea of their own role due to the involvement of male protagonists in pornography, but I think this argument is flimsy.

The flipside, of course, is the ready availability. There is no longer any need to go and hunt illicit porn, it's not illicit, it's everywhere.

Looking back now, it was all very sad. There's nothing to be proud of as you walk out of an adult book store; it's not a liberating experience, it's a very lonely and hopeless place.

To be fair on myself, I didn't actually buy much pornography, it was too difficult. I didn't know where to hide it and I was so fearful of being caught with it that I didn't want to chance it.

So I was a cowardly, dirty young man, occasionally sloping about Soho in London or the rue Saint-Denis in Paris, just looking.

I didn't know anyone I could talk to about this obsession.

It wasn't every day, basically whenever the opportunity arose, but it was over a long period.

It wasn't until I was in my late twenties that I talked about it to anyone. Chris Eymard from The Joeys was one of the first people I admitted my guilty secret to, and he was so positive and understanding. Just the act of talking about it deflated the monster to manageable proportions. It was obvious from my forays into pornographic bookshops that I was not alone. They were always full of men my age, guiltily looking at the racks of glossy magazines, and this is to completely ignore the effect it had on any women in these men's lives or, indeed, the women in the pictures.

There was a time in my mid-twenties where I distinctly remember saying, after yet another embarrassing and disastrous romance or possibly another secretive foray into a porn store, 'I can't wait until I'm a bald, toothless sixty-year-old with no sex drive.'

The reason for this heartfelt desire was because I was convinced my libido was the thing that caused me the most distress. The prospect of not being driven by these base needs was very attractive, and the notion of being a celibate monk really appealed to me, it was just the religion bit I couldn't quite grasp.

I could be seen as being lucky. Many of my contemporaries, and particularly those in show business, have had a much tougher time with alcohol and hard drugs. I never went down that path of misery, but my libido was occasionally obsessive and often joyless and hollow.

I've made it to sixty and beyond, and while there are elements of how I pictured myself at this age when I was in my twenties, a toothless, bald sixty-year-old with no sex drive, there's still a scattering of spindly grey hair on top of my head, I've got a few of my own teeth but I've achieved the last item on my list with gusto.

I'm a sixty-year-old bloke with a low sex drive and that's fine.

I'm serious. Imagine being a sixty-year-old bloke with a huge rampant unquenchable sex drive. Nightmare.

An endless desire to ogle or grope women younger than your own children.

There're plenty of examples of old blokes in that position; British heritage rock is festooned with them.

Recently the true nature of older men groping, pressuring and even raping younger women has been in the news. The Weinstein revelations did not come as a surprise to me but that didn't make them any more palatable. This behaviour has, I admit, got less to do with sex and lust and far more to do with power and the assumption that powerful men think they can get away with it.

With all this going on, it comes as a huge relief that I'm not sexually interested in young women any more. I'm not suddenly sexually interested in men either, even though my wife was convinced I'd come out when I was fifty.

No such luck, darl.

It's not that I don't notice beauty. I do appreciate the spirit and elegance of certain women, I notice and I admire them, but I don't long for intimacy like I used to.

I appreciate Judy, I stare at her sometimes when she's off with the fairies, which is quite often, and it's a constant surprise to me that after thirty years together she still fascinates me.

I feel very blessed to be this way. We've been through all the usual boring turmoil that long-term breeding heterosexual couples go through. Misunderstandings, fights over schools, rows over where the marmalade is kept, why we have a fridge that requires me to lie on the floor to see if we have any milk.

Okay, that last description may need some explanation. I was working away from home when we had our kitchen done. That in itself defines us as supremely middle class, an anxiety to which Judy is completely immune, due to being Australian.

Anyway, it was deemed a good design idea to have everything in the kitchen at the same level, everything to fit under the work surfaces. Lovely, I'm sure it looks wonderful, but it does mean we have a floor-level fridge. Which means the bottom shelf is at ankle height, which means if I'm in a stroppy mood and have to see if we've got any carrots, I literally lie down on the kitchen floor and stare into the fridge.

As you may be able to guess, Judy finds this mildly annoying. Joey the Lurcher, however, finds it mildly arousing and has been known to shove his annoying nose where the sun don't shine and start getting grippy with his front paws.

Anyway, back to breeding. I have no hesitation in saying I love Judy, I've loved her since the first time I saw her, but that was a very romantic love, fairly unconnected to the daily slog of work, diary planning, parenting, house maintenance and paying the mortgage.

The bit everyone focuses on in romantic novels, love songs, sonnets, movies and plays is that beginning bit and understandably so. It's an amazing, life-affirming experience. That first connection is so exciting and tantalising, so delicate and sensitive. The possibility that the incredibly powerful feelings you have for someone are reciprocated is rare; I've only experienced that a handful of times.

We didn't really fight before we had children, not seriously. Okay, there was the time I said something possibly offensive as we walked along Upper Street in Islington, London. I was probably trying to be funny and I pitched it badly, Judy seemed genuinely annoyed and using her left forearm 'tapped' me on the stomach. That's how she described it later. 'I just tapped you. Why d'you have to be so dramatic about everything?'

It's important to explain that this was when Judy had been a circus performer and gymnast for the previous five years, and she was built like a battle-ready Royal Marine, so a tap from Judy was like being hit by an angry bull.

I folded into a winded heap on the pavement, probably making pathetic wheezing noises as Judy kept on walking. Two very charming gay men helped me to my feet and asked if I was okay. I don't know for certain they were gay, they just seemed very gay and caring at the time. I recovered, we got over it, and somehow stuck together for the next five years until we had babies.

I had wanted to have babies for years, literally years. When Judy and I, or I should modify that, when I was trying for a baby, I worried that I'd ridden my pushbike for too long. I became convinced I'd permanently damaged my vas deferens.

My bicycle chain snapped while cycling up a hill and my

lower gentleman's equipment made violent contact with the alloy crossbar of my ultra-lightweight racing bike.

My goodness that hurt a lot, I can still feel the pain today.

So, I was trying for a baby with Judy and no baby was forthcoming, for an increasingly alarming amount of time.

Here's a strange observation, which I'm sure is not in the least scientific, but one swelteringly hot day in Australia, Judy and I sat on the shaded deck of her mother's house in Mitchelton, a northern suburb of Brisbane.

I have no idea how the topic came up, but at one point Judy's mother Maureen, a strict Catholic and yet very accepting of our non-married status at the time, said, and I quote, 'If you had a baby, Judith, I wouldn't think of it as a bastard.'

Now that may sound slightly shocking to some less religious readers, the very notion that a mother could consider her grandchild a bastard is a little outrageous. Personally, I found it charming.

Here's the thing, though: Judy was pregnant within forty-eight hours of hearing her mother say that. We'd been 'trying for a baby' for many months with no result. I naturally tied these two events together with no proof that there was any connection.

My analysis was that Judy's unconscious response to hearing these words from her mother allowed her to procreate. She didn't say, 'Oh phew, now I can get up the duff without feeling guilty,' and I'm sure she didn't even think it, but that's what happened.

It was all deeply mysterious to me.

This wonderful event convinced me further that a book I'd read not long before, namely *The Mona Lisa and the*

Wheelbarrow by an American writer called Floyd Dell, was really on the money.

Floyd Dell was part of a small group of men who lived in Greenwich Village in New York in the early 1900s, a bunch of intellectual renegades who rejected the claustrophobic attitudes to sex and marriage prevalent at the time. This was not the 1960s that everyone from my generation drones on about endlessly, no, it was the 1900s.

I think I first read about this writer in some old newspaper and I became a bit obsessed; it really chimed with a lot of things I was struggling with at the time. Men, women, sex, pornography, equality, empathy, maturity. Really complicated stuff for a young bloke.

Floyd Dell wrote a book called *Feminism for Men*, published in early 1914.

Yes, a book called *Feminism for Men* published before the First World War.

It blew my mind when I managed to read an original copy of the book in the New York Public Library on Fifth Avenue in Manhattan in 1987.

It was fascinating. I didn't know the word feminism existed then, I thought all ideas of sexual liberation, gay liberation and feminism started in the mid-1960s, but they were busy talking about all this stuff before the First World War.

I also discovered other books he had written, most importantly the aforementioned *Mona Lisa and the Wheelbarrow*. In many ways this was Floyd Dell's masterwork, an essay exploring the notion that men had to work hard to understand and therefore empathise with women.

In it he said, 'The two great riddles of the world are machinery and woman.'

He didn't mean 'a woman' or even women in general, he meant woman, the enigma, the Madonna, the symbol of woman, the smile of the Mona Lisa that Da Vinci portrayed so beautifully but probably didn't understand.

Men's struggle to understand woman was the very foundation, according to Dell, of the inequality between the genders. Men could understand machines but they didn't seem to ever understand women.

The book first appeared as a series of articles in a socialist magazine called *The Masses*. Yes, a socialist magazine published in New York in 1914. I held a copy in my hands, the staff at the New York Public Library had dug it out of their vaults and I had to wear white gloves to read it.

I devoured it and copied much of it into a battered notebook I still have. When I read it in the mid-1980s, I was powerfully moved by Floyd Dell's ideas. It felt like he was writing about me.

I had a fairly good grasp of machines, levers, cams, wheels, axles, gears. I understood those easily, but women? Hopeless. I had no idea.

My often desperate need to be accepted by women, the pain their rejection caused me, the desire I had to be with them – utterly mysterious.

However, as is clearly the case with some men, this lack of comprehension didn't make me fear, hate or resent women. It made me sad and depressed at my inability to grow emotionally to some mysterious point when I might truly understand them.

I never reached that point and Judy's sudden and easily achieved pregnancy was just another step in the dark for me.

Finally, at the age of thirty-seven, I fathered a baby boy and he was, and still is, wonderful. Born in a big tub of body-temperature water in a hospital in Worcester, Louis emerged after many long hours of labour like a little purple terrapin, just floating under the warm water with his arms and legs splayed.

Babies don't drown when they're born underwater, in case you're wondering; they're not breathing when they're in the womb so when they finally emerge they just expand and stretch a bit, floating under the surface because they're neutrally buoyant.

The midwife gently tapped him to the surface and as soon as his face reached the air he took his first breath with barely a murmur. No crying, no holding him upside-down and slapping his little arse, he just started breathing.

The midwife picked him up and put him onto Judy. He stared at his mum with an intensity I've only ever seen once again, when my daughter was born three years later.

Okay, my boy was a daily challenge over the next couple of decades leaving me broken and grey-haired, but he's an amazing young man and I love him so much it hurts every day I don't see him.

Then we had another baby, a baby girl and she is divine, funny, complicated and creative. She too was born in a tub of warm water, this time in my wife's office at our house. At the time Judy was busy working as a 'script doctor' for a Hollywood studio. She was constantly rewriting movie scripts and receiving endless screeds of notes from movie producers. She was the breadwinner during that period, I was a mere house husband. Happy times.

We had stripped out her office but left one shelving unit with a phone, dial-up modem and fax machine in one corner. In between contractions she would lean over the edge of the giant tub which took up three-quarters of the little room and read a long fax that was constantly turning out pages from a script she was working on. This was in 1996, fax machines were the biz back then and we had one with a big roll of paper so your faxes came in long reels. She would read the fax and swear heartily at what she was being asked to rewrite, and then another contraction would kick in and the soggy paper would fall into a damp heap in the corner.

The midwives later told me they thought they'd seen everything in their careers, posh women who suddenly sound like fish wives when giving birth, women who bit holes in their husband's arms, punched people and screamed blue murder. They had never, they told me with some glee, seen anyone reading a fax while giving birth.

The reason there were so many midwives present at my daughter's birth is because at the time, water births were quite unusual. The midwife who delivered my gorgeous girl had experienced them before; the others came along to watch.

I don't know what a birth is like any other way; I've only seen babies pop out underwater and float about a bit. I stayed behind Judy's head, being supportive, or, as Judy described it, 'being an annoying attention-seeking twat as usual'.

Two babies, I'm so blessed. They are both now healthy adults and contrary to their unstable parents and chaotic upbringing, relatively sane.

Here's a brief example of their challenging childhood. Early one morning, it was still dark outside, we had managed to raise my son out of bed to catch the bus to school. He's like his mother, not good first thing in the morning. My daughter is like me, up and out with no problem, boom, where's my breakfast.

So Judy and I were mucking about trying to cheer him up. I can't remember what she did but I think I may have been mincing around and very politically incorrectly behaving like a camp gay man in a 1970s sitcom.

He sat crouched next to the oven and shook his head. He said, and I quote, 'I've got a gay dad and a lesbotic mum. What hope is there for me?'

I want to state, here and now: Judy and I had never used the term 'lesbotic' before then, he didn't get it from us, but guess what, we've used it since. Wrong I know.

So do I want to meet a svelte young fertile woman and have another baby? At sixty years old? Go on, guess.

I know plenty of men who have done something like that. When I say I know them, I don't mean I've read about them in an article in *Marie Claire*, I mean I actually know them.

Men with adult children, sometimes grandchildren, meet and 'fall in love' with a young woman and it's all wonderful and then they have a baby.

I know I shouldn't judge, maybe they're really happy. Some men I know who've done this clearly are very happy and it's all fine but I know it's not for me.

*

I need to insert a small gap here, because I didn't write this book in one long session. It's taken years and there was quite a long gap between writing that last bit and the next bit.

I wrote the previous section when I was staying in Sydney, Australia. Early that morning I closed my laptop (super-early-morning writing courtesy of jet lag) and walked from Kirribilli in north Sydney to the Ultimo in the Central Business District.

I took this early morning stroll to take part in an interview on Wendy Harmer's ABC radio show. Wendy is an old mate of my wife's and we'd spent time with her and her family when we'd lived in Sydney when the kids were younger.

I followed a route over Sydney Harbour Bridge, an amazing structure that I knew a few basic facts about as I'd done a voiceover for the History Channel about the struggle to build this world-famous landmark.

That's the sort of engineering nerdery that was rattling around in my old noggin as I walked through the warm morning smog.

Yes, that's the downside to Sydney Harbour Bridge, it carries a very busy road which was choked with early morning fossil-burning cars and trucks. They love burning fossils in Australia.

Anyway, it's an engineering marvel and I even tweeted a picture of the massive nuts and bolts used in the footings of the bridge. The nuts are about the size of a human head.

'Imagine the spanner you'd need to tighten this! #massive-nuts.'

So I wasn't prepared for what happened when I was about halfway over the bridge. Australians officially love sport and I witnessed many very fit and healthy people of all ages jog over the bridge in the morning. I was used to seeing this, it was all very normal and then, I saw her.

Running towards me was someone I can only describe as a staggeringly beautiful young woman. She was tall, slender with very long tanned legs, sun-bleached hair tied back. As she passed she smiled and muttered, 'Hi,' as many friendly Australians are wont to do.

That was it, she carried on running, I carried on walking until I started to falter and had to find something to lean on.

I literally stopped breathing; it was an experience akin to being winded. I stood against the huge railings that run along the side of the footpath and tried to make it look like I was taking pictures of the *Queen Mary 2*, a massive cruise liner that was docked near the Sydney Opera House.

But I wasn't thinking about ships. I was shaking my head in disbelief that I could be so affected by the fleeting glimpse of a young woman in her prime.

Why on earth would this have such a dramatic effect on a man my age? It's absurd and indeed quite sad. It wasn't as if I was going to run after her, somehow catch up and say, 'I'm sorry to interrupt, but I'm actually in love with you. Please marry me, let's make babies.'

For starters, I can't run that fast, she was really moving and I was old enough to be her grandfather.

This desire has to be a biological anomaly. I assume that many millennia ago there would be very few surviving men of my age. Wars, injuries and disease would remove 95 per cent of men long before they reached sixty years old. It seems that human biology hasn't evolved enough to adjust male reproductive desire. If you can still desire to mate at my age – because I suppose with enough time and encouragement I could just about manage – then my self-satisfied illusion of being beyond caring is doomed.

A woman my age can no longer reproduce without major medical intervention, but old blokes can. I don't want to get too agricultural but I haven't had the snip, so as far as I know I'm not firing blanks.

Okay, the gun is a bit knackered and . . . I'll stop there.

So, even when exposed to the breathtaking beauty that this young woman on Sydney Harbour bridge had in spades, the thing I have become almost unhealthily aware of is breeding.

The whole romantic or lustful desire I used to experience when I fell in love has gone. It's been replaced with a deeper understanding of what drives us. It's obviously not just women who want to reproduce and men try to take advantage of that need. I wanted to reproduce and the desire to do so was only just below the surface. I knew I wanted babies from a very early age, I often found myself looking after other people's babies in the various squats and communes I lived in during the 1970s.

I should mention Stan, who's a fireman in his early forties now. Stan is very strong and capable. He's one of those blokes who cuts people from car wrecks or runs into a smoke-filled building when everyone else is running out. I know he'd be a very reassuring presence at such a traumatic event. He comes from a chaotic but essentially loving hippy family, his mum and dad were separated by the time he arrived.

However, for his first four years I lived with the assumption that this baby boy was my son.

Stan was born in 1976 in Bath, I knew his mother Jean, obviously I mean that biblically. We were never a very serious biblical item but it was the seventies and Jean was very organic and didn't believe in modern medicine, and that included any form of contraception.

I was young and did believe in modern medicine and contraception, but I wasn't very good at following through with such notions at the time.

So Jean got pregnant and Stan was born. I was just twenty when he came into the world and had no idea how to look after a baby. I didn't live with Jean but I visited Bath a lot when I lived in the truck.

Jean never said one way or the other that I was Stan's father; she was fairly cynical about men and once told me as I sat in her kitchen with Stan on my knee, 'It doesn't matter who's the dad, I'm his mum.'

It was very hard to know what to think. I didn't want to impose my will and get all patriarchal and claim him as my offspring, I was also in no position to give him a stable home life. I knew I'd slept with Jean at around the right time, in the beautiful cottage in Ireland where I left my dog Cabbage.

Yes, all the stories kind of tie together don't they?

What emerged after a couple of years was that Jean's exboyfriend Pete had visited her in Ireland just after I left. I had no idea this had happened until Stan was a little toddler and it sowed further seeds of doubt, making it yet harder to really commit to him. He was a lovely little lad and I adored him but his mother was quite, I'm trying to put this delicately, quite difficult. Not horrible, she was an amazing and loving mother to her children, she ran a spotless home, she was much loved by her peers, but she was five years older than me and not that bothered if I was around. I think I annoyed her and I can understand why. I wasn't much use.

Eventually I discovered I could have a blood test, myself, little Stan and Jean and this would settle the paternity confusion.

I arranged everything and met them in London and we all had a blood test. Stan was close to four years old by this time and I was worried this procedure would upset him.

I cannot imagine what that was like for him but as I remember it he didn't seem that bothered.

The blood test was quite an emotional event for me, Jean seemed very happy about the whole thing and Stan was a brave little lad when the nurse pushed the needle in his arm to take some of his blood.

A couple of weeks later I received a letter stating quite clearly that Stan was not my son.

The man who turned out to be Stan's biological father, Pete, didn't pay much heed when he was born. He'd already had children with another woman, but thankfully Pete became a great father and through all the normal difficulties of life, Stan turned out to be an amazing man.

I only told my mother about Stan after I found out that he wasn't my son. 'Well, that's a relief,' she said with her usual overflow of empathy. It wasn't a relief for me at the time, I felt very hollow when I found out.

I've just remembered an extraordinary event. Many years later, after my son Louis was born, I went to Bath to visit the people I knew there. I took Louis with me and we ended up at

Stan's flat. Sitting around the room were four or five women, including Jean, Stan's mum. They were being very nice to me and admiring Louis and commenting that it took me long enough to breed but they were happy I'd finally managed.

I put Louis on the floor to have a crawl about, something he liked doing. All the mums held their hands out and said, 'Louis, Louis, come and have a cuddle,' and, 'Isn't he a sweetheart, come here Louis.'

Louis ignored them all, crawled over to where Stan was sitting, grabbed hold of his jeans and pulled himself upright. Stan, who would have been nineteen or twenty at the time, reached down to him, looking a little surprised, and stroked his head. Louis then sat on Stan's feet and seemed very happy.

I was choking back tears a bit. I know it's stupid but it was as if this little pre-toddler boy knew there was a connection, even though there is no biological one.

By the time my own children arrived, in theory I'd had training; I'd changed nappies, I'd run a timetable of sleeping, eating and laundry. It should have been a walk in the park.

Of course, I wasn't prepared. It was a massive shock.

I had never had insomnia before Louis was born, I didn't know what it meant. After the first couple of weeks with my boy in his cot, I suffered from chronic exhaustion and insomnia, even if it wasn't 'my turn' to get him fed, changed and settled in the middle of the night.

Yes, we took turns. I want to go back to explain to my 'I want to be a hands-on dad' stupid self at the time, give myself a good slapping and explain that this really wasn't a good idea.

When it was her turn, Judy could get up, feed Louis for ten

minutes, change him, settle him and go back to bed and be asleep instantly.

I'd listen to her pottering about and gently coo-coo-ing to Louis. I'd be wide awake and stressed. The following night when it was my turn, I'd feed him from a bottle filled with milk Judy had expressed, change his nappy, put him in a clean baby-gro, eventually settle him back to sleep and then lie in bed wide awake for hours worrying about money, the apocalypse, gangs of zombies invading the village, a violent armed revolution where I'd have to choose sides, a massive meteor striking the Atlantic off the coast of Ireland, sending a fifteen-mile-high wave of death across the British Isles.

Oh, the joy.

When my daughter Holly was born we'd learned our lesson. Judy did the night feeds, I did the morning. I could get up and have everything organised very early, no problem, I slept like a log and truly enjoyed my daughter's babyhood. Lesson learned.

No one can give you advice on how to bring up kids. If they do, it's bound to be wrong, stupid or inappropriate for your own children. You have to muddle through, work it out as you go along. No amount of training can prepare you for the hardship, sure, but nothing can prepare you for the deep, profound joy.

I loved having babies, I loved having young children. Loved having young teenagers, so funny and quick-witted.

Okay, having two older teenagers was more of a challenge. If it were possible to measure the sheer weight of damp towels I picked up off the floor over a ten-year period, it would be in the tons.

The pleading wail of 'please pick your wet towels up after you've had a shower' still echoes through our now empty-nest house.

The response to these pleas? 'Whatever, old man', 'stop moaning' and 'get a life'.

The joy they bring.

It may sound like I'm obsessed with the minutiae of family life, and I was, but I've always been interested in the big picture, particularly when the small picture, i.e., my own chaotic life, seemed to overwhelm me.

I think pondering the big picture of human existence and our impact on the planet kept me sane, removed the emotional turmoil to a safe distance for a while.

About thirty years ago I started writing a big-picture novel set in the near future. Its hero was a young cycle courier living in London (I'd done the research) who spent his days delivering discreet physical packages to the uber-rich.

He was surrounded by old people, the music, the fashion and the dominant culture all dated from thirty years before he was born. London was almost empty, his own mother was very old, he rode through quiet streets of Soho and Covent Garden on a sci-fi hyper-bicycle.

It was titled *All Quiet in the West End*, and I curse myself now for not finishing it. The setting was brilliant, though I say so myself, a young man exploring a world where 80 per cent of the population were over sixty and very few people had children. Okay, it didn't have anything resembling a story and after splurging thousands of words on it I finally accepted it was yet more bottom-drawer fodder.

My bottom drawer is enormous; think the final scene from *Raiders of the Lost Ark.*

What intrigues me is how I'd been aware of the problems we are currently facing, where the majority of the population in Western Europe, Japan and America are old people and I'm one of them.

We baby boomers are retiring, there are lots of us and we own all the houses and we've got all the money. We drove the big cars and flew everywhere and ate lots of meat and clearly didn't give a tuppenny toss about what we left our children.

If you are young, you may have noticed.

So while we baby boomers are around for the next twenty years, it's hard to see how everyone will cope, because my generation, one that I believe will be seen as the most selfish and short-sighted in history, haven't even had enough babies.

Contrary to many clickbait headlines, the population in Western Europe, Japan and the USA is actually decreasing.

I don't find it easy to understand birth rates and population. Many of the figures are baffling and seem contradictory to our experience.

When I was a kid, the population in the UK was around 56 million and the national birth rate was 2.4 children. Now the population is around 62 million but the birth rate is 1.04 children.

My maths works it out like this: 1 million couples breed but they make less than two babies per couple. When the 1 million couples die, they haven't replaced themselves, they have left fewer than they started with. Add to that the fact there are a few million people who don't breed at all, so even if some women have five children that doesn't make up the short-fall.

That's sort of it, isn't it?

I think we can all agree that big families with five or more children are unusual in the developed world; I know it happens but it's not common.

I went through my address book recently and built up a list of people I know who don't have any children. It may say something about my larger circle of friends, colleagues and work mates, but a huge number of them don't have kids. I'm talking around 40 per cent of the total of a few hundred people listed, and these aren't eighteen-year-olds, they're proper grown-ups who own houses and have jobs.

This means that in the geographic area known as Europe (which includes the islands I live on, LOL) more people are dying than are being born. Multiply that by many millions and you have a rapidly falling population.

So why has the population in the UK risen in my lifetime?

Immigration.

Yes, folks, immigration has literally saved our sorry arses. Without immigration we wouldn't have enough nurses, doctors, engineers, computer programmers, sanitation workers, factory workers, agricultural workers, the list goes on and on.

If it wasn't for young people coming into the UK from elsewhere to work and settle, the world I tried to create in my potential groundbreaking, Booker Prize short-listed novel of thirty years ago would have become horribly true.

But the problem goes beyond the local, beyond the little

UKIPers and their night terrors, the decrease in population growth is a global phenomenon.

There are already whole provinces of Spain that are deserted, dead villages, empty towns, no one there. It's the same in Italy, Finland and parts of Southern France.

One very simple fact has come out of the latest research. If women are educated and there is even the most basic health care in their home country, they have fewer children and they give birth later in life.

This is as true in Copenhagen as it is in Cairo, valid in Chicago and as much as Chittagong.

Half the world's population is already reproducing at a level below replacement, the other half are slowing down fast.

Now none of this means things are necessarily going to get easier; a falling population creates as many problems as a growing one. A massive bulge in one age group with a smaller tax base from young people means we surviving baby boomers are likely to make things fairly stressful in the coming decades, and I'm a perpetual optimist.

So, should we be encouraging young women to have babies, as they are desperately trying to do in Russia? I mention Russia because they have the lowest birth rate in the world, lower even than Japan, which is often used as an example of what happens when the majority of a population are old.

I don't think so. If we are wise and sensible and take the long view (okay, that's never happened before in human history but you can dream) a smaller global population is not an altogether bad idea.

I'm glad I did some breeding, there's no question that my children made my life make a bit more sense. Maybe I should have had more, Judy certainly wanted to, she's from a Catholic family and they're meant to have loads. Interestingly, all the people she knows from her childhood have had fewer children than their parents did. She's from a family of four kids, all their neighbouring Catholic families in Brisbane had four or five children. All those next generation children have had one or two.

I sometimes tweet something wholly unconnected to population, something about renewable energy or the smart grid infrastructure and I will invariably get a reply along the lines of 'what's the point, there's too many mouths to feed' and 'you seem to forget the population explosion, there's seven billion of us now, that will double in fourteen years. We're doomed!'

The fearsome drumbeat of the 'population explosion' has been a lifelong background racket for my generation. I've always assumed it's an impossible problem but a slightly closer inspection of the fear of population growth is often focused by us, white people in the developed world, on areas like India and sub-Saharan Africa where birth rates are still in the region of four and five children per woman.

Maybe the fear is then that 'they' will take over; that these Africans and Indians are breeding 'us' out of existence.

Again, closer inspection of all the research on this topic indicates that the growth is slowing, it isn't the numbers of people being born that's falling, it's the growth in the number of births that's falling.

Birth rates are dropping everywhere and the projections by the UN and other bodies of what population will be in the years

2100 are very broad. From a high of 18 billion to a low of 6.5 billion, lower than today. Both are equally possible but the lower figure seems to be becoming more likely.

The maximum rate of change in global population peaked in the late sixties, which was when more people were having more babies more rapidly. Since then, the change has been entirely the other way, with more people having fewer babies less often. In 1968 the change was 2 per cent growth; each generation was having 2 per cent more babies than their parents. This has now dropped to below 1 per cent, and these figures include Africa, central American and Asian countries. This drop is mostly driven, it seems, by the rapidly falling populations in the rest of the world.

Forty-seven countries around the world are currently not replacing their populations; the total number of people in those countries is set to reduce in the coming fifty years.

But, and this I think is the most important fact about breeding: a mere 7 per cent of the world's population consume 50 per cent of the planet's resources. That number will include you, if you're reading this book. It includes pretty much everyone we know, walk past, live next door to.

That's what used to keep me awake at night when I had small children. I could see the change in my own life as our babies grew.

I had led a possibly unusually low-consumption life for the first thirty years I was knocking around. I used public transport, a bicycle, I was an occasional vegetarian, I didn't fly anywhere or go on holiday. I lived in small apartments with low-level heating, indeed, I often prided myself on my low-impact existence.

That all changed radically when I had children. Before long, I had a four-bedroom house with central heating, a washing machine, a tumble drier, two cars, and boy did we fly.

We flew every year to Australia, sometimes twice. My carbon footprint is immeasurably huge. If I live in a tent for the rest of my life and only eat raw vegetables I will still have consumed vastly more than an African farmer the same age as me. If I never fly again, that same African farmer will have to fly around the world for a couple of years non-stop and only eat factory-farmed beef to even begin catching up with me.

On the other hand, 50 per cent of the world's population, that includes the African farmer the same age as me, consume 7 per cent of the world's output and are responsible for 7 per cent of human-produced CO_2.

That means the remaining 50 per cent consume 93 per cent of the world's output. That's not terribly well balanced is it?

So, the question we need to ask, and it's a very uncomfortable one, is: who are the over-breeders and who are the over-consumers?

When I am introduced to do a talk about renewable energy and electric cars and the person says, 'Please welcome Robert Llewellyn, green activist,' I have to politely correct them.

I'm about as green as a Canadian tar sands extraction installation. I'm a privileged, developed-world hyper-consumer with a carbon footprint the size of an ice-free Greenland.

This state of affairs has regularly made me depressed and despondent, so much so that I occasionally have what my wife describes as an emotional meltdown where I react strongly against our over-consumption.

I say again, my generation, the Western baby boomers, have been the most greedy, short-sighted generation I hope the world will ever see. We will go to any lengths to justify our over-consumption with no thought to how this might affect future generations.

So that is what drives me. I know it's pointless saying to four hundred people in four hundred individual cars that are stuck in a massive traffic jam, 'Why don't you turn your cars off, get out and walk.' That's just silly, no one is going to do that.

But if we start to think about how we can share the riches we have a little more equally, use technology that doesn't waste the resources it requires, be a little more careful where those resources come from and the impact they have, then we might get somewhere.

I'm not overly optimistic. The only other growth as massive as population in my lifetime is inequality; that's growing at breakneck speed and shows no signs of slowing down. You don't need a graduate degree in philosophy, politics and economics to know that grossly unequal societies do not function well.

So, I hope I live long enough to see my grandchildren and I fervently hope that the world they are born into is a little less unequal than the one my children were born into. It's not looking hopeful.

'Straylya

The wall of heat that hit me the first time I landed at Brisbane Airport in December 1990 is something I will never forget. It was my first visit to that vast and exciting continent.

Judy and I had flown together from London. She had slept for about 90 per cent of the journey. I don't know how she does it; I had a window seat and didn't sleep a wink. Everything was bright, exciting, new, different and beyond anything I spent the first half of my life expecting to experience.

It is a ridiculously long flight, as anyone who's done it will agree. From the time you leave your house to the moment you arrive in Australia, you are travelling for between twenty-four and thirty-six hours. If you don't manage to sleep in that time, the combination of exhaustion and jet lag bends your consciousness in ways not possible with mere psychotropic drugs.

We were met at the airport by Judy's family, her three brothers and their partners, their children and of course Judy's wonderful mother Maureen.

I'd heard about Maureen when Judy performed her show in Edinburgh a few years before and I was slightly anxious about meeting her.

My first memory of meeting the brothers was staring directly in front of me and seeing three belt buckles; these were on the waistbands of three enormous men, Judy's brothers Mark, David and Tony.

David is the shortest at around six foot one (1.83 metres), Tony is around six foot four (1.95 metres) and Mark is a terrifying six foot seven (2.04 metres).

They shook my hand and actually said, 'G'day, mate,' to which I'm sure I blathered some inane nonsense in return.

We walked out into the sun-bleached car park through the shimmering all-engulfing heat, loaded our bags into Maureen's Holden saloon and headed off through the scorching northern suburbs of Brisbane.

We arrived at the family home in Mitchelton, a lovely cream-painted wooden house built in the 1950s, constructed on a hillside high up on wooden stumps, a very common building style in Queensland. It was so hot I could barely breathe. Up to that point, I had experienced some dry heat in California, some humid heat in New York but none of that was close to a midsummer day in Brisbane. I later discovered that the temperature that day was 39 degrees centigrade with a 100 per cent humidity. Moist.

I was instantly sweating like the proverbial and became very nervous that this family would think I was just another stinking Pom.

'Would you like a shower?' asked Maureen as I stood wide-eyed and vacant in her kitchen. I don't think it was a question, more of a gentle command.

I stood for ages under the lukewarm shower head trying to get my brain to work for a bit longer. I dried myself off and applied copious amounts of Body Shop underarm deodorant. I put on a vest and a pair of shorts and went back down under the house where the family were drinking cold beers, lemonade and eating Lamington cake.

I was dizzy with jet lag and exhaustion so I sat down and put my hands behind my head as I felt like I might fall over at any moment. Judy's two delightful nieces, Katie and Laura, both then under ten years old, squealed and pointed at me.

'Look! Robert's got shaving foam under his arms!'

I glanced down and true enough the Body Shop product, created as it was for a cold, damp climate in the British Isles, had reacted violently. Now, in the shimmering tropical environment of midsummer Brisbane, it had started some kind of unexpected chemical reaction and foamed up big time. I don't mean a bit of foam residue, this was like twin foam guns from an airport fire-fighter. Hugely embarrassing. Judy smiled flatly, ignored her annoying boyfriend and talked about something else.

After I'd removed the copious underarm foam with a paper towel we had some kind of lunch, I ate my first fresh mango and I'm sure made too much fuss about how amazing it was. Later that day, Judy's brother Mark handed me a flat piece of dry leather. I inspected it through jet-lagged eyes; it looked like a dried-out handbag with some sort of leg design around the edge.

'There you go, mate. Welcome to Australia,' said Mark, a grin just visible behind his enormous dark beard.

'Mark, for Pete's sake!' said Margaret, his wife.

The family were laughing, the young nieces were squealing and jumping up and down with delight. They all knew I was holding a squashed cane toad, flattened by a passing Ute (utility vehicle or pickup truck) and dried to a crisp in the blazing sun.

It was a lovely present but strangely enough I didn't keep hold of this particular gift. I gingerly put it down on the concrete patio beside me and continued to try and stay awake.

Like many Brits, I instantly fell in love with Australia. The natural beauty of the eastern coastal strip is so intense, so dazzling that it's hard to remain unmoved.

I could not help lying in the sun at every opportunity. It was December, for goodness' sake. I had never been hot in December in my life.

I went very brown very quickly on that first visit. I know, it's not good for you and it's very un-Australian. I was reminded of this when Judy and I went to a New Year's Eve party held by some old mates of hers in a scruffy house in Brisbane. When the host opened the door to greet us, he followed this friendly welcome with, 'Is it still fashionable to have a tan in England, mate? Cos it's not here.'

Cruel but very Australian. I'm used to it.

We stayed with Judy's mother for a while and then headed off 'up the coast' to a small town called Peregian. It's not really a town in any sense a European would recognise, more a suburban strip near a massive beach.

I had spent my life being encouraged to go into the sea when we had family holidays. It was always traumatic and uncomfortable because the sea around the UK is so damn cold!

The first time I went on a beach in Australia the notion of beach culture suddenly made sense. The water isn't just 'not cold'. It's hot, like a bath. The water is so clear, the waves are so huge, the beaches, particularly Queensland beaches, go on for miles. Literally miles of flat sand, huge seas and dazzling sun.

I was so happy waking up in the morning, pulling on a T-shirt and a pair of tatty shorts and walking barefoot across the dunes to watch the sun come up over the ocean. I always woke up long before Judy, my God that woman loves to sleep, so I went for long walks and remembered how incredibly lucky I was.

For one thing, I could just about afford the ticket to get to Australia, for another the exchange rate at the time (1990) was very much in favour of Brits in Australia. The pound was worth close to three dollars so everything seemed very cheap.

Also, I was in love with an Australian who had fantastic connections with people in Australia so I felt less like an outsider tourist. And we were living next to the biggest beach I'd ever seen.

And laundry. Oh, my goodness, I was in laundry heaven.

In the apartment complex we stayed in there was a laundry room with a couple of huge top-loaders ready for action. I washed all our clothes and hung them outside on a Hills Hoist, the greatest invention ever to come out of Australia. (It's a rotary clothes line.)

Within minutes, I'm not joking, within minutes, the clothes were super bone-dry. They went stiff with their hyper-dryness. There is nothing in the world better than doing laundry in Australia. I miss it every time I do laundry in the UK.

Later, we drove from Brisbane to Sydney, stopping halfway at a fairly grim motel in Nambucca Heads. This was when I discovered cockroaches could fly. No one told me. We were lying in bed when something quite big crawled on my arm. I turned the light on and saw a fairly chunky insect near my wrist.

'It's just a cocky, go back to sleep, you big wus,' said my ever-empathetic life partner.

I flicked it off onto the sticky red-patterned carpet and whacked it with a foam rubber flip-flop. It was like striking a battle-hardened Royal Marine with a goose feather. The wretched creature didn't even flinch but it did take off and flew right at my face!

I fell back onto the bed and Judy expressed her dismay in a torrent of expletives, mainly aimed at my fragile masculinity.

I didn't give up. I delivered several lethal blows, this time with my new R M Williams elastic-sided boot. This was more like striking a battle-hardened Royal Marine with a medium-sized twig, it had more impact but nothing like enough.

The filthy beast landed on the wall. I whacked it again, ignoring the increasingly obscene critique emanating from the love of my life, until the creature crawled between the door and door frame of the motel room, I had the door open as I was trying to chase it outside. I slammed the door and using the simple principle of leverage, flattened the innocent creature.

I have never heard a more satisfying crunch. I punched the air and swaggered about the room triumphantly. Until I saw another cockroach scuttle across the vile carpet.

It wasn't a good night.

I don't need to describe Sydney, the area around the harbour is one of the most beautiful cityscapes in the world. Judy took me around all her old haunts; she'd been living in Sydney when she joined Circus Oz and had spent her early twenties living there.

We drove to Melbourne and it was hot. Lord, was it hot. I loved it, Judy was complaining about the heat. Yes, an Australian, complaining about the heat, they all do.

Melbourne reminded me of Streatham in South London, probably because a lot of it was built around the same time. It's very flat and can be very hot, or cold, or windy, or pouring with rain all in the space of an afternoon.

I met many of Judy's friends, actors, writers, film-makers, comedians, circus performers and nearly all of them were wearing Doc Marten boots they'd bought when they were in London.

We stayed in a scruffy house in a suburb called Northcote. I had my thirty-fifth birthday there, someone made me a cake, someone else arrived with a dog on a bit of string, which promptly ate the entire cake. Lovely.

We went to my first barbecue in the garden of a lesbian couple's house in Carlton. In case you didn't know, there are a great many lesbians living in Melbourne, well, there were in the 1990s, I think it's still the same. It's a bit like San Francisco is for gay men. Melbourne is a very lesbian city.

'Place is jam-packed with lezzoes, mate,' I was told by Shirley, one of Judy's long-time mates, and a very happy lesbian.

There was another thing I learned that evening that runs contrary to many people's supposition about Australian men being drunk, loud, rude and sexist. I wish to illustrate that this isn't always the case.

At one end of the small urban garden of this beautiful house was a barbie. Standing around it were a group of men, some holding small babies, others looking after toddlers, many discussing recipes while preparing delicious salads.

At the far end of the garden was a table covered in a handsome collection of fermented intoxicants. Standing around this was a group of women, tough-looking girls who were laughing, joking and using the most coruscating coarse language I've ever heard.

'Ignore them, mate,' said a friendly bloke carrying a cute baby. 'They're just showing off, they'll calm down soon enough. D'you fancy an elderflower cordial?'

These were my kind of blokes. I've never been a big drinker but I was very thirsty, and the elderflower cordial was delicious.

Judy joined the rowdy ladies and I watched her laughing uproariously with the girls. She was obviously having a whale of a time.

For the following seven years, and again I wish to state I knew how lucky I was at the time, we spent every Northern Hemisphere winter in Australia. We flew with our baby son for the first time in 1993 – that's no picnic, but we survived. The delight of waking up somewhere sunny and warm in January and watching your toddler run about with nothing on, his little bare feet padding along the patio as he chewed something unmentionable he found under a chair, is a fond memory.

Louis now lives in Sydney and has no fear of the things that freaked me out the first few visits. Insects the size of dogs, moths the size of light aircraft, and stick insects. Give me a break. The term stick insect is a dangerous misnomer that can lull the unwary traveller into danger.

Okay, so I was thirty-seven years old and I couldn't swim. This does relate to Australia because swimming in pools and the sea makes perfect sense in Australia and it relates to stick insects – bear with me.

Judy is a very good swimmer. I don't mean she can swim about in water and not drown. She's a proper swimmer who does fifty lengths of a big pool just to warm up. Front crawl, very little splashing, superb style, swims underwater, can dive in, all the cool stuff.

I literally couldn't swim when I met her. If I had fallen into deep water I would have drowned, literally drowned to death.

So, I started having swimming lessons when Judy was pregnant with Louis. My dad couldn't swim, neither could his dad so my theory was, if I can learn to swim then I'll be able to make sure my son can swim and break the pattern.

It took me fourteen weeks of long, often distressing swimming lessons. Tim, the most incredibly patient swimming teacher, never once lost his rag when yet again, for the hundredth time, I'd be thrashing about in the pool making unmanly squealing sounds.

During the fourteenth session, I lay floating in the middle of the pool like a badly formed starfish, face down, relaxed, incredibly happy. I did one stroke and started to move, I was actually swimming.

It was an incredible moment for me. I had experienced years of dread catching the rattling old bus to the public baths in Northampton to undergo the torture of being forced to swim by a bullying games master. Years of being teased by my peers, being thrown in the deep end 'for fun'. I lived in terror of drowning. I know what it's like because I've nearly done it twice.

Going off to the lake near my parental home as a teenager with a crowd of mates, them all stripping off and going skinny-dipping, while I sat on the shore like a massive loser.

But at the age of thirty-seven I left all that behind. For the first few months I could only swim underwater. I loved it, it made me so happy to finally discover that if I wasn't holding onto the side, if my feet didn't touch the bottom of the pool, I'd survive.

The pattern of non-swimming males in my family was broken. My son could swim before he could walk, my daughter likewise. Judy had them in the pool when they were tiny babies, plop them underwater, they kick their little legs and come up to the surface with a big grin.

Neither of them remember learning to swim, they're both naturals at it, and Holly in particular is an excellent swimmer.

So back to the stick insect. A few years after I'd finally conquered my fear of water we were staying in a wonderful beach house in Queensland with a pool in the backyard. Judy's big brothers Mark and Tony were visiting with their children, a delightful noisy crowd of people in the house with wonderful food and what seemed like dozens of kids.

After it got dark, I had a swim in the pool while everyone sat around chatting and drinking beer. I was calmly breaststroking my way across the floodlit pool when something I can only describe as a flying log started skimming across the water surface and heading right towards my face. It was, I later learned, a stick insect having a drink. It did have some kind of proboscis drooping down to the water's surface as it buzzed along. I was terrified, I was in the middle of the pool and this monster was heading right at me.

It was then I realised that I had never learned how to turn corners when swimming, I could only swim in a straight line. Apparently, I made enough high-pitched alarm noises that Judy and her brothers looked over the railings of the deck that towered above the pool and for some reason they found the sight of an ungainly swimmer and a large stick insect highly amusing.

I tried to dive under but it all went wrong and resulted in a lot of embarrassing thrashing.

'Don't worry, darl,' said Judy calmly. 'Tony is a lifesaver, he can give you mouth to mouth.'

I got out of that pool sharpish and have never tried a relaxed, night-time swim in Australia since.

So yes, there are some particularly big bugs and snakes in Australia, but it's not like you're surrounded by them all the time. You might see some big fella with eight legs every now and then, but no more than you'd see a fox or badger in the UK.

Okay, there was the huntsman spider under the washing machine when I was busting for a number two early one morning. That puts some strain on your digestive system, but I survived.

In 2001 we lived in Sydney, the children went to the local school, Mosman State Primary and they loved it. We lived in a small apartment overlooking Balmoral beach in North Sydney, I was writing a book, *Brother Nature*, and spent a great deal of time arranging an incredibly complex travel schedule for the rest of the year.

After school, Louis would often take part in junior surf-life-saving practice, going out with equally tiny kids into the massive crashing waves on Manly beach as if he was going for a walk in the park. We had two pet mice in a little cage and the kids seemed very happy. I was very happy. Judy was, well, less so. It was much less of an adventure for her, and she missed England. In January, can you believe it.

We were so settled in Sydney, I would gladly have stayed for ever, but I had to go off and work.

It's one of the saddest memories from my years of parenting, after living happily in Balmoral for four months I had to fly back to London leaving Judy and the kids in Sydney. They all walked with me up the hill in Mosman to where I could get a taxi to take me to the airport. I got in the cab and looked back as I drove off, Judy was crying, so was Holly who was in her arms, Louis was patting his mother's hand, very concerned for her.

She told me later he said, 'It's all right, Mummy, I'll look after you.' He was six.

I blubbed quietly in the back of the taxi, slept like a log on the flight to London and before I'd recovered from jet lag started shooting a new series called *Hollywood Science* in the back garden of a house in Basingstoke.

While we were having lunch in the kitchen of the house one day a motorbike courier arrived and delivered the script of the *Red Dwarf* movie, which I read with great eagerness. It was a brilliant script, I still have it although the final page is missing as it was used to write a shopping list. Never leave a script in the kitchen, lesson learned.

As many readers will know we never made the film. We got close, but sadly it was not to be.

I then flew to California to shoot a new season of *Scrapheap Challenge* and after another eight weeks I flew from Los Angeles back to Sydney. That flight was a doozie, as they said in California, a day of your life just disappears as you cross the international date line. Time, day, night, none of it makes sense. There are loads of pictures of me with my young children, I know it's me because I can see this tired but happy-looking man in the photographs but I have zero memory of the time. I was jet-lagged beyond redemption for days.

In the ten weeks I'd been away from my gorgeous babies, they had grown and developed so much, it was as if I had to get to know new people. My son was so much more confident and doing really well at school, my daughter had grown so much I barely recognised her. Judy, well, she was not so good. For someone who was born and grew up in Australia and lived there up to her late twenties, she really wasn't happy there.

'My brain's gone to mush,' she said. 'Life is too easy here, everyone is just having a fucking lifestyle and no fucking life, I'm going crazy.'

So a few months later we flew back to the UK, the children went back to the local school and everything sort of returned to normal.

I often wonder what would have happened if we had decided to stay in Australia, how our lives would have panned out. It wasn't an easy decision, Judy had been living in the UK for over thirteen years and had lost touch with many of her old crowd. They had moved, had kids, changed lives, all the normal stuff. She'd made her home in England so we are that peculiar mixture. An English bloke who'd like to live in Australia, and an Australian woman who wants to live in England.

I had to go back to California for another eight weeks to shoot the remaining episodes of *Scrapheap Challenge* and *Junkyard Wars*.

Since those early days, we have spent many happy months in Australia. It's a completely unsustainable life choice, it's always felt temporary, I mean the ability to fly halfway around the planet in a massive machine that burns tons of fossil fuels. It's yet another reason that proves beyond doubt that I'm about as green as a slag heap in the Rhondda, but I'm incredibly grateful to have been able to do it.

After our children started school, and particularly as they progressed through secondary school, our visits have been shorter and more spread out. Judy still goes once a year to see her mother, I manage to wangle trips whenever I can and I stay in amazing places and meet incredible people.

One of the many things I love about the country are the contrasts, not only the geographic ones, but the political ones. Australia has delivered some amazing political thinkers, writers and activists but remains a predominantly conservative country. It seems, and I'm confident this is an incorrect generalisation, that the greatest minds that come from Australia tend to live either in London or New York. However, even in the time I've been going there I've witnessed incredible changes.

Okay, they also produce some of the most backward-looking and it has to be said, amusing political nutters.

When I was last there, a government minister stood up in parliament and waved a lump of coal at the opposition, shouting, 'What are you so afraid of? Anyone would think you had coal-a-phobia, ya drongoes!'

Lovely. But on the other hand, Australia has seen dramatic uptake of domestic solar panels. It's very apparent when you visit now. Ten years ago, I'm sure there were some trendy, wealthy people in Sydney that strapped a load of solar panels on their roof, but it was rare. Now it's the norm. Go to any Australian suburb – my goodness, they love suburbs in Australia – and virtually every roof is covered in panels.

The adoption of household batteries is also meteoric; it makes even more sense to use the sun as an energy source in Australia. But that's not all; massive solar farms are being constructed in the desert, and they really do have a lot of desert in Australia. Tesla have installed their largest-ever grid scale battery in South Australia linked to a wind farm, solar reflector technology is being installed, individual states, particularly South Australia, are going hell for leather for renewables even though the current federal government are still enthralled by the dirty great god of coal.

Electric car uptake is a little behind but it's appearing. Tesla taxi company Evoke are running a dozen or so Model S and Model X cars in Sydney and there is a supercharger network from Adelaide to Brisbane.

Australia has also made great strides towards becoming what it calls a 'reconciled nation' by acknowledging and dealing with what used to be endemic racism towards its indigenous Aboriginal people. Much like America, that other nation of immigrants, Australia still struggles with issues of equality for its indigenous people, but in recent reports, almost all the population believed that reconciliation was important and possible, and 77 per cent of non-indigenous Australians felt that Aboriginal culture was important to Australia's national identity. It's nowhere near perfect, but with goodwill from all quarters, it's getting better.

For the last twenty years, I've been working on persuading Judy to go back there permanently. 'Maybe we could live in Australia when we're old, darl?'

'Maybe,' she says. So there is hope.

My dream is to be an old man padding around in bare feet wearing baggy old shorts and a tatty *Red Dwarf* T-shirt, living in some tin shack not too far from a beach, eating freshly picked mangoes with my grandchildren. Just for a couple of years before I pop my Ugg boots.

Ten Years on the Heap

I cycled across London from Islington to Hammersmith on a breezy Tuesday morning in the spring of 1998. I was on my way to a meeting in a converted fire station on North End Road. I went up a couple of flights of stairs to the offices of a small and very new TV production company called RDF. There I met a delightful man called David Frank (the DF of RDF) and moments later we were joined by an amazing young woman called Cathy Rogers.

We talked about engineering, machines, cars, hovercraft, helicopters and steam engines with great enthusiasm. Cathy had an idea inspired by the story of what happened to the crew of *Apollo 13*: their oxygen scrubbers packed up when they were roughly 250,000 miles from earth, they were going to suffocate and there was no way of saving them.

Back on earth, a team of engineers sat in a room with all the equipment, spares and back-up kit they knew was on board the module. With sticky tape, bits of tube, cardboard food packaging and tissue paper they managed to recreate an oxygen scrubber and the instructions were then relayed to the three-man crew in space. They followed the instructions, built an oxygen scrubber and lived to tell the tale.

This escapade was recreated in the 1995 film *Apollo 13* starring Tom Hanks, which Cathy had seen earlier that year.

She wanted to make a TV series where two teams of three engineers made a machine out of bits of discarded machinery and technology within a limited time, guided by an expert over a walkie-talkie who was in a remote position but could see them. Once built, the teams would then test those machines in a competition.

I liked the idea, I was genuinely enthusiastic but as I rode back home after the meeting I pondered as to why I got to make really interesting but quite quirky TV shows which appeared and were then rapidly forgotten.

Not long before this meeting I made a series called *iCamcorder* which was originally an idea from Rob Grant and Doug Naylor, the two creators and writers of *Red Dwarf*.

Six half-hour shows for Channel 4, written and presented by me and exploring more creative ways to use the suddenly popular device, the mini video camera or camcorder.

These clunky old cameras recorded low grade video onto tapes, which were then nigh-on impossible to edit, but we did our best. We came up with all manner of tips and tricks on using your camcorder more effectively.

We had guests on the show including the legendary film director Ken Russell, who helped shoot a wedding video at an actual wedding in the Black Country. It turned out to be a bit of a Ken Russell drama as the mother of the bride and the mother of the groom had a bit of a set-to outside the church. A couple of crumpled hats on the floor and a lot of fabulous bad language. So that series was broadcast and people seemed to like it well enough but nothing more came of it.

I also made a series called *Hollywood Science* for the BBC and the Open University, where a real scientist, Dr Jonathan Hare, and I recreated stunts and events from blockbuster Hollywood movies to see if they were scientifically verifiable.

An example was the scene in the original *Die Hard* movie when Bruce Willis jumps off the top of the Nakatomi Tower when the baddies are shooting at him. Of course he survives because he tied a fire hose around his waist which broke his rapid descent.

What would happen to a human body if you really did that?

The production team procured a length of fire hose similar to the sort found in modern American buildings and we discovered that it has a certain elasticity in its cross section, to allow it to take high-pressure water, but none in its length.

If Bruce Willis really made the jump, he would reach terminal velocity, about 200kph or 120mph, long before the hose broke his fall.

At the moment the hose finally took all his weight there would be no give in the hose with the result, as Jonathan described so succinctly, that you would find Bruce and Willis splatted in separate lumps at the base of the tower.

Yuk.

Then there was *Speed* with Keanu Reeves and Sandra Bullock in the bus that couldn't go slower than 50 miles an hour or it would explode. Brilliant plot, those Hollywood folks are so clever. Keanu kicks some ass and Sandra is one tough lady who survives against the odds.

So what, we asked, are the odds of an American bus, which weighs around seven tons, jumping over an eighteen-metre (sixty-foot) gap in a partially constructed highway flyover?

Jonathan worked it out and informed me it could be done. Yeah, I know, it's surprising isn't it?

But only if the bus was travelling at over 270,000 miles an hour.

Hollywood Science was brilliant fun to make, but of course, as it was an Open University programme it initially went out in the middle of the night and was only seen by insomniac physics and engineering students.

So *Scrapheap Challenge*, as it was titled, felt very much like another one of these shows.

Ten years and around 176 episodes later when we shot the final episode next to a lake near Basingstoke, I accepted that *Scrapheap* turned out to be a little bit different.

There was the regular annual run of twelve episodes plus a couple of specials, the *Scrappy Races* where six teams built mad vehicles which we tore around the UK to take part in crazy tests at various locations, then there was *Junkyard Wars* which we made in California.

I only took part in a handful of the *Junkyard Wars* episodes but it still took up a great deal of my year.

I have dug through my boxes of papers to try and find an article I wrote the year before I started working on *Scrapheap*. It was published in the *Guardian* and expressed what could be seen as a slightly jaundiced and bitter appraisal of the 'profession' of TV presenting.

I can't find it, nothing new there, my office is in utter chaos.

That article was something I came to regret over the following ten years, not that anyone remembered reading it, but it was a bit spooky. I thought I was being brave and radical having a pop at self-important tossers who stand in front of a camera and talk, but no, I was just explaining the remainder of my so-called TV career.

If I had never planned on being an actor, I had definitely never planned on being a wretched TV presenter. They had often annoyed me. I can't remember the circumstances but something or someone must have stoked my ire enough to fuel a *Guardian* rant.

My loving wife once described TV presenting as 'the most honourable profession' but between you and me, I don't think she really thought it was.

You stand in front of a camera and waffle, that's about the skill level required. However, I admit that on *Scrapheap Challenge* I truly found my niche.

I loved what the show was about and I loved making it, even though the hours were comically long and the exhaustion experienced by everyone involved was legendary.

I have written about the shenanigans of making *Scrapheap* elsewhere (*Behind the Scenes at Scrapheap Challenge,* Channel 4 Books, 2001); suffice it to say it was an incredible experience.

I learned a great deal about engineering, but also about team dynamics and how to cooperate creatively. The teams that could do that well would invariably win; the teams that internally competed with each other would often come a cropper.

For the first four years on *Scrapheap Challenge*, I worked with Cathy Rogers, an incredible woman who is so clever there are no means yet devised to measure her intelligence. She is also charming, happily married to the lovely Jason, who also worked on the show, and mother to three wonderful children.

We made the first three series in England and the fourth in Los Angeles. This was because in 2001 we also started making *Junkyard Wars*, an American version made for the Discovery Channel.

I know: in Britain it's a Challenge, in America it's a War but the show was exactly the same. We flew the British teams out to California and took them to a very hot and dusty scrapheap in the San Fernando Valley. This was a very different experience to making the show in the UK. For a start, in the San Fernando Valley, it never rained and it was hot, very hot. Metal gets very hot when it's in direct sunlight all day in California, something many British teams learned the hard way when they forgot to wear gloves when scavenging in the vast scrapheap we were using.

We throw away a lot of stuff in the UK but believe me, we're amateur wasters in comparison to the USA. That scrapyard was so big you couldn't see the other side of it, it just disappeared into the haze.

For me, the most memorable episode, possibly ever, was the one we made in 2002. The flight special.

It was to commemorate the one hundredth anniversary of the first mechanical manned flight by the Wright brothers in 1902.

Three teams, British, American and French, were challenged to build period flying machines in two days using traditional tools and materials. Basically wood, string and canvas.

I really wanted them to carve their own propellers out of wood and use lawn-mower engines but we had to abide by certain aviation rules laid down by the FAA, the Federal Aviation Authority in the United States, who had eventually allowed us to test the planes.

This meant we had to use brand-new microlight engines and brand-new propellers for safety reasons which, when you think about it, isn't such a bad idea. A hand-carved propeller spinning at Lord knows how many RPM that starts to fall to bits could be quite dramatic. It would make good telly but it might just kill someone. Fair enough.

So the following two days were the quietest I had ever experienced on the heap. Normally, there was a lot of noise from grinders, metal saws, welding equipment, large men with unusual facial hair smashing some large lump of metal with a big hammer, but not on the flight special.

It was really quiet. It smelled wonderful as the teams shaved the timbers they were using with hand-held wood planes.

Slowly the shape and design of the planes appeared. The French team recreated a version of the Blériot Flyer, the first plane to fly over La Manche, otherwise known as the English Channel.

The American team recreated an early American design that had originally been built by a bicycle maker. They used steel tube soldered together like a bike frame as a crude fuselage and wooden wing structures.

The British team created a bi-plane based on a design cooked up by a *Scrapheap* stalwart, Dr Billy Brooks, a hang-glider test pilot.

Yes, you read that correctly, Billy tests hang gliders for a living. He literally jumps off cliffs with some aluminium poles and canvas strapped to him to see if he can fly. At the time of writing he is still alive and he is an extraordinary man.

On day two the planes were really starting to take shape, although the teams had an enormous amount still to do. By lunchtime, they had mounted their newly unwrapped state-of-the-art microlight engines. They wanted to test them but the French and American teams couldn't get them started, while the British team engine started first time. This may have had something to do with the fact that one member of the British team was an RAF engineer who knew a considerable amount about engines.

There was much discussion among the French and American teams. They decided there was a fault with their engines, phone calls were made, a disaster loomed until a British team member casually walked up to their engines, pulled out a small safety tab and started the engine first time with very little effort. She smiled at them, and casually walked back to her own bay.

A generous serving of humble pie was then consumed, not that I mentioned it again and again on camera for the following few hours.

By the end of the second day there were three things that looked quite like aeroplanes in each build area. It had been very hot and it was very late as we had overrun as this was a very ambitious project. We'd never done anything like it before.

The following day, the planes were loaded onto an enormous American big-rig truck and we followed this unusual cargo on a very long drive from Los Angeles to the Mojave Desert. I won't go on about how hot it is in the Mojave Desert in July other than to say you really don't need a coat.

The day after this we gathered in the dawn light in the middle of a vast area of white salt flats. Distant mountains could just be seen on the horizon and the vast blue dome above us was totally cloudless. The teams were busy from first light, adjusting their creations. As the sun came up we all gathered around a Clint Eastwood look-alike who was the representative from the FAA. He explained how we had permission to fly the machines but only to a height of 50 feet. They were classified as experimental aircraft and there were very strict safety rules we had to adhere to.

Before long, the American team started their engine and did a practice taxi run to see if their very basic controls worked. A pickup truck with a camera mounted on the back drove alongside as the machine gathered speed, and boy, did they gather speed. At one point, the driver of the pickup truck realised they touched ninety miles an hour and still the American machine stayed resolutely on the ground. In fact, the wing design was a brilliant method of keeping the craft attached to the salt flats: the faster it went, the deeper the little wheels dug into the pristine white surface.

They clearly needed to do some major adjustment, but it's worth pointing out that the American test pilot was a very brave man. He was a genuine test pilot who had flown just about every aircraft you've ever heard of but he did admit this was possibly the most terrifying.

Next, the French team fired up their engine and the Blériot Flyer started to move off. This looked a little more hopeful when the tail skid left the ground and it seemed like it might get airborne. It kind of bounced into the air for a few metres and then landed again but there was, for a second or so, something that resembled flight.

Dr Billy Brooks then sat on the child's beach chair that was tied to a long plank of wood that made up their fuselage, in front of him was a sawn-off broom handle attached to the plane with a strip of leather to give it manoeuvrability. Tied to the broom handle were four bits of string, which were in turn attached to the control surfaces on the wings and tail of the machine.

This half-baked creation only had one wheel, so two members of the British team ran alongside as the plane built up speed to keep the wings from digging into the salt flats. The plane continued to move faster as the two teammates let go and before anyone was ready, I'm talking camera crews, the sound department, the director, the man from the FAA, me, anyone, the damn thing got airborne.

I mean seriously airborne. It went up in the air. It actually flew, like a proper aeroplane.

I was standing next to the director who was doing some quite impressive swearing because he wasn't getting this on camera. This wasn't the actual test, which was due to take place in the afternoon, this was just to see if the machines could move.

Part of the crew that day were the pilots of a very beautiful powered glider that was designed to film birds in flight, a very quiet and sleek machine that could fly at low speed due to its enormous wingspan. As Billy flew further away the two-man crew ran towards this aircraft, not unlike fighter pilots on an airfield in Kent during the Battle of Britain. They eventually got airborne too, but by this time Billy Brookes and the British plane was happily sailing away into the distant sky.

I don't know how you judge how high a plane is flying, especially in the unusual environment of the Mojave Desert, but even with my lack of experience I was guessing he was at more than fifty feet.

I turned to look at the man from the FAA. He was standing with his head in his hands. I think he may have been swearing under his breath. Many Americans tend to be less sweary under stress than the foul-mouthed British crew who were effing and jeffing with wild abandon. The FAA man got back in the air-conditioned cab of his enormous pickup truck and pulled his cap down over his eyes. He clearly didn't want to see anything more.

By the time the beautiful powered glider with the amazing cameras caught up with Billy Brooks we started to get some information about his well-being. Billy had no method of communicating with the ground other than waving as he flew around in large circles way above our heads.

'Tell him to land!' screamed the director to the crew of the spotter plane. Okay, there were other words in the sentence bellowed by the director. I won't give an exact quote, I'm sure you can imagine what they were for yourself.

Their voices came back clear over the radio. 'We have gesticulated to the pilot by repeatedly pointing in a downward direction.'

'What's he doing?'

'He is smiling and waving, sir,' came the humourless reply.

More swearing from the director and then, 'How high are you?'

'We are currently level with the British aircraft at two thousand two hundred feet and climbing gently,' came the reply.

Thankfully, about twenty minutes later Billy landed the machine perfectly and was clearly very pleased with it. For the first and only time in *Scrapheap*'s history when we did larger international challenges, the British team won. It was almost awkward.

As we were packing up later that day Billy revealed a model of the plane he had flown. This was all off-camera as the camera crew had already left for the motel we were staying in.

The model was not exactly the same but a fairly close rendition of the sticks, string and canvas-built machine he'd flown in.

'I built this just to see if what we were trying was going to work,' he said.

'Oh, Billy, that's amazing, we should have filmed that,' I wailed.

'I didn't want to show anyone in case we couldn't make the plane I had imagined,' he said with a big grin. 'But here's the thing. Watch this.'

He launched the model with a powerful throw. It immediately spun and crashed into the ground.

'And I didn't want the team to see that,' he said, his grin even bigger.

Mad as a box of spanners.

The following six years, my trusty co-presenter was the equally impressive Lisa Rogers, and no, they're not related. Lisa and I became firm friends. She's a wickedly funny woman, bright, quick and always kind and generous. She now has two lovely daughters and lives in a beautiful house in Wales.

One of the possibly not extraordinary things about *Scrapheap*, and something that has nothing to do with what was broadcast, is the number of Scrap-babies there are in the world. It must be down to the fact that it was a long-running show that employed a large group of young people in the production team. There is a veritable crowd of couples who met during the production run, stayed together or married and had children. It's possible someone has counted them all, the resulting babies I mean, but there are many dozens.

Is it okay to count babies in dozens? Maybe it's considered rude, anyway, there's a metric shit tonne of them.

But the hours, oh my Lord, we did very long hours.

We shot all the series in real scrapyards around the south of England, starting in a grubby pile of discarded trash near the M4 flyover in West London. The site is now the glistening head-quarters of the pharmaceutical giant Smith Kline.

The first series was the learning series; the plan was to shoot the entire process in one day. We'd start when it was still dark and we shot this in midsummer in England when it gets light at about 4.30 in the morning. We'd finish well after midnight the following day, something around twenty hours of non-stop activity.

It broke people. I cannot believe we did it and, more importantly, that no one got seriously hurt. A reminder to both myself and the reader that I was knackered but all I was doing was watching the teams and talking, the teams themselves were incredibly busy trying to build something. I don't know how they kept going. Of course, they were young and really enjoying themselves so I suppose that helped.

I do remember being so tired after a long day filming the build process in the sweltering yard when we moved next door to an aggregates store. For the uninitiated, an aggregates store is just a patch of dusty land with huge piles of stones used in road building and construction work. From big lumpy rocks at one end down through various grades to sand at the other, there were huge conical piles of aggregate in neat rows.

I discovered through careful testing that if you lie down on five-millimetre aggregate it's very lumpy and uncomfortable, one millimetre is too fine and you slide down the side. However, three-millimetre aggregate is perfect, you lie back, your body weight makes enough of an indentation on the sloping pile to support you, and you can go to sleep.

I did. I slept for an hour while the teams tinkered with their machines and the lighting crew placed their lights and the camera crew placed their cameras and everyone talked and drank tea and ate takeaway pizza.

I was woken at three in the morning by a kindly production assistant when the test was ready, it was spectacular and noisy and a team won, I can't remember which, and as the sun came up we finally packed up and went home.

I clearly remember driving my old Land Rover Defender

through the empty streets of West London with the low sun blinding me. We'd been on the set for just over twenty-two hours.

That, ladies and gentlemen, is the true glamour of the television industry.

The following two years we recorded the show in Canning Town, East London. That was a proper East End scrapyard, the sort of place to discover a body in the back of a dumped Jaguar. No, they actually did discover a body in the back of a dumped Jaguar; okay, it only happened once when we were there and we only knew because we saw police cordons and men in white overalls in the distance.

Oh yes, and someone was murdered in the local pub with a sawn-off shotgun, but other than that it was a lovely area.

I would arrive at the yard at around six in the morning. There would be a hurried breakfast, pull on the costume, get my helmet and goggles, look at the opening lines and shoot the opening sequence. There was enormous pressure to get this done because we needed to get the teams up and running before 10 a.m.

They really did have ten hours to build their machines. Pretty much everyone knows that the people who make TV are shallow manipulative liars, it's all done with mirrors and Photoshop and dodgy backhanders.

But for real, the teams on *Scrapheap Challenge* really did build the machines and they did it in ten hours.

The reason for this time limit was simple: we could only work the poor camera operators for that long. The budget was always stretched and we learned during the first series that if we didn't have cameras running the entire time we'd miss something, usually a catastrophe or a breakthrough. This missing moment would cause the director and production team to get quite depressed.

What this meant was that once the teams started building, there were eight cameras running non-stop covering the two teams for the entire ten hours. Four would be on the shoulders of our wonderful camera crew, four more locked-off cameras mounted high on the set.

The team that made sure these cameras were running all the time had their work cut out. There was constant activity in the camera department and each hand-held camera had two operators. They would do one hour on, one hour off for the entire ten hours.

Then there was sound, that was also incredibly complicated. We needed to be able to record sound anywhere on the site, with eleven radio mics that needed to be on all the time.

The only person who worked on every single episode of *Scrapheap Challenge,* other than me, was Paul Meredith, commonly known as Mr Med.

He sat in his big sound van all day and mixed the sound coming in from all the microphones, also turning them down when contestants took a 'comfort break'. Mr Med is very discreet because people who are not used to wearing microphones commonly forget that someone can hear literally everything they say or do.

Discretion is paramount. I know this from many years' experience.

I learned it very early on from my very first TV production, *Edinburgh Inside Out*, 1985. I was wearing a radio mic at a large event one evening in a huge hall in Edinburgh.

After a while I went to the gentleman's toiletry area and while I was relieving myself, a Channel 4 executive I'd met a couple of times entered and did likewise next to me. It was fairly apparent both from the force of his flow and the fact that he was leaning against the wall as he relieved himself that he was, to put it politely, heavily relaxed.

Okay, he was hammered, pissed out his brains, drunk as a Lord.

'What the fuck are you doing here?' asked the executive, who for reasons about to become apparent, will remain nameless.

'Shooting a thing called *Edinburgh Inside Out*, for your channel, mate, you should know about it,' I replied with gusto.

'The fuck is that? Sounds shit. It's not the thing that XXX has commissioned, is it?'

'Yes, that's the one,' said I.

'He is such a fucking wanker,' said the executive. 'I dunno how you work for the twat. Every idea he's ever had is utter shite.'

'Okay,' said I. 'Fair enough.'

I re-joined the crew to see some concerned faces. The other Channel 4 executive, the one who'd just been called a 'wanker', was sitting in a folding chair with headphones on. He'd heard the entire exchange. As young folks said in about 2015, 'Hashtag Awks'.

I seem to remember the drunk executive who'd been urinating beside me went on to work for someone else shortly after this incident.

So I knew to unplug my mic cable if I wanted privacy, so did lovely Lisa, however we also liked to entertain Mr Med back in his sound truck. He was party to some of the most scurrilous and disgraceful gossip ever uttered by two relatively well-educated people who should know better. A torrent of filth would be an apt description.

One of my party tricks was to leave my mic plugged in when I went to the toilet. Just a standard wee, nothing number-two-related, but I needed to keep my energy up so I would then grunt and groan and swear under my breath as if I was straining in an unhealthy constipated way, muttering things like, 'Jesus Christ, that looks like a Jacobean chair leg!' just before I flushed.

Mr Med would later comment that such antics were unnecessary and I should act my age. Yeah, right.

One fateful day a small group of Channel 4 executives were visiting the *Scrapheap* encampment to see how we were getting on. I'd had breakfast with them and they were all very excited; it must have been an amazing place to visit, a self-contained world of creative madness.

Later they were chatting to Mr Med, standing by the door of his sound truck as he explained in a mature, professional manner how he managed the mass of audio data coming into his huge mixing desk.

At that precise moment, I could be heard in the toilet fifty metres away, grunting and straining and complaining that what was happening was 'unnatural' and various expressions to the effect that what I was seeing in the Portaloo bowl was 'beyond the laws of physics' just before he could slap down my fader.

I was later severely admonished by the sound department, but they assured me they had the recordings backed up.

It was all very silly, but it was stupidity such as this that kept us chipper. The in-jokes and long-running gags among the crew were equally stupid and, to an outsider, possibly worrying and politically incorrect. We didn't do much political correctness on *Scrapheap*.

As the light faded and the twentieth cup of tea was drunk, many of the regular production crew would become genuinely concerned that the teams were not going to complete their machines in time. The pressure on the teams was unimaginable; they definitely didn't do it for the money, they were so driven and focused and we'd all get sucked into their concerns.

In the ten years and hundreds of machines built on the heap, I can only remember one team who genuinely didn't build much of anything. Ninety-nine per cent of the teams we had were either very good or utterly breathtaking in their ability.

The one team who weren't proved the point. At the end of the build there was a crisis in the production office. I was standing in the doorway of the porta-cabin listening to the conversation.

'They really haven't made anything. There's some metal lying around in the build area, they're very funny but they haven't made anything, they just talk.'

I wandered into the build area to see if anything had happened. There was nothing to show. I talked to the team off camera, all their plans had gone wrong, they couldn't find what they needed on the heap, it was a disaster.

'It looks so much easier when you're watching it at home,' said one of the broken team members.

Eventually, the *Scrapheap* engineering team carried in various bits of metal, some corrugated iron sheets, a couple of old wheels and tyres and using the work bench as a base, piled things up to look vaguely like a machine.

I then had to stand a full twenty metres away outside the build area and lie to the camera.

'I cannot believe they've actually done it!' I said enthusiastically, the camera positioned in such a way that I partly obscured the distant creation. 'They pulled it out of the hat at the last minute and finished their machine. Will it work, will it fall to bits in seconds? Join us after the break when we go for the big test!'

Lies, total television fake news.

The following day, the engineering team led by the inimitable Hadrian Spooner built a machine for the team; they did a fine job (you'll notice I'm not saying which challenge this was), and when we all gathered in a distant field to test the machines the following day we lied even more saying they'd done an amazing job. This team who had effectively cheated for the first time on *Scrapheap* promptly blew up the engine and failed to complete the challenge, which was something of a relief.

But seriously, that was the only time in ten years such a disaster happened. Every other one of the countless contraptions built on the show were built and tested by the teams with either zero or very little help from anyone other than the obligatory health and safety equipment.

If the machine was a vehicle or needed protective shielding or a roll cage of some sort, our in-house engineers would add those but other than that, the teams did everything.

Talking of health and safety, I should mention Grandad. One of the problems faced by TV productions that could put contestants, or indeed presenters and crew, in danger was insurance.

We were amazingly lucky on *Scrapheap*. Some of the machines we constructed were genuinely dangerous; some of the teams would push these botched-together masterpieces beyond the limit, and yet amazingly enough no serious injury or death ever occurred. Okay, if there had been a fatality no doubt it would have got in the news, but there was certainly the chance of something disastrous happening.

In order to mitigate against this, insurance companies insist on there being a qualified health and safety person on the set at all times.

This is where Grandad came in. He was a very well-qualified retired health and safety officer, but he was quite old and a little bit deaf. I don't wish to denigrate his skill and experience, he was a kosher H&S officer, but his slight frailty meant we could get away with occasional risky behaviour that may not have been acceptable had we followed the rules to the letter.

If a team were stripping down an engine and dripping oil and petrol all over the ground next to someone who was welding, Grandad (that was his call name on the walkie-talkies) would be called in.

'What d'you think, Grandad. Is this safe?' an anxious producer would ask.

'Oh yes,' he'd say, 'just use a bit of common sense. Put a bit of straw down to soak up the spilt contaminants, bit of sand, it's fine.'

Straw, soaked in oil and petrol under the feet of someone welding, marvellous, we'd carry on regardless.

On one occasion, I was sent to chat with Grandad while the crew built a small explosive device for an introductory sequence, just a small fireball exploding in the middle of the yard.

The directors knew it might be mildly dangerous and having Grandad inspect it could waste valuable time so I was sent to ask Grandad if he wanted a cup of tea.

He walked with me to where the tea urn was kept just off the set. I asked him about his grandchildren. He had quite a few and was busy telling me about the day they'd spent at Chessington Zoo when I heard a low 'whooompa!'

Over Grandad's shoulder I could see an impressive fireball and thick clouds of black smoke rising from the middle of the vast scrapheap we were working on. He didn't bat an eyelid, just carried on talking about how the grandchildren loved the camel ride.

On another occasion, Lisa had to climb quite a tall building at a derelict site we were using to test machines. The idea was that a camera crane would get a close up of Lisa introducing the show which would then pull back to reveal where she was.

Grandad was naturally concerned for her safety. Lisa was pregnant at the time and needed to clamber up an impressively long ladder to gain access to the top of the tower. Grandad climbed up the ladder first and then lowered a stout rope down to the ground, someone from the team then tied this around

Lisa, under her arms so if she did slip, a retired health and safety officer standing at the top of the tower would make sure she didn't fall.

That was the plan, and it worked. Lisa, who is a fearless and very capable farmer's daughter, shimmied up the ladder like a young goat on a mountainside. She did the piece to camera and then using the same safety procedure climbed down, Grandad carefully feeding out the rope as she descended.

Just before she was safely back on the ground Grandad, who was still up the tower, presumed Lisa had finished her descent and threw the rope down. The rope, which was long and heavy, fell on Lisa's head, causing considerable pain.

We all rushed to see if she was okay. She was laughing so hard she couldn't speak for a while. After all the arrangements and the safety talks, she suffered a minor head injury caused by Grandad, who as far as I recall never knew there was a problem. After he climbed down the ladder he walked back to the tea urn without a second look.

After I'd done the show for seven years, I had become very aware that *Scrapheap Challenge* had completely taken over my life. For the ten years previous to working on the show, I was used to a far more flexible diary. I would work on *Red Dwarf* for eight to ten weeks, incredibly intense work, non-stop, utterly exhausting, but then I would be free to follow my own projects for a year or more before we made another series.

Scrapheap was very different. We would be making the show from spring until autumn, and then I'd be doing voiceovers for weeks afterwards. It took up too much time, that was my lament when I went into discuss my next contract.

I explained that although I'd become a TV presenter, it wasn't something I wanted to do; I genuinely never wanted to be on the telly.

The man from Channel 4 smiled at me. 'That's exactly why we want you to do it,' he said. 'We don't want someone who wants to be on the telly, we want someone who's interested in the machines and the teams. That's why we hired you.'

So I agreed to do another three years and I'm very glad I did. The last three years on *Scrapheap* were by far the most enjoyable and the best organised. It was a very complicated show to make, it involved so many people and so many departments that very often we would overrun and work late into the night.

Enter Dom Bowles, who had directed a couple of episodes of the previous series but for the last three years took over as producer.

I really hit it off with Dom. He was often foul-mouthed and noisy, which was the perfect thing for *Scrapheap*. He made the show run like a well-oiled machine instead of a rusty old banger and very often, we'd actually finish when we were meant to.

It still took up an enormous amount of each year I worked on it, but I really enjoyed those last few years. The crew, production team and everyone behind the scenes were a bit like a family, we spent so much time together and had so many adventures and mishaps. It's a very hard thing to replicate in normal life.

I certainly miss the wonderful people who worked on the series over the years but have no regrets that I'm not making it any more. Ten years felt like a long time when I finished working on the show, and it still does.

I really hope the show is revived in some form; it had an enormous impact on a whole generation of young people who grew up with it. I cannot count the number of amazing engineers I've met who tell me they never missed a show when they were growing up. I've spoken to lecturers in engineering colleges who stated that they had an enormous increase in applications when the show was being aired; it caught people's imaginations, showed them that the complex technology we are surrounded by has been created by people; it's been planned, adapted, developed and adjusted to make it what it is today.

We have lost touch with how stuff is made and where it comes from and I think *Scrapheap Challenge, Junkyard Wars* and the many other shows I've worked on, *How Do They Do It?* and *How Stuff's Made,* have all helped people understand a little more of the world around them.

Living in the Future

Last year I got in my Tesla Model S 85 and drove down the narrow lane from our house.

The Tesla is an electric car; it doesn't have a petrol engine, it's not a hybrid. The car has an 85-kilowatt-hour battery under the floor. The battery weighs nearly a ton.

To put 85 kilowatt hours of electricity into context, it uses about the same amount of electricity as the average semi-detached three-bedroom house in the UK uses in four to five days.

The battery had been charged from 100 per cent solar power during daylight over the previous three days.

I know this because I have a sophisticated app which came with the car. This app also controls the Tesla Powerwall home battery mounted on the wall of the garage.

The 13.3 kilowatt hour Powerwall battery had been empty when I woke that morning. This was because I drained what remained in the battery from the previous day into the car. We have yet to use the entire contents of the battery to run the house, but it's summer as I write this, it doesn't get dark until quite late.

The Powerwall battery was recharged to 100 per cent capacity by midday so I used the excess solar output to charge the car.

I'm still getting used to this new and constantly improving arrangement but in the few months since the house battery was installed, 89 per cent of the electricity we've used to power the house, office and cars is from the solar panels.

The remaining 11 per cent was from the grid, but we only used grid power at night to top up the Nissan Leaf, another electric car.

At night we pay an off-peak tariff of 6p per kilowatt-hour. This change has resulted in a massive reduction on our electricity bill, despite the fact that due to two electric cars we are way above average electricity consumers.

That day I drove the 98-mile journey to Heathrow Terminal 5 using autopilot for the majority of the journey. Autopilot is a feature built into the Tesla, a combination of cameras, sensors and Lidar (laser radar), which means on main roads and motorways the car can drive itself. I mean literally drive itself. It keeps the same distance behind the car in front, steers, slows down and speeds up in harmony with the traffic flow.

I'd like to point out that I always keep my hands on the wheel and my eyes on the road. If I don't apply some pressure to the steering wheel, the car starts beeping warnings at me, the dashboard starts flashing and eventually, if I still don't rest a hand on the wheel, the hazard lights will come on and the car will gently slow to a halt.

This autopilot system has improved during the two years I've used it; it effectively learns the road by using data from other

Tesla cars that have travelled the same route. For long motorway journeys it reduces stress to the point I don't notice the kilometres sail by.

When I arrived at the Heathrow Terminal 5 pod parking area, I parked the car using the Tesla 'summon' feature, which means I can get out of the car with the driver's door opened to its full extent, close the door and remotely drive the car into the rather narrow parking bay using the app on my phone. Yes, you can move the car from outside using your phone, its sensors stop it from hitting anything and it steers itself into the correct position.

I then had to walk all of fifty metres to the pod station, I pressed one button on the welcome screen and a fully autonomous electric pod opened its doors for me.

I climbed inside and the pod drove me along a raised carriageway right under the flightpath at Heathrow, and then right inside the Terminal 5 building. Electric cars can be used in buildings as they don't emit any toxic gasses.

I checked in using an automated system, went through security like a normal person, and flew to Paris for the day to test drive a frankly ridiculously fast electric hot hatchback concept car.

I'd like to be able to say this is a normal day for me, but to be fair it was fairly unusual.

It was when I got out of the car at the airport car park and used the app to reverse it into the parking space then got into an autonomous pod that it hit me.

I am living in the future.

But, as the writer William Gibson stated so beautifully a few years back: 'The future is here, it's just not evenly distributed.'

So, if I am living in the future, this is not quite what I'd hoped for.

A future where the majority of the global population still live in poverty, often combined with ignorance and fear, while a minuscule minority live in solar-powered houses and drive electric cars, using technology that could revolutionise the equality, prosperity and longevity of the human race.

I'm not talking so much about financial inequality, although obviously that has a large role to play in this; I'm talking energy inequality.

What on earth can we do about that? It's hopeless, the complexity and expense of changing the way we generate and use electricity, the way we import and refine billions of gallons of oil. The way we import and burn billions of cubic metres of gas.

How on earth can anything be done about that?

And what about the developing world and the expansion of the middle classes in Africa, China and India who have spending power for the first time? They too want refrigerators, phones, electric lights and cars, all the things we take for granted.

How can we possibly create enough power to supply these rapidly expanding demands?

Would large corporations building coal-burning power stations in Africa and India help the world's poor?

Somehow that doesn't sound like a good idea. They've tried it in the past and it's always a disaster. Power plants like those need around-the-clock maintenance, they require billions of tons of coal, the companies who install them ensure they make a profit but the electricity is unreliable and restricted to developed areas with a reliable grid connection.

So what could work?

Solar panels and batteries.

Seriously?

What is already working in many locations in Africa and India are small-scale solar panels attached to batteries that provide light at night. Vast numbers of villages and small towns still have no reliable grid access. Up to now, electricity, if it exists at all, is supplied by diesel generators, large, inefficient noisy machines that need fuel which has to be regularly transported over long distances to keep them running.

But countries like Africa, South America and India are adopting solar at unprecedented rates.

Why? Because it's cheap and reliable and small communities can afford it.

The combination of solar and small-scale batteries creates a system that is a complete and viable alternative to kerosene lamps or diesel generators.

This revolution started in the developed world. Solar photo voltaic cells were invented in the 1960s. They were incredibly expensive and were used mainly by NASA in various forms as a way of harvesting the sun's energy for satellites and the International Space Station.

Over the past forty years they have steadily dropped in price, not 1 or 2 per cent, no, a 99.5 per cent drop which makes them accessible to more and more people.

But the sun doesn't always shine, even in Africa, and what about during the night?

Can it all be down to batteries?

I would like to suggest that renewable energy and batteries are going to take a very big new role in our lives in the next twenty years, in ways that are emerging and expanding very rapidly.

But let's be honest, there can be nothing less spectacular to look at than a battery.

It's a dormant object, sometimes a small round cylinder, sometimes an ugly box next to a petrol or diesel engine with two nodules sticking out of it. Batteries don't make a noise, there's no moving parts, no pistons, crankshafts or valves. There's no brass bits you can polish, they don't need 'topping up' with oil, water or antifreeze. They just sit there doing whatever it is they do and they don't look any different when they've finished doing it.

However, the more I've discovered about new battery systems both in cars and homes, the more convincing the argument becomes.

Considering that I spent the first fifty or so years of my life happily living in a fossil-fuelled economy, joyfully driving around in often very thirsty powerful cars, this change of heart may seem sudden and confusing. I'm not entirely certain when the idea dawned on me that something was changing, but one key event happened back in 2001.

I had a short ride in a hybrid car. Mundane as anything now, but back then I'd never heard of anything like it, and I was slightly baffled as to why anyone would bother. What was wrong with normal cars? I'd grown up with them, they were just cars.

A hybrid car felt a bit like a solution looking for a problem. We'd done road cars, what about flying cars or genetically engineered thought bubbles that transport you through space-time with zero energy requirements. Where were they?

I was in California making *Junkyard Wars* when I first rode in a hybrid car. After another long day recording the show in the midsummer heat of Los Angeles, one of the production crew gave me a lift back to my apartment when we'd finished shooting.

I took no notice of the car when I got in, it was just a boring dusty car. It was only when the driver pulled away from a set of lights on Sunset Boulevard that I noticed something peculiar.

The car moved forward like it was being pulled along by a wire, there was no noise, no vibration, no changing engine tone as the driver built up the revs to produce the required torque to move. It just glided off silently.

'How the hell d'you do that?' I asked.

'Oh, it's a hybrid,' said my charming driver in her sing-song Californian accent.

I had no idea what she was talking about. We're all used to the word 'hybrid' now, but back in 2001 the only time I'd heard that word used was to describe an apple tree. Hybrid fruit trees have been around for centuries. Using the root stock of one tree, you graft on the shoot from another tree and hey presto, you get a new tree. My dad showed me how to do that when I was a kid. But a hybrid car?

When we arrived at my apartment block just off Sunset in West Hollywood, I asked my driver to pop her hood. This is a perfectly respectable thing for a man in late middle age to say to a young woman he's only just met.

She did pop her hood and I had a look at the complex bit of high-quality engineering Toyota had produced to create the now ubiquitous Prius. It is a really clever system that made it possible to link a petrol engine and an electric motor in perfect synergy.

Now, sixteen years later there are two electric cars in my garage. A Nissan Leaf and a Tesla Model S. I haven't bought petrol to put in a car in years. I did buy half a gallon two years ago to power my old petrol lawn mower but now I have a Bosch battery electric lawn mower so my direct investment in refined fossils for transportation is now zero.

Other than flying. I'll get to that in a moment. Oh yes, and trains, okay, and the bus, no wait, the bus was electric, anyway, onto all those in a moment.

Not only are there two electric cars in the garage, there are sixteen solar panels with a maximum output of 5.2 kilowatts on the south-facing roof of the building I'm writing this in. They are currently feeding into the Nissan Leaf because the house battery, a Tesla Powerwall 2, is already full. It's been a sunny day, so far the panels have produced 28.04 kilowatt hours of electricity, more than most houses will consume in one day.

What is a kilowatt hour? You may be more familiar with the term 'unit' which is how it's often described particularly on electricity bills.

A kilowatt hour is enough electricity to run ten 100-watt lightbulbs for one hour. The average three-bedroom house in the UK uses 20 to 25 kilowatt hours in a day.

Because I can now use all the power the solar panels generate either in the house or cars, the amount I buy from the grid is negligible. I have never wanted to 'go off the grid'. I just want to dramatically reduce the amount of electricity I take from the grid. What I have been able to do though is never use grid electricity between the hours of four in the afternoon to midnight.

In four months since the system was fitted, not one solitary watt. The reason I'm happy about this is we have peak demand for electricity in the UK in the early evening. The solar PV and battery have removed our house from this demand; the nationwide demand in that period is now reduced, by one household.

For me this isn't only about economics although clearly the cost reductions are useful. This is about seeing if this kind of system works and then extrapolating what this would mean if batteries like the one running my house became ubiquitous.

My single battery won't make any difference nationally or even locally. The fact that our house has reduced its yearly demand for electricity by around 75 per cent will make no difference to the wider world.

But imagine for a moment if every house had a similar system installed.

Imagine if every school, hospital, factory, warehouse, supermarket, government building had similar systems installed.

Then it would make a massive, dramatic and very disruptive difference. It would throw well-established industries a curve ball that they might not survive.

So in some ways my personal journey over the last ten years may be a portent of what's to come. I have slowly moved from being a casually enthusiastic petrol head to being an obsessive volt head. I won't get too granular on the step-by-step journey, petrol car to hybrid, hybrid to pure electric, pure electric car to solar panels, solar panels to domestic battery. It's a journey that has been well documented elsewhere.

However, I would like to discuss the long-term implications of renewable energy, batteries, computer power and sensors. The connection between these new technologies is very strong, it's essentially the same technology but some of it has wheels and seats.

As I'm sure you're aware, electric cars are still more expensive to buy. I won't go into the details of how much cheaper they are to run right now. But here's how that is changing.

When I went for a ride in that hybrid car back in 2001, it cost well over $1,500 to build a battery that could store one kilowatt hour of electricity. As of 2017, that cost is nearer $280 per kilowatt hour.

In 2001, a 5.5 kilowatt hour peak solar panel installation would cost around £25,000. Now it's close to £3,000.

These massive cost reductions are due to many things. With solar panels it's down to production scale: companies around the world are churning out literally millions of solar panels every week. The technology has improved, they are now more efficient and last longer (twenty-five to thirty years).

Improved battery chemistry and an enormous increase in manufacturing base is reducing the cost of batteries. Some of you may have heard of 'the gigafactory' being built by Tesla and

Panasonic in Sparks, Nevada. This is a truly gargantuan build-ing with floor space of over half a million square metres (5.5 million square feet).

Tesla proudly boast that when it's completed it will have the single biggest footprint of any building on earth and there are already plans to replicate the gigafactory in Europe and China.

Each year, this single factory will produce 35 gigawatt hours of storage (a gigawatt hour is a thousand megawatt hours. A megawatt hour is a thousand kilowatt hours), which is equiva-lent to the current total global production capacity. That is, every battery maker on earth, Panasonic, LG Chem, BYD, Sam-sung, AESC, and many others combined produce about that much battery storage each year.

With one factory, Tesla will double the global output.

All this to make batteries? Can this really be sensible?

The demand for batteries is so huge and the growth in demand is so enormous that all over the world, companies are increasing capacity and investing billions in production.

When I mention these facts to people, I mean ordinary people who aren't obsessed with the rapidly emerging new energy matrix, they seem slightly baffled. Batteries are so dull and boring, what sane person would show any interest in them?

I often wonder if, in 1904, there were people like me talking about the new-fangled motor car. I choose 1904 because it's generally accepted that this was the year of 'peak horse'.

There were more horses used for transport around the world in 1904 than ever before. Yes, they had steam trains and steam ships, there were certainly early versions of the motor car in existence but they were a very rare sight and prohibitively expensive, unreliable and often dangerous.

By 1913, in most cities in Europe and North America, the horse had almost completely disappeared.

Thirteen years is all it took for the huge industry that supported all those horses to disappear. The feed merchants, saddlers, carriage makers, blacksmiths, horse breeders and of course literally thousands of people employed to remove the many tons of manure from the streets of cities around the world were gone.

Those jobs just disappeared.

It wasn't a 100 per cent change, big changes never are. There were still lots of horses around, particularly in rural areas, but within twenty years the world was unrecognisable.

This transition from horse to car was in a fairly typical time frame for the historic period. Somewhere between fifteen and twenty years and we've seen this adoption of new technology repeated time and again over the past hundred years.

The radio, refrigerator, television, telephones all took around twenty years to complete their adoption.

It wasn't until the mobile or cell phone was introduced that we witnessed a much steeper adoption curve, the so called 'S' curve.

I had to have the concept of the S curve explained to me by someone in marketing. They love S curves in marketing, it's their bread and butter. When you have a graph with a bar rising up in a straight line from left to right, that's a linear progression. It depicts a gradual and predictable increase. That's how I would imagine a graph would look like if you saw the adoption of the TV, phone, radio or car.

In fact, it's never a linear increase.

All these technologies were adopted very slowly at first, they're expensive, the general population can't see the point, they seem fad-like, silly, overly complex and frighteningly new. Then they reach a point where it makes economic sense to change and the adoption becomes almost vertical.

The Toyota Prius (the car I had a lift in back in 2001) is a really good example. When the Prius, the first mass-produced hybrid car, was launched in the 1990s, very few were sold and almost all of them were in California.

When the car was launched in Europe a few years later, the uptake was dismal. I was one of the early adopters but I was one of very few. People didn't trust it, Jeremy Clarkson on the BBC's *Top Gear* hated the Prius with a passionate fury. The automotive press were universally dismissive; the Prius, said the knowing men who write about cars, was a dud.

Very slowly the sales increased but at a glacial pace until around 2007, when a few taxi companies adopted the car. They very quickly discovered that a fuel cost reduction of around 40 per cent made a very big difference to their profitability. As a result, more people experienced being in the car, the adoption rate increased creating an almost vertical line on the graph.

Toyota, who sold a few thousand Prius cars in the first five years, have now sold over 10 million worldwide. Virtually every Uber, every taxi company and millions of individual owners currently drive them. They have become a very common sight in every city I've visited.

That was a standard S curve taking something like fifteen years to be fully drawn. The cell phone's S curve was around five years. In developing countries you'd almost have to describe cell phone adoption as an 'I' curve. One year no one had cell phones, the next, pretty much everyone had them.

In 2015, I stood in a shantytown in the middle of Mumbai surrounded by hundreds of smiling, barefoot children and a great many of them were holding smart phones. There was no running water, no sanitation or paved streets, but there were cell phones and satellite TVs everywhere.

They are transforming the economies and social structures of these countries faster than any previous technology.

I should explain I didn't just casually drop into the shanty town, I was filming a programme about Indian trains for the BBC. The BBC love making programmes about Indian trains. And cooking, and singing competitions.

So, this is the theory behind the coming adoption of electric cars and renewable energy systems. All the signs are pointing to the fact that we are now at the foot of an S curve of mass adoption. Sales of electric cars have been growing, but very slowly.

This year (2017), they have seen a significant increase but I'm too sceptical to say this is the start of mass adoption. However, the area that can be said to be at the foot of a high level of mass adoption is solar and wind generation. The installation of renewable technology has dramatically increased over the last couple of years and is now making massive in-roads in many countries around the world, including the UK.

Here's a rather stark example. The controversial Hinkley Point C nuclear power station that is currently, or might be currently, under construction will, if it's completed on time – which no nuclear power plant ever is – but if it does get completed, will produce something around 3.5 gigawatts. That's a lot of electricity; it will work around the clock while producing minimal CO_2, day and night, summer and winter.

Today, in 2017, there are 13.8 gigawatts of solar already installed in the UK; it will no doubt be over 20 gigawatts by the time you read this. This system, as we all know, is not always producing electricity, it's seasonal, it doesn't produce anything at night, but when it is producing electricity it's the equivalent of three and a half Hinkley Point Cs. And it's cheaper, and there's no waste to deal with for the next thousand years, and it's distributed all over the country, and it is often locally owned, and new solar farms are now being built with batteries attached meaning their energy flow can be regulated and harmonised with the grid.

Okay, that's a long list but worth mentioning.

What is clear is that electric cars and renewable energy are linked disruptive technologies. They go hand in hand alongside artificial intelligence, autonomous cars and trucks, sensors and associated computer development. Only a few years back it was impossible to see all the implications resulting from the re-emergence of electric cars.

I say re-emergence because they are certainly not new. In 1908, electric cars outsold internal combustion cars so they've been around for a while.

I had my first electric car in 2010. It was called the Mitsubishi Innovative Electric Vehicle or iMiev. It was based on a small petrol-powered city car Mitsubishi made for the Japanese market. They took out the engine and fuel tank, replaced it with a melon-sized electric motor and an 18-kilowatt-hour battery pack. This little car had a range of around seventy miles on a charge, not quite the one hundred miles range the Mitsubishi sales teams suggested, but it was a great car, a funny little thing I drove for 12,000 miles that year without a problem.

Back then there was zero charging infrastructure in the UK, no rapid chargers anywhere except at the Mitsubishi office and yet I found it a very useful vehicle. I charged it at home using a specially fitted standard UK three-pin plug. I drove it around the local area, shops, school runs, errands. It was simple to drive, very reliable and incredibly cheap to re-fuel.

That 12,000 miles cost me around £150 in electricity. An equivalent-sized petrol version would have cost £1,440 to cover the same distance. Add to this, the car required zero servicing as there's nothing to service, no oil changes, filter changes, spark plug changes, timing belt inspection and replacement, catalytic converter service, clutch wear, gearbox oil, no emissions tests, nothing.

In 2011, I bought the first-generation Nissan Leaf. This was the first mass-produced, purpose-built electric car on the market. The Leaf has a 24-kilowatt-hour battery under the floor of the car and a range of around 90 miles on one charge. By the time I got this car there was a steadily growing rapid charge network emerging around the UK.

I have driven all over the country in my Nissan Leaf. At first it wasn't easy, there were certainly times I was waiting while the car charged and I'd far preferred to have been doing something else, but I can say in all honesty 90 per cent of the time it really wasn't an issue.

I drove from London to Edinburgh in one day using the then recently completed London to Scotland rapid charge network.

It's a stupid thing to do, it's much easier and quicker to catch the train but it's perfectly possible to do this journey in an electric car.

And this is in a car with at best a ninety-mile range.

It's much easier now with most new electric cars having a range of over 150 miles on a charge and every motorway services in the country fitted with rapid charge stations.

Then I made a rather rash move. In 2015, my wife was discussing various topics with our children who at that time were both living in Australia. It was an early morning Skype call and she was a little bit cross with her offspring. My daughter had been working in a cafe in Brisbane and wanted to pack it in, she was also asking if I could pay her rent. My son had been doing labouring on building sites in Sydney and he wanted to do something else. He'd stopped working and was asking for money.

Now my wife is a very patient woman, particularly with our children; actually, now I mention this, she isn't very patient with me but that's possibly understandable. Anyway, this is what she said and I'm quoting her verbatim.

'Both of you get off your lazy arses and get back to your jobs. Your father has worked hard for you all your lives and he deserves a Tesla.'

End quote.

As soon as she said this, I went online and ordered one.

Three months later, I turned up at the Tesla showroom in Hounslow, West London and took possession of a brand-new Tesla Model S.

It's by far the most extravagant purchase I've ever made. It cost about the same as the house we bought in 1992, although I lease the car, the monthly payments are nothing short of embarrassing.

My stoically patient financial advisor recently pointed out that this car is my pension. He didn't mean, 'That's a wise investment, Robert, when you retire you can live off the Tesla.' No, he meant, 'You've screwed up big time, you may live to regret this.'

Hey ho, it's too late now, and to be honest, although it's put an unpleasant strain on my fiscal planning, I'm very proud to be a Tesla driver simply because what this upstart company have done is singlehandedly give the complacent automotive industry the night terrors.

Every posh carmaker you've ever heard of will release an electric car in the near future; by the time you read this they probably already have.

Every engineer who works for every posh car maker I have ever met all repeated the same story. As soon as the Tesla Model S came out, the company they worked for bought one and tore it to bits in their research departments.

They wanted to know how it was possible to build an electric car that cost much the same as the high-end models they were producing. An electric car that could travel from 250 to 300 miles on one charge and look good enough for traditionalists to admit it was a fine-looking machine.

Tesla have shown beyond any argument that electric cars work, they can do the job conventionally fuelled cars can do and do it better, faster and for longer.

We drove to Italy in 2015 and Sweden in 2016 in the Tesla; it was a doddle. The maximum distance we covered on one charge was 265 miles, which we completed in France.

These long-distance trips have been made possible by an impressive network of Tesla Superchargers that cover the USA, Europe, China and Australia. These chargers currently offer the fastest recharge any electric car can accommodate.

To explain what a Supercharger does it's worth comparing it to a 13 amp, three-pin wall socket we use in the UK, the thing you plug your kettle into. A standard domestic socket delivers up to 5 kilowatts, which results in adding between four and five miles range to the car in one hour.

The Tesla supercharger can deliver up to 150 kilowatts if the battery is empty enough, adding over 500 miles range in one hour.

Recharging a Tesla from 5 per cent to 80 per cent of the battery's capacity takes about twenty-five minutes, giving you a further 180 to 200 miles range.

The appearance of these superchargers has happened very quickly and it's still expanding.

Not only superchargers, the UK rapid charge network has expanded: every motorway service area in the country has a 50-kilowatt rapid charger installed, many of them have two or three outlets.

But all these changes are irrelevant to my argument; it's the wider impact this technology has that really interests me.

How will the new technologies of distributed solar, storage and electric vehicles affect the wider world?

The National Grid in the UK only really came into existence

after the Second World War. One single, centrally managed network of power stations, transmission lines, substations and local networks took many years to build. The village I live in didn't get mains electricity until the early 1950s.

The whole design of this network was to deliver power all over the country from a small number of massive power stations, very often constructed on the coast or near rivers as they require huge amounts of water to operate.

They also require huge amounts of fuel which was cheaper to transport by ship. In London, for example, Bankside (now Tate Modern), Battersea and Lots Road Power Stations were built on the banks of the river Thames to allow the coal barges to dock and unload next to them.

Nuclear power plants are generally built on the coast or near large lakes to give them access to water. In order to distribute the power from these enormous plants, a massive network of wires strung up on huge pylons was installed all over the country.

Electricity always went from big centralised generating systems out to towns, cities and villages across the land.

Solar panels only started to appear a few decades ago. They were rare because they were very expensive but once again, like batteries, as their adoption began to increase, the price started to come down.

In 1977 the cost of manufacturing a solar photo-voltaic panel was $77 per watt. When you consider that the average panel today produces 265 watts, you're talking $20,000 per panel. If you recall, I have sixteen panels on my roof so in 1977 they would have cost £320,000. Not very economically viable.

Today the cost to manufacture the panel is around 6 cents per watt meaning a panel costs around $170. From $20,000 to $170 is what I would describe as a significant price drop. All the predictions I've seen are that the price will reduce by a further 50 per cent by 2020.

That, dear reader, is disruptive technology in waiting, and that is what is giving the fossil fuel industry the determination to hang on at all costs.

As of this year, 2017, the cheapest electricity produced anywhere on earth is from large-scale solar. Okay, it's in Dubai in the desert near the equator but it's still the cheapest. The company that installed the massive solar farm are selling, unsubsidised and at a profit, wholesale electricity at two cents per kilowatt hour.

There is no nuclear, gas, coal, oil, hydro or even wind generation that is remotely close to that cost. There never will be. Solar is here to stay and it's cheaper, cleaner, quieter and easier to install than anything else currently available.

It's also developing very rapidly: new types of solar panels are more efficient at turning sunlight into electricity. New designs and materials are being adopted to make solar panels aesthetically less challenging.

There is a large school in Copenhagen, not exactly near the equator, that supplies 50 per cent of its annual electricity consumption using solar, the entire building is clad in solar PV, including the walls and windows.

But here's another very important point that is relevant to both electric cars and large, centralised electricity generation.

For 90 per cent of the time, we don't use the cars we own.

The generally accepted statistic, which I first heard from engineers working in the automotive industry, is that 90 per cent of the time, 90 per cent of the cars in the world are dormant, switched off, parked.

Doing nothing.

One of the most expensive items we buy is used around 10 per cent of its useful life. Imagine owning a house which you only lived in for 10 per cent of the year, that's about thirty days. It might be normal if you're a Russian oligarch or Chinese billionaire with a house in Kensington and Chelsea but for most of us that's not an option.

Imagine if an airline or shipping company only used their investments in aircraft or ships for 10 per cent of the year, they'd be bankrupt in a day.

So how has this ridiculous state of affairs come to be normal? And when people ask me how long an electric car takes to charge I have to be polite and explain the variety of ways you can charge a car, when what I really want to say is about 15 per cent of the year and always when I'm not using it.

Okay, that's cars, more on that in a moment, but then there's big electricity generating stations. I had always assumed that they are all running 24/7. They must be because when I flick the switch, the light comes on.

In the case of nuclear power plants, that's true, they run twenty-four hours a day, you can't turn them up or down and it's a very complex and costly process to switch them off. As a wonderful old nuclear engineer explained to me once, 'A nuclear power station is either working at a hundred per cent or you are trying to overtake me as I run away from it.'

He was being humorous in case you were wondering. Statistically, nuclear power plants are incredibly safe, with a couple of massive, terrifying and very long-term disasters as the exceptions.

But in the case of coal and in particular gas-powered generators, they don't run all the time.

However, the owners and operators are paid all the time. By us, the consumer.

They need to be on standby for large periods of time because we, silly humans, don't consume electricity at the same rate through the day. We produce peaks and troughs, high demand and very low demand because we're wasting time sleeping.

Con Edison, a major power company in the United States, have recently revealed that one-third of their generating assets are used a mere 6 per cent of the year.

That is a massive generating capacity doing nothing for 94 per cent of the investment's lifetime. These plants are on constant standby to help cover peaks in demand.

That is not only a catastrophically inefficient use of infrastructure, it's also very expensive and is one of the biggest reasons we have to pay so much for electricity. A big commercial company isn't going to build those plants unless it's economically viable, you don't need to be an economist to understand that a 6 per cent utilisation isn't a very sensible way of 'sweating your assets'.

So we all pay for that downtime. If you hear people suggesting that renewables can only be used because of government subsidy, while that is becoming increasingly rare due to dramatically falling costs, it's also ignoring the fact that conventional generating systems are one: very inefficient, two: very expensive, particularly when they are in standby mode, which many of them are a lot of the time and three: offline for many months at a time in order to service and repair them.

Conventional generating systems are subsidised to the hilt, billions of pounds of our money is spent on keeping billions of pounds worth of generating capacity on standby.

It's a subsidy in every possible meaning of the term, a huge one; about 95 per cent of energy subsidies go to conventional methods of generating, about 5 per cent goes to renewables.

I should also point out that a massive slice of that 95 per cent goes to looking after the many thousands of tons of highly toxic and inherently dangerous nuclear waste we've got lying at the bottom of massive pools in Sellafield, the UK's nuclear waste processing and storage facility.

So how can we get around this?

Legislation? Probably not going to happen, and if and when it does the changes will already be underway.

The introduction of smart metering, demand side management? That could help but it would also require big changes in the habits of the general population which, if we're being honest, isn't going to happen overnight, not until there's a crisis.

One way we can get around this is, you've guessed it, batteries.

This, I predict, will happen much faster than either I or indeed the big energy-generating companies expect or are prepared for.

For example, in the last month I have used zero, not less, but literally zero power from the grid between 4 p.m. and 9 p.m. in the evening, traditionally the peak period in the UK.

We haven't changed our daily habits, we are cooking, using the washing machine, water heating, the lights are on, okay they're all LEDs but they're still on and we use zero grid power.

We do that because we have solar panels and a battery.

Now, some caveats. I'm writing this in the summer, the solar panels are producing between 25–35 kilowatt hours a day. In the winter, this will drop to 5–10 kWh a day, nothing like enough.

But, in winter we can charge the battery overnight using off peak, cheaper and also cleaner electricity. Night-time generation is generally wind and nuclear, particularly in the winter. It is universally accepted by everyone I've spoken to that electricity in the system between midnight to around 7 a.m. is the cleanest we produce, and it's getting cleaner all the time.

This not only saves us money, but it also means that we won't use electricity from the grid in the peak period, which is the most likely time we burn coal and gas to generate power. We are reducing strain on the grid, not increasing it, same with electric cars, we only charge them at night in the winter.

So, to simplify the argument further, if, and of course this will take years to install, but if every house in the UK had batteries installed, we would need far less generating capacity and we'd use it far more constantly, which would be far cheaper.

We wouldn't need to pay the likes of Con Edison to maintain a third of its generating capacity and only use it 6 per cent of the year.

This would require grid management and smart charging of those batteries, meaning they would be charged when demand was low and discharged when demand was high, smoothing out the peaks and troughs that we currently see every day. This more level use of electricity would create massive savings, regardless of the power source. We'd need less, not more power stations, and they'd be running for far greater periods of time. We wouldn't need such huge assets on standby costing us a fortune.

A change that big would be a massive disruption to our power systems. It will mean without doubt that some companies, household names, will go out of business. It will change the way the national grid operates. No one truly knows what the full implications of this change will be, but it will be big.

With the energy network as we understand it today, there are a handful of players with billions. Building a new centralised power plant costs billions; if you include the expense of getting that power to where it's needed, you're talking many billions.

The rapidly emerging renewables industry has changed the shape of energy economics due to the fact that new companies start generating electricity using mere millions. Large solar farms, wind farms and offshore wind turbines require a fraction of the expenditure needed to build a huge centralised generating plant. These systems are more widely distributed and need less newly installed grid connections and long-distance distribution networks.

But that is still less than half the story because of a completely new paradigm: energy generators which need thousands. It costs a few thousand pounds to install roof-top solar, a few thousand to install a house battery.

So globally you are talking a mere ten to twenty companies

that can afford to invest billions in centralised generating capacity.

There are already many hundreds of companies who can afford to spend a few million on large scale solar or wind farms.

However, globally there are literally millions of people who can afford to spend a few thousand on solar panels for their house.

That is a game changer. Very soon, millions of thousands will outweigh the few tens of billions. The big players are in serious trouble and they know it.

How am I stating all this with such confidence? Because I attend, either in a speaker's role or as a facilitator, many conferences a year where energy companies, car makers, large engineering companies, software engineers, universities and manufacturers meet to discuss this very topic.

These entities know it's coming, the government is five steps behind as usual, but even they know it's coming. Are any of us ready for these disruptions?

No, not in the least.

Will it make a mess, will some systems fail while others succeed?

You bet.

Will solar companies, wind turbine manufacturers, micro-grid operators go to the wall as the new paradigm emerges?

Of course they will.

Will new mega-corporations emerge, companies that haven't even been founded yet?

Obviously.

Will we, the people who rely on a stable, constant supply of electricity benefit?

Possibly, if we are noisy, active, knowledgeable and aware of what's going on, yes, we will.

And not just crazy early adopters like me who decide to invest their mis-sold Personal Protection Insurance refund on a new-fangled battery; I mean everyone who pays for electricity.

But seriously, and this is going to be more controversial, this is just the start.

Imagine a world where everyone can move about just as easily as we do now using cars, but there are less cars.

I'm not talking a few less, I'm talking around 80 per cent less.

Imagine a city street that is currently jammed up with parked cars on either side completely car-free. I'm suggesting zero cars parked on the street.

Imagine a city with no traffic congestion, no toxic gases coming from sooty tailpipes, no car parks, smaller narrower roads with wider, quieter pavements.

It doesn't sound too bad, does it, and it's being considered, planned for, discussed and argued over right now.

It's the combination of electric autonomous vehicles, distributed generation and storage of electricity and modern power metering that will cause as big, if not bigger disruption and change to the way we live than the industrial revolution did two hundred years ago.

So fewer cars, all of them electric. Where will we get the power to charge all these machines?

Well, one thing rarely mentioned in the scare stories that will litter the press for the next five years is the fact that an electric car isn't a car as we understand them today.

It's a computer and power storage system on wheels.

The Tesla Model S, for example, has an on-board computer that is connected to the 3G network all the time. Yes, Tesla knows exactly where I go, how fast I travel, where I charge, where the car is parked and I have to trust them with that data.

At the moment, this machine is considered to be 'my car'. I lease it, so technically I don't own it, but it is my responsibility. However, I am hoping to live long enough to experience moving around in a car, when I want to, where I want to, without – and this is the important aspect – owning it when I'm not using it, which, as we have heard, is 90 per cent of the time.

If I have to wait around for the car I want to use to arrive, that puts a crimp on my 'freedom'. It may be a small price to pay but if this is the case, adoption of this technology will be slower.

However, if and when I need to use a car and it appears before me in a few moments, I'm talking under a minute, what's the big deal? I then use that car, either driving myself or being driven by a fully autonomous vehicle, until I get to where I'm going. I then get out and leave the car which will then go off and recharge itself if it needs to or start moving someone else.

Sounds far out and unlikely?

I thought so when I first heard about such systems four years ago. Since then, the amount of research, investment and technical competency in this area has grown exponentially. There are already thousands of fully autonomous cars on the road; companies like Google, Apple, Bosch, Siemens, BMW, Nissan and many others are busy developing fully autonomous drive systems.

I have been driven around London in a fully autonomous Nissan Leaf. There was a driver behind the wheel but he didn't touch anything. We drove along narrow side streets, busy main roads with pedestrian crossings, traffic lights, roundabouts. We drove onto dual carriageways, past schools with 20mph speed limits, all of which it managed with ease.

Not once did the car falter, not once did it break the speed limit. It read road signs, judged the speed and direction of other vehicles, cyclists and pedestrians. It also followed a route put into the satnav without hesitation. After the first few moments of feeling slightly alarmed as I watched the steering wheel make dozens of small adjustments as we travelled along the road, I soon came to trust the machine. It was a far better driver than any human being, it didn't get distracted or bored, it didn't read texts or fiddle with the sound system, it could see everything around it, to the side, behind as well as up ahead.

So, this stuff is coming and the normal fears pop up instantly. What if the system has to make a life-or-death decision? What will all the people do who currently earn their living as professional drivers? What will happen to the current automotive industry that sells cars, not miles? What will we do with our over-developed road network that will no longer be needed? What will happen to the global oil industry on which a huge section of our economy, our pensions and government income depends?

I have no idea. Something will happen, many things will change, disruptive technology like the steam engine two hundred years ago, the internal combustion engine a hundred and twenty years ago, commercial air travel seventy years ago, all caused profound changes to the way we live.

Some of it will work, some won't, but I think we have now passed the point where this stuff is a maybe. This stuff is a certainty, it's going to happen anyway, regardless of what I say or what Trump says.

It's cleaner, it's more long term, it's sustainable, it's exciting because the technology is developing so quickly. That's all true, but the most important aspect is it's cheaper.

If you're in the least bit interested in following these developments I have been making a series about this subject for the past eight years. It's called *Fully Charged* and you can find it on YouTube and Facebook under the title 'fully charged show'.

The increase in interest and awareness of these emerging technologies and systems is reflected in our subscriber numbers and view counts.

It took two years to get an aggregated 1 million views when I started making the series. We now regularly get over 2 million views a month.

It took three years to reach ten thousand subscribers on YouTube. We now have over a quarter of a million.

Of course, these increases could be entirely down to the handsome chiselled features of yours truly, the charisma and charm I exhibit so naturally.

I somehow doubt that. I think it's because we explore as many aspects of these changes as possible, and occasionally get to drive amazing and groundbreaking cars.

Josh Joshi and the Great Divide

Nationalism, isn't it great?

Feels like it was a bit dormant for most of my life but it's back big time.

Agreed, it survived in ugly little pockets, shaven-headed thugs waving Union Jacks in the 1970s, shouting racist nonsense.

Britain First, the National Front, Column 88, the list is long and dull. Angry white men demanding their rights, while living in a country whose social structures were designed by and built for white men.

Then early this century along came the acceptable faces of extreme nationalism: Farage, Johnson, Gove and most frightening of all, Rees Mogg.

Uniformly white, middle-aged and privileged men who still don't have enough power. Poor sausages, it must be terrible to be that deeply inadequate.

It's not just in the UK. Hungary, Poland, the Netherlands, the United States, among others, have all seen a rise in extreme right-wing nationalism.

If you've got this far in the book it will come as no surprise that I have always found nationalism, regardless of which country it was coming from, to be the most stupid, short-sighted and pitiful human emotion.

There currently seems to be no acknowledgement of the long period of the British Empire, the burden that our equally short-sighted colonialist forefathers bequeathed us.

Why are there Pakistanis, Indians and Africans living in the United Kingdom?

Because of the EU?

No, because we, the British, used to own their countries. We extracted huge wealth from their homelands, and as the empire crumbled after the Second World War, many of the people we ruled were classified as British citizens.

There is a very simple truth revealed by the party first, country second decision made by a PR executive who was briefly prime minister.

It is ignorant and wrong to suggest that everyone who voted to leave the EU is a racist.

I know people on both left and right who voted that way for perfectly legitimate reasons. There is a great deal wrong, corrupt and inefficient about the governance of the European Union.

However, every racist bigot in the UK *did* vote to leave the EU. All of them.

So, if you voted to leave for perfectly legitimate, well-thought-out reasons, you have to accept this ugly truth: the racists are on your side and this is your burden to carry.

Yes, overt racists only make up a minority of the people who voted to leave but they exist. They are ignorant, dangerous and always, always angry.

The fundamental idea behind the formation of the EU in the late 1940s was to stop the many and various people in Europe having wars with each other. From the beginning of recorded time until 1945 there was always a war somewhere in what we now classify as Europe.

Most of these conflicts were small. We won't have heard of 90 per cent of them, but there was always some jumped-up little nationalist who wanted more power, more land or to get rid of gypsies or Jews or Muslims from their sacred little patch.

It's happened hundreds of times, it always fails, and always ends up causing terrible suffering and destruction. Nationalism is the single most stupid, short-sighted and ugly political movement human beings have invented that always – check your history – always ends up being a right mess.

So, I was busy thinking about such reactionary and extremist notions as I started writing what was going to be my next book.

I've managed to launch three books with Unbound: *News from Gardenia*, *News from the Squares* and *News from the Clouds*.

They make up a science-fiction trilogy set two hundred years in the future where most things are a bit better. It's no utopia: the human race is surviving, and the technology is amazing but we still have plenty of problems.

The reason I had a rant about nationalism earlier has a direct connection to the thinking behind the books. I set them two hundred years in the future for the precise reason that if we haven't got over nationalism by then, we will just live in the same state of perpetual war that the little eager-beaver nationalists like Rees Mogg love so much.

The experience of creating these books was wonderful, the Unbound folks are amazing, what they've done in the world of book publishing is incredible.

So I wanted to do it again.

After attending a YouTube conference a few years back where I was the oldest attendee by several decades, I was inspired by the young people who were, I later discovered, YouTube stars. Kids with 20 million subscribers and a substantial income from pre-roll advertising revenue.

I wanted to write about them.

I was also fascinated by how London had become this insanely wealthy megacity that seemed to be sucking the lifeblood out of the rest of the country, despite the BBC's attempts at shifting the cultural focus by moving a small part of its production facilities to Manchester.

Having moved out of London twenty-six years ago, I had a slightly different perspective and started to imagine a world where London became politically separated from the rest of the country. I started a thought experiment as to how the country might look in fifty years' time.

The two things, YouTube stars and megacity London, began to coalesce and I started making notes. I came up with an idea: a young man in London in 2067 who is the equivalent of a YouTube star, online almost his entire life, and how a rampant free-market society might develop.

The background to this story described how megacity London was politically separated from the rest of what is currently the United Kingdom. I had decided that the rest of the country would be a slightly shabby but humane, mildly socialist, Corbynesque almost-democracy with a reasonably good health service. That was about as much thought as I'd put into it.

It was going well, I was getting really excited by the idea.

Then the EU referendum happened.

The entire notion I had created for this book fell to bits overnight. I don't claim to fully understand the benefits or otherwise of the vote to leave the EU, but what really struck me, and proof if it were needed that I live in a different country to many people around me, was where many of the people who voted to leave the EU lived.

Not in London, which I had been painting as a bastion of free-market brutality and unparalleled greed.

Londoners voted overwhelmingly to stay in the EU.

It was the rest of this island, which I had been planning to portray as a slightly crumbling, vaguely socialist humanitarian state.

How hopelessly wrong can you be? Clearly, I can be very hopelessly wrong. Although maybe not.

I have now spent time with numerous MPs who are riddled with difficulties, MPs on what was both sides of the divide.

A Labour MP who voted to remain in the EU, while his constituents in the north-east of England voted overwhelmingly to leave.

A Tory MP from London who is a vehement leaver whose constituents voted overwhelmingly to remain.

What a tangled web we weave.

Then Trump happened.

Since then, we have seen a rapid rise in nationalism, racism, homophobia and general reactionary white male rhetoric. Fed, as it has been for the last twenty years in the UK, by a handful of off-shore billionaires who control the printed press, newspapers that are only read by old white people who, as we discovered, vote.

These 'normal people', whoever they are, 'are sick of having political correctness rammed down their throats', according to the likes of the Murdoch press. Isn't that a brutally ugly turn of phrase? The extremist press is good at that sort of rugger-bugger bully-boy phraseology: 'rammed down our throats'.

Who, I bother to ask, has rammed anything anywhere? There has been a slow cultural shift away from the old habits of racism, sexism and homophobia. It's taken my entire life to slightly change; when I was young all I heard from the entire culture that surrounded me was a continuous stream of racist, sexist and homophobic bigotry.

That was normal. Anyone who questioned that was immediately subject to abuse, bullying and social exclusion.

I suppose all we can infer from this vile swing towards nationalism is that 'normal people' – the people who, according to the extremist press, voted in droves to isolate this damp island from our civilised neighbours – want the natural freedom to be bigots.

They demand the freedom to go back to the 1950s when you could use racist terms without a second thought. You could mock homosexuals, beat them up with impunity, you could live in a Benny Hill world where women were either vile bossy hags or sexy ladies whose clothes seem to drop off.

These 'normal people' are demanding the freedom to happily live under the illusions that white people who are born in England are better than anyone else.

As you might be able to gather, I was a bit depressed by it all and the prospect of writing a humorous science-fiction novel came to feel increasingly pointless.

I am aware there is discussion in literary circles that writing fiction of any sort other than murder mysteries and cop dramas is fairly pointless, as these two categories have more chance of being made into long-running TV shows.

But now it seems that we are living in fiction. Our new rulers are con artists, criminals or profoundly in-bred, weird little men with posh accents.

When I foolishly mentioned some of these thoughts on Twitter, I was deluged with furious responses from angry Brexiteers who called me a 'libtard' and 'snowflake'. Proof, they bellowed, that I was part of the liberal elite who didn't know what life was like for 'normal people' who had to live next door to brown people.

It is an interesting observation that the individuals who are the most rabid supporters of the UK leaving the EU, the people who won the vote, are furiously angry all the time.

Everything makes them livid, they are always screaming with the injustice of – wait – of them winning the Tory referendum?

So I stopped writing science fiction and wrote *Some Old Bloke* instead.

However, I promised the wonderful supporters on Unbound that I'd include the first chapters of *Josh Joshi and the Great Divide* as the end piece to this book. So here it is.

Chapter 1

On the day Josh Joshi left his apartment complex on Berwick Street, exactly 83.6 per cent of the population of London would have been unable to answer the simple question: 'Who is Josh Joshi?'

They wouldn't have a clue; his name would mean nothing.

He set out with the clothes he was wearing, a small backpack stuffed with a party outfit, and a peel slapped to his face. He was off to yet another celebrity shindig where he could be certain everyone would know who he was.

The remaining 16.4 per cent would have known exactly who he was, where he lived and what he was doing at any time of the day or night they happened to check up on him.

It's worth stating that 16.4 per cent of the population of London was an impressive number. During this era, London was a hyper-city with a population approaching 65 million.

No one entity within the multi-layered London economy seemed to know the exact population figure; it was huge, there was no dispute about that, but there were no agreed-upon figures.

Multiple news outlets referred to it as 'the city of choice for the 65 million free citizens and the thought leaders of the globe', but finding accurate figures remains impossible.

The sea borders were very porous around some of the less reputable southern corporate docks; there were areas of the city where people from all over the globe arrived day and night without any official intervention or data registration. With no central authority keeping tabs on numbers, most of the incumbent population accepted that London was just very big and very crowded, constantly busy and increasingly expensive to survive in.

So 16.4 per cent of Londoners knew Josh Joshi's face, and his face was everywhere. His reputation was such that his location was continually logged by millions of peels in the city, and possibly billions worldwide.

Hiding was not something Josh Joshi considered. He didn't really know what hiding meant.

He lived in public to an extent that his emotional and financial well-being were entirely reliant upon being seen. He was embedded in the very breath of the city. Josh was London and London was Josh, that's how he felt about it.

Of course, everyone has to have down time, even Josh Joshi. This was partly the reason he'd gone out on a limb and taken a lease on the Berwick Street apartment.

Living in Soho Town wasn't cheap. The membership alone was over a hundred thousand a year, then there was the lease, the power and connectivity charges, the support charges, the waste disposal charges, the security charges and, obviously, the food charges.

In total, Josh paid over a million a year to live in quite a modest abode. A handful of delightfully appointed square metres was the place he called home.

He'd bought the twenty-year lease from Gruber Gashet, who claimed he was a direct descendent of the man who had built the house in 1685. A fellow called Henri Gashet Guber proudly showed Josh a contemporary etching of the man, a Huguenot fleeing the persecution and murder of his people in France and Belgium.

While the original house had indeed been built in the seventeenth century, the building Josh lived in was very twenty-first century. Merely the facade survived, exquisitely blended nanofibres from the newly grown building made any join between ancient and modern subatomic and invisible to the human eye.

Josh had lived in the delightful but cramped building for a mere eighteen months on the day he left.

He had originally moved in with Source Dunbar, a forty-year-old image consultant and fashion model who looked not a day over eighteen. There was great peel activity during this change in his life. He was thirty-seven when he'd moved to Berwick Street, and like most people of his and previous generations, he had lived with his parents his entire life.

Millions of his followers lived vicariously through this transition, dreaming of one day doing the same thing.

Very few Londoners could afford to leave their parental home, if indeed they had a parental home, in the city. Although he earned a substantial income, Josh still had to save, borrow and beg in order to pay the first year's rent upfront, part of the deal he did with Gruber Gashet.

For a while, he and Source were propelled by the sheer energy of enormous levels of attention. Attention was the fuel that gave her life and he was not going to miss the chance to ride in her enormous wake.

The level of increased attention Josh received from moving in with a well-known socialite and brand cheerleader was beyond his wildest. Non-stop events, parties, openings, launches, and star-studded dinners.

He and Source got on well enough on the surface; she was an adept and professional lover and fulfilled every dream Josh had ever secretly nurtured. He was essentially a shy and reserved man with a great line in patter, but he wasn't very confident in intimate situations. He found a woman as wanton and explicit in the bedroom as Source Dunbar a little overwhelming but she clearly tried to have a kind heart when away from the lights, attention and adoration she craved.

He was therefore confused when once his lust began to fade, the more time he spent with Source the more he felt lonely and miserable.

She was momentarily notorious, her looks were startling, her face and figure frozen in adolescence by the latest in beauty chemistry. She would live on to be the oldest teenager in human history and through grim determination maintained her social and media position into her late nineties.

But, when not in the glare of massed ranks of peels, they had nothing in common and barely spoke to each other, and it wasn't long before she found someone more her style. A man of fifty-five who looked like a twenty-year-old. Beauty chemistry became a topic Josh riffed about regularly.

'Youth freaks and teen wannabes,' he called them. 'Pointless and a bit disturbing, no?'

This sudden parting was cushioned by the fact that Source wasn't a member of Soho Town so she couldn't get into the club without him. She was a member of Shoreditch Village, a slightly cheaper area that, according to Source, young people preferred, and as far as Source was concerned, she had been twenty for two decades.

'Vacuous' was how Josh described her during a rant about how much she'd meant to him. 'Nothing, she meant nothing to me. Does that sound harsh? Good. I feel harsh. I may change my name to Harsh Harshi.'

Although not an obviously attractive man, Josh had charm and wit on his side and was deluged with offers from all over, but for the following year he had kept himself very much to himself.

He didn't need Source or anyone else to be that close. When he was on his own he didn't feel lonely, but then again he wasn't alone very often.

In the peculiar world he inhabited, he was one of the big players, a streamer, a dreamer, a high achiever.

Josh Joshi spouted streams around the clock, producing between fifteen and twenty a day. They were mostly short, sometimes lasting less than a minute, but his followers seemed to love them.

Josh had 170 million global subs with hourly hits in the billions. His streams were energetic, funny, instantaneous commentaries on the vibrant culture of the London he loved.

For three years, Josh Joshi was the right man in the middle of the right city at the right time. He knew the right people, the loud funny people, the pushy opinionated people who knew everyone worth knowing. Josh was one of them, he knew he was one of them, but he also knew, because he'd seen it happen so often, that he was as vulnerable to churn as anyone.

London churned like nowhere else, the churn-over was frenetic, unpredictable and unmanageable. With the mere touch of a peel he could be dropped, finished, not so much a 'has-been' as a 'not-seen'.

The feeling of imminent disappearance from his much-vaunted position made every step along Berwick Street mildly uncomfortable. He was itching to stream, something he couldn't do from the confines of his club. All external contact was blocked, peels were dead floppy plastic, cameras banned, no peelcasts allowed because many well-known people lived in Soho Town and anyone caught staring or peeling at an A-lister would have their membership revoked without hesitation.

In Soho Town, communication between members was permitted but he could only use Soho talk. The one place he could get a global connection within the confines was in the high tower on Shaftesbury Avenue and that had stairs, a deliberate attempt by club authorities to discourage external comms.

As always, he had to wait until he was outside the club. He understood and even agreed with the policy; it meant that for the time he was in Soho Town he could switch off, calm down, sleep and recuperate.

His unending desire to stream wasn't about money, he had the trust income from his father's onshore account, it was about access, acceptance and acknowledgement. He relished it, bathed in it, he was conscious of it all his waking hours.

Josh was in public to such an extent that even when alone, when his peel was offline and thrown on the inducer, he found himself performing.

He would perform commentaries as he made a sandwich, took a shower, performed basic bodily functions. He was in some ways constantly rehearsing for the real thing, coming up with concepts, quips, turns of phrase he could use on a future peelcast.

As he walked north along Berwick Street no one turned and looked at him, they may indeed have recognised him, may have followed his peelcasts but no one would acknowledge something so uncool in Soho Town.

Josh walked towards Harry in the entrance lodge onto Oxford Street. Harry was an old man, over seventy, Josh guessed, although he had a thick crown of real hair, dark and lustrous, his face a mixture of absurdly youthful vigour and deep tiredness around the eyes.

Harry was a regular on North Gate security; Soho Town had no old-school electronic systems surveillance, no tags, cameras, facial recognition, no iris scanners, palm scanners, gait analysers or movement sensors. It had old men like Harry.

Old married men, men who were well paid and regularly vetted, men who had free accommodation and food, family quarters and security within the enclave.

These men where theoretically unimpeachable, unreachable, beyond corruption. They had too much to lose and the job was relatively easy if mind-numbingly boring.

If Harry didn't know you, you didn't get in. Even if you were with someone Harry knew, it was entirely at his discretion that you would be allowed in.

Every gatekeeper had complete control of the gates, no negotiating, no special pleading.

No one could hack their way into Soho Town, there were no back doors, no clever work-arounds. It was personal, it was human contact. All new members had to spend time with the gatekeepers, they had to get to know them. This was how Soho Town kept its security intact: using un-hackable, un-bribable and generally uninterested human beings like Harry.

'Afternoon, Mr Joshi,' said Harry, giving him a discreet nod.

'Afternoon, Harry. You well, sir?'

'I am indeed, Mr Joshi. You off to one of your shindigs are you?' he asked as he pressed the gate release.

'Got my fat suit packed and ready to wobble,' said Josh.

This line received no visible response from Harry the gatekeeper, the gate swung open silently and Josh took a deep breath and stepped out into the chaos.

Chapter 2

As soon as Josh left the quiet, tidy confines of Soho Town the atmosphere changed dramatically. On one side of the entrance, a private club enclave covering five hundred acres of what had been the West End of London in times long gone, all was peaceful, ordered, tidy, clean and expensive to live in.

But one step past the security gate took you onto Oxford Street, a shanty-town bazaar packed with thousands of people trading, shouting, hawking, performing and hassling, either that or it was people moving as fast as they could through the milling throng to get anywhere but the insanity and danger of the crowd.

Josh didn't need to walk through this maelstrom, he could have had an auton pick him up in the private lane that ran under Soho Town, which would have taken him onto a clean, quiet raised private highway that wound through the outer towers.

However, his credibility required that he live among the deafening bedlam of the real London; he was Josh Joshi and this was his home.

He brushed his peel and went live for the first time that day.

Over his right eye the view count symbol went from yellow to darker yellow to green. Green signified over a million viewers, it was suddenly worth a commentary.

'Hey, yiddily poop, it's the Joshmeister here, navigating through the urban jungle, oh viewsters.'

Millions of people were now seeing what he was seeing. 'Yes, bros and sistreenies, I'm doing a bit of essential schlepping and shopping because, you guessed it, it's another shindig for the Joshington, a noughties humpty bop, this you will have to see to believe, it's going to be a jobble wobble joy.'

Josh Joshi was determined to keep at the front, keeping his head above the mire. He found he needed to be reminded of just how vile the mire was, he had convinced himself if he didn't experience the full mire at regular intervals he'd grow lazy and before he knew it he'd suffer the churn and be up to his neck in it.

It was all too easy to live in a bubble in London, that's why he claimed he loved 'life on the streets'. Most of the people he knew, people who could afford to live in a confine, never went into the city real; they protected themselves from the stinking throng outside the bounds.

Most spent their entire lives in their enclaves; the most they would see of the mire was through the window of a speeding auton as they transmitted out to the airport.

As Josh was experiencing, there was a lot of mire in London, everywhere you looked there was mire piled upon mire.

It was perfectly possible to thrive in London, millions did, they lived in their confines and earned money, ate good food imported from around the world, got in and out of the city with little difficulty, but they paid for those privileges to a degree that was beyond the imagination of the majority population.

However, with all the restrictions, justifiable fear on the streets, pollution, stench, decay and endless miles of towers, those few lucky people knew in their bones they were living in the one city on earth that really mattered.

Merely waking up in this massive, sprawling metropolis was enough for them. They'd made it; they were inside, where it counted. As far as they understood, an understanding that was constantly reinforced by the sheer gargantuan numbers of people living there, everyone wanted to live in London no matter where they came from.

London was a city of freedom. It was creative, exciting, exhausting, crowded, noisy and endlessly entertaining.

It was also cruel, unforgiving, brutal and hopelessly exclusive for those who did not have money and connections, but that didn't seem to stop people wanting to be there.

In London anything was possible, that was the magnetic attraction for millions around the world. London sold itself with the dream that anyone could be rich beyond comprehension, anyone could live the life of such deep, manicured glamour that hunger and poverty became mere concepts, things you might witness in passing but never experience.

London was the epicentre of the world, all eyes were focused on the city, at least that's what it felt like for Josh Joshi and his cohorts. But Josh felt a bit special. He was different from his peers, he knew what life was really like on the streets, he liked the look of fear he could induce when describing his off-confine adventures to a group of manicured lovelies at a club bar.

'Amazing people,' he'd say. 'Brilliant creative people doing amazing things. Yeah, poor, smelly, dirty and maybe a bit dangerous, but you can't fault their creativity, ingenuity and determination to make something of their lives. If they live long enough, which of course most don't.'

The small gathering at the bar would shake their heads. Many of them did charity work, raising money for orphan homes, community hospitals and free schools for girls.

Josh didn't do any charity work for anyone. If hassled at a benefit event he would post a few hundred on the entrance tablet so his name was on the list, but what he saw on the streets told him clearly, 'This place is beyond charity.'

As he squeezed himself through the crowds on Oxford Street he brushed past a large pile of cloth that started to move as he passed. A human face was inside, eyes half open, mouth moving.

Without hesitation Josh put his hand over his right eye to block the view. His view count would drop off a cliff if this was streamed. No one wanted to see the detail of human hardship.

The big picture, the chaotic background was fine, not that sort of vile detail.

If you were sitting in a high rise, lounging on furnishings with a peel slapped on your face, the chance to see the wild outside could be invigorating, amusing and entertaining. Close-up detail of a human cloth pile, wrapped in endless cast offs, unwashed for possibly years, was over the line.

Josh quickly brushed his peel. 'Anyone seen this? So cute, yeah.'

He fed in a commercial stream and in doing so immediately auto-transferred sixty big ones into his onshore. Instead of his field of view, his transmission showed a crowd of screaming young women, or to be more accurate, a crowd of people who resembled screaming young women. Some of them could have been fifty, some of them undoubtedly started out in life as men.

'I cannot believe I've actually touched Josh Joshi!' said one of these over-excited fans waiting outside the spectacular Richmond Hippodrome entrance ramp. Her face was ecstatic under the harsh lights. 'He was so lovely, he held my hand and said hi to me like we knew each other and—'

The image died. 'Enough about me, now, what d'you think, about me?' said Josh using one of his regular catchphrases.

He would later admit it wasn't actually one of *his* catchphrases, it was one his father had repeated to him over and over when he was a child. Josh knew it was a joke at his expense when his father called him out for talking about himself incessantly when he lived with his parents.

His father, Rupe Joshi, would regularly remind Josh to remember he was no more important than anyone else.

This oft-repeated statement annoyed him. His dad was old and stuck in his miserable little unknown life. Josh had experienced his own importance for long enough to know his father was wrong.

He pushed past another gathering of ordinary muggins and a corporate officer from BipTic who was talking to an absurdly tall woman.

Josh scanned the local zone and moved towards the wall of a crumbling building, he then aimed his head at the scene.

'We have a situation in sector nine,' said Josh, adopting a crude rendition of an American accent. Had he wanted, he

323

could tune into a stream of comments coming in at thousands per second but the noise on the street was so overwhelming that it would be too much even for his highly attuned ears.

There was no sector nine. Josh had hundreds of similar quotes, bon-mots and gags he could call on to comment on what he was seeing or doing.

The BipTic cop was asking questions of the tall woman who, Josh commented, 'Does stand out a bit, mean-to-say where the frickatory does she come from? Mars, or some covert low-gravity off-world breeding colony?'

There were no off-world breeding colonies, covert or otherwise, it was just another quip.

For a beat, he tuned into his comments stream. Big laughs, screams of 'I love you, Josh' and 'Punch the cop, see what happens!' Comments being bellowed into peels from all over the world, some people probably in their beds late at night, some in the immediate area saying they were rushing towards him.

He tuned out again, he was on a roll.

He stood staring at the stand-off between heavily armed corporate officer and tall woman in cream sheer cloak but it all looked a bit pedestrian, no stun being used, no screaming and thrashing.

'Seen this?' he asked, brushed his peel and his stream cut to security footage of a lion, an actual lion that had escaped some rich idiot's confine and got into a pharmacy. He'd logged it just before he left to use at a time like this. When in doubt, cut to a clip.

Millions of snippets just like that filled the streams; if you searched for Josh Joshi, the response was a data burst of eye-crashing intensity. Josh knew how to pick the right snippets and sprinkle them into his peel-streams. He was a master chef at stream concoctions; he wasn't merely an actor, he was a creative genius.

There's no way of defining what he did. He was Josh, that was enough. There was none other, except maybe NotJosh.

This requires a short explanation because although the technology was fairly basic, the cultural significance is harder to grasp.

NotJosh was an utterly indistinguishable fully autonomous digital rendering of Josh. Even Josh admitted in a stream he wasn't sure which was him and which was NotJosh when he watched his own streams, a habit he tried to avoid.

The NotCorporation had launched version three of Not and it suddenly became ubiquitous. Everyone could have a 24/7 presence with their Not if they could afford the stream fees. No need for scheduling or hastily prepared streams: if you had the following and could pay the Not fees, you could be on every peel for ever. You didn't even need to be alive.

Josh was very pleased with himself when the NotCorp PR team got in touch, he didn't acknowledge publicly or even to himself that it was Source Dunbar and her relationship with NotCorp that had facilitated the deal.

Previous to him meeting Source, no one at NotCorp had heard of Josh, they would never have approached him, but that was the story he told at the time.

'NotCorp have got me, they are strangling me with their contractuals. I'm going to be replaced by NotJosh,' he screamed once the deal was in place.

He managed to spin the story that NotCorp had literally bought him and they were going to kill him and replace him with their software NotJosh. He even staged a mock kidnapping and terror alert, which for a while made NotCorp anxious.

However, the resultant spike in streams, the massive increase in subs and the consequent sales leap made NotCorp very happy.

They wanted him to continue to promote the Not notion and he did so with gusto. He explored everything he could do with NotJosh as soon as the product was released.

Within hours he was making a hugely popular string, a series of interwoven short pieces called JoshNotJosh. Everyone loved JoshNotJosh. Young women wore JoshNotJosh animated emblazoned clothing, some people even had touch-animated JoshNotJosh tattoos.

From this frenzy of activity, he rapidly secured lucrative commercial deals. A soft drink brand, originally called simply 'NotJuice' was quickly rebranded 'JuiceNotJuice'.

Produced by food giant Notxious, a shell company owned by NotCorp.

Josh was an integral part of the relaunch. JoshNotJosh suited the product well as JuiceNotJuice was clearly not juice, rather some chemical residual substance in liquid form that tasted like soap.

Not soup, soap, a nice scented soap, not some cheap knock-off brand. JuiceNotJuice was an acquired taste, laced with sugar and caffeine and a lot of other chemical waste products, it flew off the shelves.

Literally.

JuiceNotJuice packaging used an extreme lamina-phobic coating; if you wanted a carton you simply entered the store, brushed your peel having previously stated, 'I'm thirsty for soapy JuiceNotJuice.'

This activated the area of the shelving unit immediately under the pack and due to the angle of the shelf and the coating density of the pack, fired it at the recipient. The effect appeared to be highly amusing to young people as sales were catastrophic and the resultant intestinal damage to the consumer was forcefully ignored.

Josh sniffed one carton and never even tasted the product. He didn't need to, he lived in Soho Town where the juice still came from actual fruit growing on actual trees in the township's spacious multi-storey greenhouses.

But his use of JoshNotJosh had catapulted him into the A-list.

His JoshNotJosh streams were hugely popular, he would argue with NotJosh so it looked like he was arguing with himself.

Anyone over the age of forty would be unable to make sense of the noise as the speed of delivery left older ears stranded. NotJosh and Josh spoke at the same time but said slightly different things; it looked like identical twins sitting next to each other, speaking over each other, Josh waiting until NotJosh started talking and then talking over NotJosh, causing software bug outs and major amusement.

With ever-increasing popularity came ever-increasing pres-sure to buy his service. This meant increasing chaos as Josh was not a well-organised man. Eventually he had to hire an independent stream producer to deal with his business relationships.

Marci Jones-Jones was her name. She was in her forties but looked not a day older than twenty-five. Marci had run numerous streamers with varying levels of success from her parents' home in Neasden but before long they were all discreetly dumped. Running Josh and NotJosh became a full-time occupation.

Marci was on his case day and night, she earned her 10 per cent and because Josh was a walking mint, that 10 per cent rapidly afforded her a fiftieth-floor apartment in the increasingly popular northern suburb of Cockfosters. When she turned thirty-eight, she finally managed to move out of her parents' cramped home in Ongar. However, as the pressure of the exorbitant rent, the power and connectivity bills, and the food and transport costs amounted to a monthly Queen's ransom, she had to keep him going and this was getting increasingly difficult.

Marci appeared in a sub screen below his stream.

'Josh, the Koreans,' she said when she finally felt him acknowledge her.

'Why is Josh so popular? Why does his manager interrupt when he's streaming? Only you viewsters know the answer to that one. I'm down, I'm gone, and here's NotJosh to bore your pantaloons off, you lucky yobblers.'

He flicked the peel and Marci took over his right eye. Through his left eye he could see the street ahead of him, in his right eye, a crystal-def image of Marci.

The eye seeing the image of Marci was closed and yet the image still had startling clarity.

Josh had grown up with peels, a thin transparent gel sack that wrapped around the wearer's head, generally covering one eye and one ear.

'Slap and forget' was one of the early advertising slogans. Users simply slapped the gel sack onto their face and it auto-placed itself over either the right or left eye and ear, whichever the user chose.

Josh's parents found them nausea-inducing, hot and very uncomfortable. In fact, most of the older generation could not abide peels. They complained of motion sickness, headaches and nausea when the augmented reality system kicked in.

Josh, however, was the embodiment of generation peel. Introduced when he was seven years old, the peel went from tech embarrassment to ubiquity in six months.

He was given one by his father when he turned ten and had never looked back.

Even saying 'never looked back' was dated; Josh could, if he wished, look back. A peel had all-round image sensors so he literally had eyes in the back of his head if he wanted. He could also look back at his previous experiences, as the peel had play-back facilities from the day it was first engaged.

'I'm on my way to the party,' he said. 'No way am I going to schlep all the way up to Amersham. It's a right shithole, why didn't they come to see me in town?'

'Look,' said Marci, she was busy doing other things and her annoying cat kept walking in front of her peel. He was irritated by the way she slapped it on the wall in front of her instead of wearing the damn thing and looking in a mirror like normal people did; she sent his audio to a wireless speaker out of the dark ages and he could hear a vague echo of his own voice.

'They insist you go to see them,' she said eventually, as if she was checking something. An image of an old-school TV studio flashed into his eye for a moment. 'They have a studio and they want to interview you for a stream to Korea. It's cool, it's all olden days' stuff. You love all that, Joshy, and they're forking out a serious fee.'

'Yeah, well, I can't go today. I've promised I'll show at the porky party and I'll get some good ints. This is what I do, Marci, I hang out with A-listers, yeah? Top people, funny people, interesting people, yeah? Not some crap Koreans and their old-school shite.'

With another finger slide he dropped the call from Marci, killed the NotJosh feed and came live.

'That's enough, NotJosh, shut your pixels, you demented apparition, this is MeatJosh using my crude bipedal stack to transport my enormous brain and even bigger personality across the fetid streets of this wonderful city. Yes, folks, it's Josh Joshi, coming to you live from the Mary of the Le Bone, in the London Town. It's all happening today, I'm off to party, it's porky night at the Vamparium. Come and see me wobble up the red carpet if you're in the area, except you probs won't know which of the porkers is me. It's going to be porkelicious. I'll be togged up and ready to wobble. It's going to be a mad-fat-mash-out!'

He saw in the peel's lower third that Marci was calling again but swiped her off and carried on walking towards Marylebone

High Street. The crumbling side streets were a little quieter than the main Oxford Street drag, but there were still hundreds of people walking about.

At certain times of the day and night the streets would become choked with 'cuisers', people who earned a pitiful crust delivering cuisine to offices, studios, homes and hotels. The notion of shopping for food had long since faded, everything was delivered and, in London, due to the nature of the place, the crowding and chaos, the best and cheapest way of delivering food was by human.

Many of the streets in the NoHo area of London were giant kitchens with street-level pick-up systems and fast-moving queues of cuisers waiting for their next delivery.

Highly computerised and incredibly efficient, the big operations could send out two hundred meal packs a minute.

Josh knew to avoid these streets as they were a terrifying maelstrom of running, cycling and shoving cuisers desperate to deliver, return and repeat.

The street he chose was lined with betting shops, strip clubs and bars on either side, all jostling for attention with their glaring come-ons, each ugly projection changing to a personalised invitation as Josh passed.

Unlike Soho Town where everything was toned down, quiet and refined, the streets of this part of London were a tangled hotchpotch of small businesses and tatty shop fronts, all lit with garish sheet lights and throbbing imagery. He could easily double-eye his peel and remove all this ugliness using AVC (assisted vision cleanse) but he kept one eye on the dirty reality around him.

He had dressed for the journey, his clothes a uniform dirty grey, which blended in nicely with the majority population, his unshaven appearance made him almost invisible among the sauntering masses. The only giveaway were his shoes, a new pair of pre-lace-Thumpers which anyone under thirty would know cost serious money.

Pre-lace-Thumpers were not something anyone could afford out of the confines but he had planned to walk across a wilder part of the city and wanted something on his feet that wouldn't let him down.

Some of the streets were likely to be contaminated and the aqua-phobic coating on Thumpers was legendary, literally stomp in dog shit and not a trace would be left. Of course, dog shit wasn't a big problem as there weren't many dogs in London but many streeters, the term used for the millions of homeless, used certain side streets as 'dumping grounds'.

This was strictly against the rules in many sectors but street people knew the areas where such rulings were barely enforced and camera surveillance was ignored.

As he wound his way past a particularly garish pharmacy-strip joint he turned into the rough end of Marylebone High Street.

He had arranged to meet Duff McGloughlin, a churned peeler who had moved into live performing and corporate relations. Their meet up was in Chin's private club at the northern end of the old high street, a dingy joint that had a genuine air of the old world, as opposed to the much safer, tidier and cleaner air of the old world in all the bars and clubs in Soho Town that Josh normally frequented.

Duff had pre-booked one of the private rooms so they could get ready for the porky party, a time-consuming and complex process.

Josh could easily have got ready at home and taken an auton direct to the Vamporium but that wasn't how he rolled. He didn't want to get soft, street life was about being sharp, noticing threats before they became unavoidable; his peel helped as it scanned for visas flickers and scam-mongers with dodgy credentials and highlighted them in red as he approached.

But that was never enough. High-end street hoodlums knew about this and went naked – not naked in terms of clothing, but naked regarding identifiers. If you saw someone on the street with random holes in their clothing, this was because they had brutally removed all tags and sensors. No security system would register them, they wore distortion masks invisible to the human eye and to all but the most sophisticated sensors, they represented a palpable danger.

His journey therefore involved genuine risk. It wasn't that the streets were actually very safe but the confiners' paranoia kept them away; in fact, the streets were really dangerous and someone with the wealth and connections Josh possessed was a rare and valuable target.

However, he was a wily street traveller and moved fast, keeping a weather eye out for trouble.

Before long he arrived at the door of Chin's but walked straight past. It was possible some nefarious streeter had got wind of his carefully encrypted arrangements and was waiting nearby. The direct walk by was a classic, throw them off balance, make them doubt their sources.

He got to the end of the street where the rumble of trams on Euston Road was deafening and crossed to the other side to make a return pass. No one seemed to be hanging about, just the normal chaos. He flicked his peel to scan and did a brief check up and down the street, no red marks, no orange triangles, looked okay.

'This is strictly business,' said Josh as he brushed his peel and looked at his reflection in the shopfront he was standing by. His audience could see him but he positioned himself and set the focus to haze so any detail behind him was blended flat and data free.

'As I always do, to protect the privacy of my clients, I am off peel for the next twenty. Yes, moan and groan all you like, you won't find me, you can't track me but just think, I could be walking by your abode in broad daylight and you won't know. That's exciting isn't it? It isn't? Hey, NotJosh, is that exciting?'

Without pause NotJosh appeared. 'Yeah, baby, that's exciting, but I know where you are and I may tell everyone.'

'And I may re-boot your sorry ass with an inside-out face, you muppet. Just do some of your poems, that'll keep everyone enthralled.'

'You hate my poems,' said NotJosh.

'Exactly, that's why I asked you to do them. Everyone hates your poems. They hate you too and that's the way I like it. Laters, dweebs, you know I love you.'

He squeezed the corner of the peel until it killed the send, darted across the street at a slow jog, the peel's sensors judging distance and speed of the multiple bicycles whipping up and down and guiding him safely to the door of Chin's.

Chapter 3

Inside Chin's it was dark and cool. Josh moved swiftly through the fairly dodgy clientele and up the narrow brown painted stairs at the far end of the room.

'Aha, stick boy Joshi, you made it,' said Duff McGloughlin. He was pulling a misshapen body suit out of a bag as Josh entered the musty room.

'All right, Duff, what you been up to, you lanky piss streak?' said Josh, finally relaxing and stripping off his peel.

'Just got back from Bonnie Scotland,' said Duff. 'Had a brilliant time, great crowds, lovely food, copious beverages. You should go, they'd love you there.'

Josh smiled. 'Why does everyone want me to leave London?'

'Sorry, who wants you to leave London?'

'I dunno, management.'

'Marci Jones, she wants you to leave? Why? What's happened?' For a moment Duff sounded genuinely concerned.

'I dunno, money.'

'Fucksake, how much money d'you need?'

'Opportunities, the usual batshit. You know what she's like.' He imitated her voice, all breathy with an almost unpleasantly wet sibilance. '"Josh you could do really well in China, they want you in Korea. They really really want to meet you in Rome." Why would I want to go to bloody Rome, or Korea or bloody Scotland? Sounds like a right shitpit.'

'No, you're wrong, pal. Scotland's fantastic, I might go and live there, it's very different, seriously,' said Duff, slightly aggressively.

That annoyed Josh. Duff always knew better about every-thing, it was another reason they'd stopped working together.

Duff was only a year older than him but always patronised him, always corrected him.

'Yeah, well, a different shitpit doesn't mean I want to go there. I don't need to go there, I'm doing fine in London town, man.'

'Have you ever been out of London?'

'No.'

'Seriously, you've never left the city?'

'No, I'm fine here. Got a nice place, do what I want to do. I'm dead lucky, I'm not complaining. I love it here.'

'Yeah, but, well, it's a bit restrictive, isn't it? The weather's shite, the food costs a fortune – not that that would worry you – it's crowded as hell. There's a whole world out there.'

'A whole world that's a nightmare. Why's it so crowded here? Cos anyone with any sense wants to come and live here.'

'I know, yeah, I've heard all that before, but that's just the corporate brain suck, you don't really know until you've been out. Sure, there's proper shitpits on the island. Great England is a nightmare, Wessex, I dunno, mad town, never been, Wales is always raining apparently, but Scotland, seriously, it's ledge.'

Josh pulled his own fat suit out of his back pack and shook it.

'When you see Scotland, how it's run, how they do things there, how they get on with everyone, how the schools work, the hospitals, the lack of crime, it's so different. It's like history, you know, when you read history about old societies and stuff.'

'Dunno anything about history.'

'They do in Scotland, seriously, they really know history, even the kids. They know how we ended up like this.'

'Like what?'

'Well, London, you know, it used to be just a city in a country, England.'

'What, Great England?'

'No, just fricking England, that's what it was called before,' said Duff as he pushed one leg into his fat suit.

'Yeah, I know that.'

'So you did do history when you were a kid?'

'Yeah, well, I had to do a course, my folks bought me a course when I was ten. Didn't pay much attention, just spoke what I read.'

'Okay. So London used to be the capital of England.'

'Yeah, okay. I remember.'

'But there was more, there was a United Kingdom too.'

'Where was that?'

'Here, I know it's confusing, the Scottish peeps understood it. The whole island was like, one place, all together.'

'Seriously?' said Josh. If he'd ever known this, he'd completely forgotten it.

'Yeah, but then it went to shit and everybody split off into little bits, Great England, Scotland, Wales, Wessex and here. All separated and independent and different. That's why it's worth going to Scotland, I tell you, it's nicer than here and they've got the bridge now.'

'What bridge?'

'To Denmark. It's a frikkin' massive bridge, a tube over the sea. Takes two hours in an auton.'

'What's Denmark?'

'Josh, you massive twonk!' said Duff with a big grin that annoyed Josh further. 'It's like another country, there's loads of other countries. Denmark, France, Spain, I don't know, there's loads.'

'Yeah, I know that, I've seen a map, just don't know all the names, yeah?'

'Okay, so each country has different things, like Scotland's got a parliament.'

'What's that?' asked Josh out of habit rather than genuine interest.

'Like a place where they argue stuff, a government, yeah? People vote and if the boss has screwed up they have to frick right off and you get a new boss.'

'Sounds stupid.'

'It's complicated, they explained it to me but I didn't really understand. Anyway, the companies don't own everything.'

'What? How does that work?

'The country owns it; well, the government, I think that's who owns stuff.'

'What stuff?'

'Well, the place, the roads and buildings and trains and bridges. And the schools and hospitals and like a really, like really ancient city.' Duff nodded as he said this as if to emphasise it further. Josh sighed. He didn't need to hear all this stuff about Scotland.

'I'm talking medieval old,' said Duff. 'Way older than anything here. Amazing castles and houses and stuff. Mountains, rivers, they've got everything, for real. I didn't wear my peel all the time I was there, didn't want to miss anything.'

'Yeah, brilliant, Duff. Scotland sounds brilliant. Let's get ready, we're going to be late.'

'Yeah, okay, this won't take long. You ready to pile on the kilos?'

Duff had remained one of Josh's few friends over many years. For a brief period in their youth they had co-peeled, creating joint streams that some older followers remembered with affection, but those days were long gone.

Although Josh had never said it to his face, he felt Duff was a burden he wasn't prepared to carry; his vertiginous ascent to hyper hits would never have taken place had they stayed together.

Happily for Josh, Duff didn't seem that bothered. He'd moved down to the South Coast and generally had a good time, living in a tent for most of the year, just doing the odd stream and getting the odd treat through his association with Josh.

The Noughty Humpty party was one of those treats, a themed gathering at an exclusive enclave by the park. Duff would never have been on the guest list for such an event so he was happy to be Josh's plus one.

The idea was inspired by old images of the early part of the century when many people appeared to be enormously over-weight. It had been a source of huge amusement when Josh was a child. He'd never seen anyone remotely as fat as the ones in the pictures. Everyone was very slim, either because of chemical treatments or that they didn't really have enough to eat. The vast majority of thin people were that way because of the latter.

So for this party everyone was encouraged to don a fat suit. They listed a string of companies that rented them by the hour, the fees were ridiculous but the choice was fabulous. Josh had gone for a very fat man in a shell suit, with a hoody. It was a look he had stared at as a kid, a big fat bloke with his belly poking out of a garment originally built for sports people, active slim people. He found it hysterically funny.

Both men struggled into the fat suits and stood up staring at each other. They burst out laughing.

The material hung off their bodies in highly unattractive folds, they both looked ridiculous, like a toddler wearing his dad's trousers.

'*Trois, deux, un,*' said Duff and they both pressed the hip-mounted button. Instantly their body suits expanded and morphed into grossly obese people, the fabric of the clothing covering the suits creaked under sudden pressure.

They checked each other out, their bodies had been trans-formed into bulging blubber sacks, the shaping of Josh's lower stomach was brilliantly sculpted, literally hanging over the skin-tight light blue trousers. The legs and arse enormous under the stretched old-school shell-suit material. Only their hands, feet and heads gave the game away.

They pulled on skin-colour matching fat gloves complete with chewed nails, and stood into wide, bulbous fat shoes, which tightened autonomously.

'And now, the *pièce de résistance*!' said Duff, unfurling a small transparent sheet that he pressed to his face just underneath his lower lip.

The material wrapped around his face and gently inflated, making what had been a lean face on top of a massive body slowly change its shape. His face looked huge and swollen with multiple double chins.

Josh was laughing so much at the transformation before him he couldn't hold still enough to perform the same face-distorting exercise. Duff finally waddled close, their massive stomachs squishing together and pushing Josh backwards.

'Stand still, you big lardarse,' said Duff.

More hysterical laughter from Josh; he'd been looking forward to this party for days.

Duff carefully held the fat face in place and Josh felt the material wrap around his face and neck. It inflated instantly and then Duff burst out laughing.

'You massive porker,' said Duff. 'Who ate all the pies?'

'We ate all the pies!' they said in unison.

For a moment, Josh felt happy and relaxed with Duff. They had known each other for a long time and he didn't need to keep up any pretence. Duff knew him before he was massive and didn't make a fuss about it. Josh smiled at his old friend, there was no jealousy, no bitterness from Duff. He seemed happy with his minor success and never expressed resentment towards Josh.

If he was a recognised face in London, Josh Joshi was massive in Asia. Many Asians had told him during his streams that he was 'massive in Singapore!' and 'Massive Josh, we love you in Jakarta!'

This was the reason, Josh assumed, behind the desire the Koreans had in discussing potential patronage deals.

According to Marci, he and NotJosh had a great future promoting products in the Far East. The NotJuice deal had been a global campaign, and apparently his multiple faces flashed on billboards from Beijing to Kuala Lumpur.

Josh's response to her suggestions about the Koreans was immediate. 'I don't want to go there.'

He observed the silence from Marci. This was no peel glitch, she just sat expressionless as if she was waiting for an auton. Eventually he expanded the thought.

'I'm not leaving London, Marci. No way am I going to bloody Korea or Hong Kong or Malaysia any of those shit ditches.'

'You don't have to go anywhere,' she said patiently. 'You can do it all from London. That's the whole point, dearest.'

Her desire for him to meet these Koreans weighed on his mind; he felt uncomfortable even thinking about it. What were Koreans like? He had no idea, but something about this approach felt dubious. Marci had never explained what company they were from, she had never met them, they were just Koreans.

He tried to put it out of his mind as he waddled after Duff up a short section of Marylebone High Street. Every step was exhausting as the massive fat suit restricted his movements.

'No one can have been this fat,' said Josh as he gasped for breath. The suits were supposed to have cooling elements in them but either they weren't working or the weather was too hot for them to have any effect.

From March to October London was a sweltering heat bubble and on that day in mid-May, daytime temperatures were in the mid-thirties.

'You've seen the pictures, they were all super massive,' said Duff who, likewise, was finding moving through the streets to be a struggle.

Josh had noted that their exaggerated appearance was getting many glances from other pedestrians; they had been shouted at by a gang of lads hissing past in an auton as they waited to cross the busy cross-town Hang Seng Road.

He could finally see the crowds gathered outside the Vamparium club that faced the huge fence surrounding Regent's Park.

Josh, not being a member of the Park Club, had no auton access to the surrounding roads and wasn't prepared to pay the ridiculous visitor's fee when he could walk up the path for a few hundred.

He slapped on his peel and started streaming. He clicked his fingers at Duff. The fat gloves made a ridiculous flabby sound which made them both laugh, but Duff knew what was needed and brushed his own peel so he could get a split-feed going on. In Duff's feed his full, wobbling mutton arsed body could be seen jobbling along the pavement.

'Check out the bumper Josh, this is how it is from now on,' said Josh to his already huge audience, 'and yes, don't bother saying it, I did eat all the pies. Every pie on the face of this fricking planetoid.'

They finally arrived at the edge of the huge gathering outside the club. Autons whooshed in, deposited their obese cargo and whooshed off again, nudging numpties out of the way with their inflated pedestrian guards.

Three women got out of an auton that pulled up beside Josh, three massive women in tiny miniskirts and weight-bearing cleavage tops supporting pairs of ham-sized mammaries. Huge legs the size of tree trunks covered in blue blotches which rubbed together as they waddled, their bulbous feet squeezed into ridiculously flimsy high heels.

'There's a sight not seen on these streets in fifty years,' said Josh as he zoomed in to the women waddling and giggling in front of him. 'Okay, they ate some of the pies, I couldn't manage all of them.'

The crowd opened up as they approached, revealing the extra-wide red carpet leading to the impressive portico of the Vamparium club.

'Oh Lord, look at the crowds, boys and girls,' he said as he waddled along. 'It's red-carpet time for the Joshmeister.'

He brushed his temple in a gentle downward motion, the peel created a title for the stream, 'Red-Carpet Time for the Joshmeister,' and he immediately saw the numbers climb.

'Hey, Josh,' shouted a male voice. He couldn't see anyone he recognised until a vast spherical figure in a shiny black suit emerged from the throng. It took his peel a moment longer than normal to recognise the figure, but soon the name appeared.

Hampton Granger, 3,009,426. The number referred to his stream subs. Josh had over 150 million and as he'd lost a couple of million in the previous month, the low figure Hampton had acquired made Josh feel momentarily more secure.

But then Hampton was only a minor peeler who had somehow managed to wangle an invite. The realisation that this party was possibly less exclusive than he'd been led to believe jolted Josh's security.

'Excuse me, boys and girls, while I humour this has-been,' he said to his peel audience, then, delivered in a depressed monotone, 'Hey, Hampton, who ate all the pies?'

'I ate ALL the pies!' shouted Hampton passionately, his bulbous face barely recognisable, his multiple chins stretching inhumanly as he grinned.

'Isn't that original? Take it easy, Hampton. See you, wouldn't want to be you.'

Josh moved swiftly forward through the scanning arch and onto the red carpet proper.

'It's Josh Joshi!' a voice suddenly boomed over a public-address system. 'Ladies and gentlemen, Josh Joshi is here. You might not recognise him but it's the Joshmeister himself!'

Another gargantuan figure loomed out of the gathering of bulbous tubbies posing and cavorting on the red carpet in front of him.

Even with a full fat body suit on, Josh recognised him instantly: Patrice Blindacre, host of Perpetual Springtime, a corporate stream with a seemingly bottomless budget. Patrice was genuine big time, a massive global star, and Josh felt his lower back relax a little. Patrice had recognised him through the fat face and inflated body get-up and announced him to the crowd.

Patrice was sporting a full-face peel over an enhanced full-face mask which loomed over a massive fat suit. Josh linked his stream to Patrice's. He was already linking Duff's so he was now sending out a multiplicity of streams and his numbers were rocketing.

Patrice Blindacre was over two metres tall in his stocking feet so the fat suit he was wearing could barely be described as human scale. He was the size of a family shack in an East London shanty.

'You look great, Josh. Very nice get-up, welcome to the noughties!'

'Thank you,' said Josh. 'I've just been out for three curries, with two Peshwari naans for dipping, a big bowl of onion bhajis rounded off with a dozen doughnuts, a delicate pile of waffles and cream topped off with an extra helping of high-fat chocolate ice cream. Is there any catering? I'm quite peckish.'

This statement received a huge, overblown laugh and enthusiastic round of applause from the big crowd held back behind the red ropes either side of the broad red carpet. Josh waved at the crowd, blinked and checked his numbers, he'd just topped 100 million. He was right: Marci didn't have a clue. He'd have to get new management who understood his pull. He still had it, he was Josh Joshi, he was massive in London and that's what counted.